The Gaffer's Shorts

Acknowledgments

The Divinity pulled it off in six days. Then he took a one day break. Since then, no work of any worth has been created out of a void. This book is the product of my life experience. Much of that experience was invested in scientific endeavors. Thus, I had the privilege of associating with many heavy duty intellects. Not everyone in science is like that. In fact, most are not. I was also compelled to associate with some of the biggest dorks you could imagine. I could not list all of either category even if I could remember them. The interesting thing about this is, I cannot say which associations were the most useful to my development; dork or intellect.

There were, however, two people whose influence on this book were very direct in that they encouraged me and made real contributions in the form of ideas and corrections to my efforts. First is my wife who reads, sometimes reluctantly, everything I write, making corrections and suggestions. Without her, there would be some outstanding blunders herein. In addition she looks after my health and well being while I muddle along. Thank you Mrs. Gaffer!

The other is Linda who has been my friend, my sounding board and my sage advisor. I have leaned heavily on her for encouragement, understanding and advice. She has never failed me. I don't think she knows how to fail. Thank you Linda!

In addition, I have some wonderful friends who generously gave their personal time to proof read and correct this work. My heartfelt thanks to Dave, Eunice, and Robin.

About Wesoomi

By the Editor

Wesoomi (Wes-oh-me) is the name of our publishing firm. It is a coined word, having no meaning until we created it. However, we wish to think of it as having meaning beyond the formal name of our firm. We would like it to carry the meaning of these concepts. Unusual, different, uncommon, funny, clever and even peculiar. To this end, we have devised a myth. "Myth: An imagined or unverifiable person or thing."

The myth:

These are paraphrased excerpts from *The Legend of Wesoomi.*

In a small village, South and West of the big water lived a tribe of hunters and tillers of the earth. A simple and gentle people, they often fell victim to raiders from the North and East. Their harvest was often stolen and their finest young men and women were carried off.

Came to this tribe, one day, a medicine man aesthetic. The gentle people accepted him and he helped by healing boils, driving out evil spirits and other like services. He often wandered the woods, and though the people of the village had warned him of the wild fungus Wesoomi, that which brings shaking and death, he did partake. Perhaps because of his diet, the aesthetic did not die, but his thoughts were affected. He began to see things.

These visions interested him and he continued adding the fungus to his diet until he partook of nothing else. Each day new visions thundered around in his head, changing what had been there and he was completely changed. He began to see how all things were and how all things came to be. This is how he came to know how to make himself disappear from one place and appear in another. In humor he played some pranks on the simple villagers. The people of the village began to call him Wesoomi and they feared him.

Wesoomi, seeing their fear, took care and soothed them by his behavior. He entertained the children with simpler tricks and games. He also sat with the elders and instructed them in the crafts of building and the arts of growing and hunting. These things increased the wealth and happiness of the village. All looked forward to the harvest festival.

Sadly, on the eve of the festival, came a raid of warriors from the East, taking away the young men, most of the harvest and the loveliest of the maidens from the village. Then, in sadness, Wesoomi also instructed the people in the art of war. He taught them the concepts of position and mobility. He showed them the advantage of high ground, speed, surprise and early warning. When the raiders came again, they met with disaster and the people became masters of their own land. The village prospered and the raiders from the East and North feared to come.

Wesoomi, seeing his work was done, took leave to rejoin the aesthetic community whence he had come. His name lived on in the land as a mark of behavior. It came to mean "He acts like he ate funny mushrooms. He is Wesoomi."

Now this is how we want our customers to think of us. We do the unusual, the peculiar, the funny and clever. We eat the funny mushrooms and live. We are what is called a small press. We are not one of the giants. We do not need to sell a million books or tapes to break even. We do not need celebrity names on our books. We do not produce the mass market twaddle. We can and will produce special interest titles for thoughtful people. We are Wesoomi.

The Gaffer's Shorts

Willie Gaffer

Wesoomi Publishing

FIRST U.S. EDITION

ISBN: 0-9653732-1-5

Wesoomi Publishing

P. O. Box 656

Ortonville, MI 48462

Contents

Start Here

I named this introduction *Start Here* because I really want you to read it first. I once started reading a science fiction book by an author I had previously admired. I read about 150 pages before I realized I was reading the babbling of a senile old man. I kept hoping it would come together. I finally put the darn thing down. I hold the author blameless, but I never forgave his agent or the publisher for wasting so much of my time. I don't want that to happen to us. I think you have a right to know, right off, if you are not going to like me. You should not have to waste time getting indignant. It should come easily. These first few paragraphs should do the trick.

I do not consider myself senile. However, it is possible that my mind is badly warped. You may call it twisted. As a result, some folks will think this is a weird book. I do not have a problem with that. I'm not sure it's an unfair assessment. I hope that will not keep you from enjoying the pieces I present.

This is a book you can put down! However, I believe many of you will pick it up again as soon as you get some loose time. You can read it in an airport, an airplane or a car, assuming you are not the driver. You can also read this book in a bathtub or a hot tub, though it seems a shame you would be alone in the hot tub.

What you have in your hand is an assembly of short pieces by me (Willie Gaffer). There are stories, essays, thoughts, limericks, humor, songs and verse. While some of these stories I tell are local, I believe the issues are common to all locales. The stories, even the true ones, may be slightly enhanced. I do claim poetic license. Each piece is complete within itself. Some will make you laugh, some may bring a tear to your eye and some may make you stop to think. Some may bore you. A few may make you want to grab my neck, yank my head down and flatten out my nose with your knee.

This book is for thoughtful people with a humorous appreciation of the irony and silliness which surrounds us. Although it has rowdy and raucous parts, it also presumes a certain joy of knowledge, learning and subtlety in the reader. I expect you to know things. If you don't know, I expect you to want to look it up. Throughout, I presume quite a bit about your knowledge and thoughtfulness. Without that, some of the pieces will be mysterious to you and some of the humor will seem pointless.

I hope parts of this book will make you think. Whether you agree or disagree with me is irrelevant. If you know I am wrong and can prove it, I expect you to write and tell me. It would be mean spirited to leave me in ignorance. I don't like being wrong and I do strive for accuracy and truth. However, if I could not risk being wrong I could never have written this book. The point is, I have thought about and enjoyed what I have written here. I hope you will do the same.

Some of this book is intended to be funny and some of it, serious. I hope you will be able to tell the difference and not laugh at everything in it. A few, perhaps many, of the stories are not my stories at all. They are stories told to me as true by great storytellers I have known. They may or may not be true but I feel they are good stories worth retelling. I have not used real names. I would like to give proper credits, however, the people who related the incidents would probably prefer I do not.

In fairness, I do feel I owe these folks a debt. Therefore, for the people who know me and recognize their story in this book, please stop by. I will be happy to share with you a large pepperoni pizza and a pitcher of beer of your choice. My treat, of course. I will do this so long as you choose a decent beer and not one of the two American media monster beers. Pick any other beer and I'll manage to choke down my share. If you do not know me, you must go to the person who borrowed your story and related it to me for recompense.

When you pick this book up, you can use the table of contents to select pieces or you can start at the front and mark your place as you read through the book. As to marking your place, this is the only use I have ever found for those things called sticky notes. They will not fall out. They mark your place effectively and when you peel them out there is no damage to the book. I have found them especially effective for doing research. While God, in her infinite wisdom, has given me only two thumbs, she has supplied me an infinity of sticky notes. It's much easier to write on sticky notes and, unlike thumbs, they are eminently disposable. Always write on the note before you take it off the pad.

If you have got this far, you either think you might like me or you are hoping to find grounds for a fraud suit. In either case, please read on while I tell you a little about myself.

It's traditional to put a note about the author in the front of the book but, for the sake of modesty, it should be written by someone other than the author. Since I do not know any literate folks who would be willing to do that, I left that part of the book out. Now I can throw modesty aside and talk about myself, me, Willie Gaffer. That's not my real name, but what do you care. I expect what you care about is whether or not I can entertain you. You hope you will enjoy reading this book. I hope so too. Since we agree on that, I conclude you will want to know what kind of person is talking to you.

What we are is determined by many things, not the least of which are the conditions of our birth and early environment. These, mitigated by our ongoing experience, are the main forces which determine what we believe and become. There were a great many beautiful things which happened in my life. I was born into a large family of caring people. Though it was not always perfect, I always had a place where I belonged. I also had a twin, so I never knew loneliness in my youth.

The up side of a big family is, no matter how bad you screw up or how down and out you become, there is someone who will take you in, feed you, let you rest, then boot your butt out to try again. My family is like that. They are the source of all the good things in me.

There were also many trials. I dwell here on the trials because I think of them as things which made me stronger as they were overcome or, at least, survived. Here are just a few of the trials I remember and survived.

At age thirteen, one single incident influenced the direction of my thoughts and philosophy forever. I was beat up viciously, with a club, by two adult school teachers, in school, because I smart mouthed one of them. My parents supported the teachers as was the custom at the time. They did not ask to hear my side of it. Things do change. The pendulum has swung. Recently, teachers have been imprisoned for much less than what those two thugs did to me.

I learned a lesson from the beating. Interestingly enough, it was not the lesson they intended to teach me. The thugs thought they had taught me respect for authority. What I learned was quite the opposite. It fixed in me, for all time, a generalized contempt for power and a particular contempt for those who exercise power. The suspicion of power was already present but that beating put it in concrete. Since then, my position has been continuously reinforced by my observations. I have never seen power exercised in a completely honest way. My theory has never failed. In my experience people who have power will eventually abuse it.

Years later in Korea I was shot at and terrified. I lay on my face in a depression a few inches deep and cried while cannon shells exploded around me and shrapnel zipped over my head. A few days later I saw a row of dead men laid neatly on the ground. These were called the enemy and the corpses were being methodically searched for what was called intelligence. They didn't look like enemies to me. They looked like dead boys. All of this for oil?

A few years ago, I was conned and robbed by a scum bag who is still walking free because the Oakland County prosecutor does not want to be bothered. The state police took all of the evidence on the pretext of investigating the case. After dinking me around for over a year, they sent me a letter which made it clear nothing was going to be done.

Four years before that, I was almost killed by an incompetent HMO doctor. I still suffer from the effects of her bungling and arrogant assumptions. She was a young snot who had me down as a whiney old man after drugs. I finally got around her by paying doctors outside the HMO to help me. When the surgeon who saved my life sent her a courtesy memo outlining what he was doing for me, she did not even have the decency to come to the hospital to see me. That is how my HMO assigned, primary care physician behaved.

Do not read this as an indictment of the medical profession. Rather, read it as an indictment of the money grubbing HMO industry. It was the heroic efforts of many excellent, real doctors which restored me to some degree of health and functionality. There was a time for about two years when I was certain I was going to die. I have had two heart attacks, four major surgeries, an angioplasty, a bleeding ulcer and night terrors.

There is no reason you should care about any of this. I don't mind. I just want to show that I have had many good adventures and many misadventures. Some caused by luck, some by errors and some, more than likely, payoffs from previous incarnations which I don't remember. Some joyous, some life threatening, some humiliating and some just terribly embarrassing. Here are a few of the life philosophies and understandings which I gained from my experience.

First, survival requires the development of a creative sense of humor. I had to do that. It's all that kept me going for a long time. It is for others to decide if I am creative. If I am, it will quite often manifest in the form of humor.

Second, I have developed an enormously deep sympathy for underdogs and people who have been hurt, insulted or have just lost their way somehow. Whether it's a citizen being cheated by a person in power, being insulted and jerked around by a clerk in a government agency, being chiseled by an insurance claims adjuster or being bullied or beat up by a law officer or other bully, matters not. Even if it's a down and outer living under a bridge, I care.

Third, I have also developed an absolute and abiding contempt for people who take advantage of power to cheat, steal or just enjoy jerking folks around. I have contempt for people who take credit for good things which happen and explain why the bad things are not their fault. Most corporate executives and high government officials do that. I have contempt for people who take credit for the efforts and successes of others, from the dork teacher who explains to everyone how the Gaffer was her student in his formative years to the two bit manager who replaces the signature on a report done by his underling with his own. I have contempt for those who exercise power in a mean spirited way. I have contempt for the people who gravitate to positions for the purpose of exploiting them in some way; shabby little people; clerks, claims adjusters, tax examiners, bullies of various persuasions, judges, prosecutors and, most of all, the managers and politicians.

Fourth, I have great disrespect for people who are lazy and derelict in their implicit and explicit commitments. Those people who wait until they have no options left before they act. Those people who will not take the final step in a task. Those people who will not do the little things they know they ought to do. You know them. It's the engineer who will not document his work or who documents it so poorly that it's useless. It's the neighbor who lets his grass grow out of control until it rains and then uses the rain as the excuse. It's the software company marketing undocumented products which don't quite work. It's the person who can always explain why he couldn't do what he ought to have done.

Fifth, I have a deep seated terror of bible thumpers, gun crazies and other sociopaths. I firmly believe that the only difference between a sociopath and a psychopath is an opportunity which could occur at any time. It could occur while I am within range and there is no defense or precaution possible. I believe the transition from sociopath to psychopath is simply the point where the person believes he can do something criminal without being caught. He has no conscience to stop him. Only law!

Sixth, I have a deep and abiding faith in the ultimate justice of the universe. We say it in many ways. "That which you sow, that also shall you reap." "What goes around comes around." "The chickens always come home to roost." "Cast your bread upon the waters." "Your sins will return to punish you." It's something we know.

All of this, I believe, will come forth in the writings which follow. Come! Take a walk with me.

Roasting Chestnuts

At one period of our union, my wife worked in Flint, Michigan and I worked in Dearborn. It was a bit far for commuting, so while she stayed at our home near Flint, I kept a small place in Taylor. We would take turns visiting each other on weekends.

The big question in Taylor, Michigan, is what to do on a Saturday night. After you get bored with bowling, country rock and bar fights, there is not much left. Taylor is not an inherently elegant or romantic place.

We are not into bar fights and had done the country music dancing on Friday, so here we were on Saturday. I figured we may as well do our best right at home so I went shopping. Behind the jugs of vintage Ripple and Thunder Valley, I found a couple bottles of very good Bordeaux. I also got steaks and other fixings. Then, in a moment of inspiration, I decided to get chestnuts. I didn't have a fireplace but, heck, an oven should do the trick.

Things went well and it looked like it would be a moderately successful romantic evening, so I set the chestnuts to roasting while I opened the second bottle. We were sipping away when the first explosion occurred. No one told me you are supposed to pierce the chestnuts before you roast them.

I rushed into the kitchen and that's when I made my fatal mistake. It had not been bad until then and the damage could have been contained. In a panic, I jerked the oven door down and pulled the rack out just as the chestnuts began going off in earnest. The first explosion had only been a warning. The rest was like one of those very long strings of Chinese fire crackers.

I remembered my military training and dove through the door, hitting the living room floor as I rolled clear of the shrapnel which was flying everywhere. I had expected my wife to help but she was rolling on the floor in hysterical laughter. For myself, I did not see anything the least bit funny. I am sure she did not realize the danger

I was in. She has never been hit in the butt by a high velocity chestnut.

After the final explosion, we waited a bit before we went in to survey the damage. There was not much nut meat remaining for eating. Much of it was strewn over the floor, but there were a remarkably large number of pieces embedded in the walls and ceiling. I mean embedded, not just stuck on. I had a tedious task of scraping, filling and painting ahead of me.

If there is a moral to this tale, I suppose it is, "Never roast chestnuts without piercing them."

A man set a tray of chestnuts
to roasting without making cuts.
The oven did roar.
He opened the door,
and almost lost more than his nuts.

Alley Cats

People have asked me if I have always been funny. I answer, "Heck yes! When I was born the midwife took one look at me and couldn't stop laughing. My mother had to get out of bed and slap her a few times."

Not many people know I was one of twins. My brother was the one they kept. I was found in a trash can and raised by alley cats. I finally got back in the house when a cat dragged me through a basement window. Mixed in with all the other sisters and brothers, I was not noticed until Mom handed me a cookie one day and I commenced to purr. By then I was too big to fit in the trash can.

You know you are slipping when you can remember what happened fifty years ago but you forget to zip your pants.

Cataract Surgery

I had been thinking and fretting about my vision for quite some time. Most of what I do, and love to do, requires the intense use of my eyes. I write and writing also requires reading. The problem was, my vision was getting progressively worse. I thought I was going blind. In fact I was.

I finally got up the nerve and asked my doctor to refer me to a specialist. The good part is, some of my vision problem was caused by clouded lenses. The condition is called cataracts. It's correctable through surgery, wherein the natural lens is removed and replaced with a fixed focal length plastic lens. With the support of Mrs. Gaffer, I decided to have the procedure. Cataract surgery is a unique experience which I recommend only if absolutely necessary. Here is what the first one was like for me.

Mrs. Gaffer drives. We hurry up to the hospital and wait. After the normal hospital delay of about 1 ½ hours, I am prepped for surgery. The procedure was scheduled for 11:00 a.m. It occurs a little after noon.

The only pain is the inconsequential prick of inserting the IV. The nurse says, "That's the only pain you will have today."

I don't believe her but, it turns out, she spoke true. They keep pumping "Don't Give a Damn" juice into the IV. There is a view of the doctor standing over me to put in the nerve block but I don't remember him doing it. I don't care.

Next I am bundled up, taped, tied down and locked in place. There is no wiggle room. Usually, in this condition, my nose would begin to itch. This time it doesn't. My left eye is covered. My right eye is out of my control and looking directly into a brilliant white light. I hear and feel sound and motion. I hear people conversing.

Suddenly a hole appears in my field of view. I feel nothing. A few minutes later I hear the sound of a sonic probe going buzzap, buzzap, buzzap. My field of view is gradually disappearing. Soon there is only shadowy grey, like having my eye closed, though I know it is not. I catch myself holding my breath and start to breathe, carefully.

After a few minutes, I see a flash and my field of view has returned. There is some wiggling, some mild pressure and flashes of light. Then things become relatively stable. I see the white light again. More wiggling.

A little later, I hear the doctor say, "We'll be finished in about five minutes."

He is not talking to me. I am counting time though. There is an automatic blood pressure device on my arm which inflates every ten minutes.

Sure enough, before the next inflate, the tape and trussing is being removed. My left eye is uncovered. Instruments pull back and I can see the doctor's face.

He says, "Look to the left."

I do.

He says, "Look to the right."

I do.

He says, "Umhmm. Good! Everything went fine."

He is talking to me. I try to smile but my face doesn't work too good. I probably grimace. The doctor puts a patch over my right eye. Then he walks away.

After an hour in recovery, I get wheeled out to the curb where Mrs. Gaffer picks me up. She drives me home. Except for follow up, that's it. The whole procedure took 45 minutes.

There was a time of terror the following day. We went to the doctors office to get the patch removed and check my eye. My vision was completely blurred. I could not see at all clearly out of the right eye. It was much worse than before the surgery. I panicked.

Thank God for Mrs. Gaffer. She took me home and took care of me. It turned out, the blurred vision was temporary and normal, caused by swelling. I looked in the mirror. It's no wonder my vision was blurred. My eye looked like I had the mother of all hangovers.

Four days later, I can see better from the right eye without glasses than I did before with glasses. There will be inconveniences. My old glasses do not help. I must wait for the eye to heal before getting new glasses. That's six weeks. So, I close one eye sometimes and the other one at other times and I can, sort of, see. OK! I'll handle that. I can set my word processor screen to display 16 point type. I can see that.

Now for the other eye.

Jack Leg

Jack Leg, the carpenter, was good at his trade. He did careful, professional work and had a well earned reputation for quality. This is how he lost his reputation and his livelihood.

One day Fred Stead, a cousin of Jack's, arrived in town with a pick up truck and a small trailer containing his few possessions. He had just inherited a ten acre parcel of land from a deceased grandfather. He went to Jack and asked him to build a little shed for his trailer on the lot.

"Just give me something quick and dirty to keep my stuff in," he said.

Jack was reluctant but Fred was a relative and after some cajoling, he gave in. He nailed some plywood and sticks into a temporary shed for Fred's trailer. He then went back to doing work for pay. Jack did not know that Fred moved into the shed and left his trailer out in the weather.

Fred was not skilled but he managed to get a job at a nearby furniture store in the stock room. He unpacked much furniture which sometimes came in wood crates. Soon the little shed on his land grew a rickety appendage. Then another and another. Even on a ten acre parcel, the bizarre assembly of crates, sticks and plywood became conspicuous. It was in a rural community with limited codes and enforcement. Thus, his neighbors, though angry, could do nothing. They did confront him however.

"You're ruining our property values," said one.

"No one wants to live near this shack," said another.

"Why did you build such a ugly, sorry thing?" demanded a third.

Fred looked very sad. "I'm real sorry it looks so bad," he said. "I wish it was better but it's not my fault. That's the house that Jack Leg built for me. You know! You'd think he'd have done a better job for his own cousin."

Word got out quickly. It wasn't long before people driving by would shake their heads and say, "That's the house that Jack Leg built."

Gradually Jack's business began to fall off. People just didn't call him any more. No one ever told him why and he never figured it out. He died a bewildered man and his name became a synonym for inept, careless tradesman.

There is a lesson here. Never, never do a quick and dirty anything, even for yourself, but especially not for hire.

If your work is building anything at all, sooner or later someone will say to you, "Give me something quick and dirty just to get this job done. Then we'll scrap it and do it right."

If someone says that to you, just say, "NO!"

If you agree to do a quick and dirty or "just temporary" it will not be. It will live almost forever and your name will be welded to it. There will never be time to do it right. It will be extended to do things which it has no foundation to support. It will be added to and extended until it becomes totally untenable and collapses of its own weight.

When it does, folks will not say, "That's just that quick and dirty job Fred Stead, the idiot boss, demanded. It should have been scrapped long ago." They will say, "That's that piece of crap that Sam Sucker, the professional, built. He ain't much of a craftsman. He's a Jack Leg."

Whether you write software, design circuits or build cabinets, matters not. If you are a professional, you must take a long term view of your career. You are better off being fired for insubordination than to put your name on something you know is not right. Even in bad times, it's far easier to find employment that it is to put the shine back on a tarnished reputation.

Cats and Birds

Last fall, I put a bluebird house on a pole near our garden with some hope. Early this spring, my effort was rewarded. A beautiful pair of bluebirds made a preliminary inspection and were about to take a lease for the summer. Mrs. Gaffer and I were very pleased.

The following day, I looked out the window to see Mrs. Gaffer's cat sitting on top of the bluebird house looking down through the hole. In that pose, he looked, just a bit, like a vulture. She rushed out and grabbed the cat but it was too late. The birds had moved on. They had discovered they were in a bad neighborhood.

This was very frustrating for Mrs. Gaffer. We had both thought her cat was going to die a few weeks ago and she had paid the vet almost $300.00 to save the brute's life. Now she almost wished she had not done that. It was a moment of weakness which passed. She did forgive the cat. It was also a tough moment for me.

In spite of all the medication Mrs Gaffer pushed down his throat, the cat could not eat, walk or stand alone. He would kind of crawl to where I was working and look up at me. I would pick him up and place him on my lap, whereupon he would commence a ghastly, death rattle purr. He seemed content to die, so long as he could do it on my lap. Minerva, what a chore you have given me this time.

I remember sitting before my computer with the cat on my lap, trying to work on this book with tears running down my face. I was sure the stupid damn cat was dying. He did not die. One day he started eating on his own and, in a few days, came to a full recovery. Eight to go.

Last week, much to our happy surprise, another pair of bluebirds happened along. For some reason, the cat was not about and they actually signed a lease for the summer and moved in. We kept our fingers crossed. We need not have worried. Yesterday, Mrs. Gaffer noticed the cat beginning to climb the pole. Two bluebirds also notice. A big fat pregnant mama, and a very mean spirited papa. They came out of the house and went right for the cat's eyes with razor beaks and claws. Mrs. Gaffer will tell you, that cat got off that pole in one big hurry. She laughed till she jiggled. It was a true *David and Goliath* episode.

It's now very clear why bluebirds survive. They are tough. After taking on the cat, they gave us a bonus by taking on a couple of squirrels which were trying to access the bird feeder. I used a 300 mm zoom lens to get some pictures of the birds. I did not want to get too close after seeing their determination. It's clear, they are here for the summer. Very nice! Bluebirds of happiness.

Now pasta fajioli was a cat,
who thought bluebirds juicy and fat.
As quiet as a mouse,
he climbed to their house.
Fierce bluebirds did cure him of that.

Abstinence is easy when you're hung over.

For absolution, try prune juice and prayers.

Limericks

Children and lecherous adults seem to be better at writing limericks than ordinary adults. This may be due to the raucous and vulgar nature of most limericks we encounter. Many of the ones we find written on viaducts and overpasses were obviously written by children. Young horny men, with their glands at maximum production, also seem quite good at following the form. It must be so, because we find the very best examples on the restroom walls of taverns. The remarkable thing is the degree of fidelity to the structure and form in these graffiti examples.

A limerick is a form of poetry. I can write words on paper and call them a limerick. Anyone else can say the words are not a limerick but they cannot prove it. Poetry, and all art, is like that. There is no international tribunal with absolute authority in art. Therefore, anyone can write words on paper and call them a limerick just as anyone can write twaddle on paper and call it poetry. Anyone can fling paint at a wall or cut out paper dolls and call it art. We are helpless to prevent the fools of the world from supporting the charlatans of the world. What I can do is define what I will call the perfect limerick.

Because the limerick is usually vulgar in nature, we tend to think of it as non-art. However, the perfect limerick, like the Japanese Haiku, is a very demanding and difficult art form. Unlike much poetry and alleged poetry it has a very rigid structure, style and rhythm. Any slop or carelessness of form will destroy its effect.

The first requirement is that the entire story be told in exactly five lines. There is no such thing as a two stanza limerick. In addition, lines one two and five must agree in rhyme and rhythm. Likewise, lines three and four must agree with each other. This all seems very simple but, even in these basics of form, many of us fail.

There is no advice to give on rhyme. If it's not there, you do not have a limerick at all. Never mind a perfect one. The difficulty, of course, is in finding the word with the correct rhyme which will also convey the meaning we intend. Some great poets have been known to spend days to get exactly the right word.

Creating the agreement in rhyme, though difficult, is less difficult that holding the correct rhythm. Looking at rhythm, in the example on the next page, we find that poetry is similar to music. The only difference is, in music the rhythm is separate from the words. In poetry the words, or more properly the syllables, are the rhythm. Each syllable represents exactly one beat; no more and no less. We do not have the license that music gives us where we can double time a two syllable word or stretch a single syllable out over several beats to make it fit the rhythm. Especially in the limerick, no such license exists. I will refrain from a discussion of the so called free verse at this time.

The particular rhythm of the perfect limerick is similar to the musical 3/4 notation in quick time. In this sense, lines one, two and five consist of exactly 3 measures or 9 beats. Lines three and four consist of exactly 2 measures or 6 beats. Each beat represents exactly one syllable. As an option, the ninth beat of lines one two and five can be a syllable or a rest so long as all three agree. The same is true of the sixth beat of lines three and four so long as both agree. These are the only options. Aficionados of binary arithmetic will notice that two variables will allow four permutations of the form.

If all of this were not enough, the closing line of the story, line five, must not only complete the story satisfactorily, it must also present a twist on meaning or phrasing and/or a plausible surprise. No cheating here. This is not an option. It is the most essential requirement of the piece. It makes the limerick a limerick and not just a short ditty.

I have created the following example to demonstrate the form. You may say anything you wish about the demonstration as art. You have that absolute right. In addition, you may agree or disagree with this entire discussion but here it is. I have placed the example on a musical score to show the relationship between rhythm and syllables. Each line begins with an upbeat to give the proper emphasis. I had to resist a powerful urge to add melody to the score. I know of no law against that, however, I believe it would change the limerick to a ditty. One would be reminded of Irish Jigs, Hornpipes or even Popeye the Sailor Man. The Popeye tune does fit the limerick form.

Now, having said all of the above about art forms, there is one more point. Art is as much for the pleasure of the creator as for the victims. If you want to write or sculpt or fling paint at your barn, for your own pleasure, no one can stop you. You have an absolute right to do it, at least in the United States, with the possible exception of Pennsylvania. Part of that state seems to have some sort of religious law which requires all barns to be alike. Since they don't try to export it, it's their business.

Other than that, although people can criticize what you do, no one can prove it's not art if you say it is. The worst they can honestly say is it's bad art and even that is subjective. So let's enjoy doing it.

Hell

There is a common myth about hell which has to do with fire and brimstone and corny stuff like that. Hell is really much worse than that. Hell is a movie theater where you are front row center. Everyone who ever knew and respected you is there around you. Everyone who thinks you are special and everyone who thinks you are not is there. Everyone you ever tried to impress is there. The feature movie is of you, with perfect sound and lighting, on all those occasions when you thought you were alone and no one could see or hear you.

Don't you wish hell was just eternal flame?

Does anyone take the newspaper editorial pages seriously? If I ever become editor of a magazine or a newspaper, no one without a sense of humor will be allowed to write for it. It is a great deal easier to tolerate silliness than to tolerate people who are so serious about everything that their turds come out in little hard cellophane wrapped balls.

What's pure and virgin white on the outside and purple on the inside?
Holy Mary, full of grapes!

On Selecting Aftershave

I think it's getting more difficult. I don't want to smell like a saddle, even if it's an English saddle. My aura should be more subtle than that. Old Spice had a reasonable smelling lotion and a cute ditty about the logo on their bottle which I liked. Somewhere along the way they dropped the ditty and their advertising got contemptibly sexist. I didn't hurt them by stopping my business. Their sales went way up when they appealed to the high school sophomore sexual mentality of the average American male.

For a while I just used witch hazel but that smells awful. I tried mixing various herbs and spices with various alcohols but I always ended up smelling like a cheap saloon. I was in a dilemma. I don't want to smell like a brute. Nor do I want to smell like a French prostitute. There is too much mass marketed, over priced toilet water. My son finally found an aftershave for me which I think is outstanding. The problem is, it's only available in a few exclusive men's stores. It's un-advertised and quite expensive.

For me, going into one of these stores is kind of uncomfortable. I stand humbly before a clerk who is dressed infinitely better than I am. I try to keep from looking up his nose and genuflecting. It's hard to keep from handing him my credit card and begging, "Please, just fix me up." I know this guy is thinking I ought to spend at least two grand just to look human, and I'm actually spending about 50 bucks. I sure wish I could order this stuff by mail.

Years ago I was hired by Ford as a computer specialist. I started work in their Dynamometer Lab in Dearborn. I had heard rumors about Ford but the reality stunned me. I knew I was in a deep swamp when, on the first morning, I said to one of my peers, "Good Morning." and he said, looking furtively about, "What do you mean by that?"

Clara

On the facing page is my Aunt Clara. I never knew her. She never got out of that bed. She died shortly after this photo was made of what was then called dropsy. The symptoms we know of indicate she had rheumatic fever. Rheumatic fever is a bacterial infection which affects the entire body and, if not treated, can cause severe heart problems resulting in death. Now, with modern drugs, the disease is eminently treatable. It is heart breaking when children die. It's much worse to find out, a few years later, that we simply did not know enough to save them at the time. Clara was born too soon.

I found this photo in a large box of my mother's memories. Clara was her sister. The photo was what we call black and white but it had turned brown with age. It took many attempts and several hours of computer techniques to get what I have here. On the final enhancements, as I watched Clara take form on the computer screen, I particularly saw her eyes and it hurt my heart. She knew she was going to die. You can see it.

Another thing happened as the computer brought Clara to life. I imagined what she would have to tell me. I thought about how her life was and how it could have been. Then, through my heart, I heard her speak to me. This is what she said.

It isn't fair - you know!

I should have grown up to be beautiful.
I would have been homecoming queen. I would have ridden in a parade,
on the back of a brand new Studebaker touring car.
Yes I would!
Right down Michigan Avenue.

At the dance, all the boys would want to stand in line,
just to sign my card and dance with me.
I would have more boys than dances.

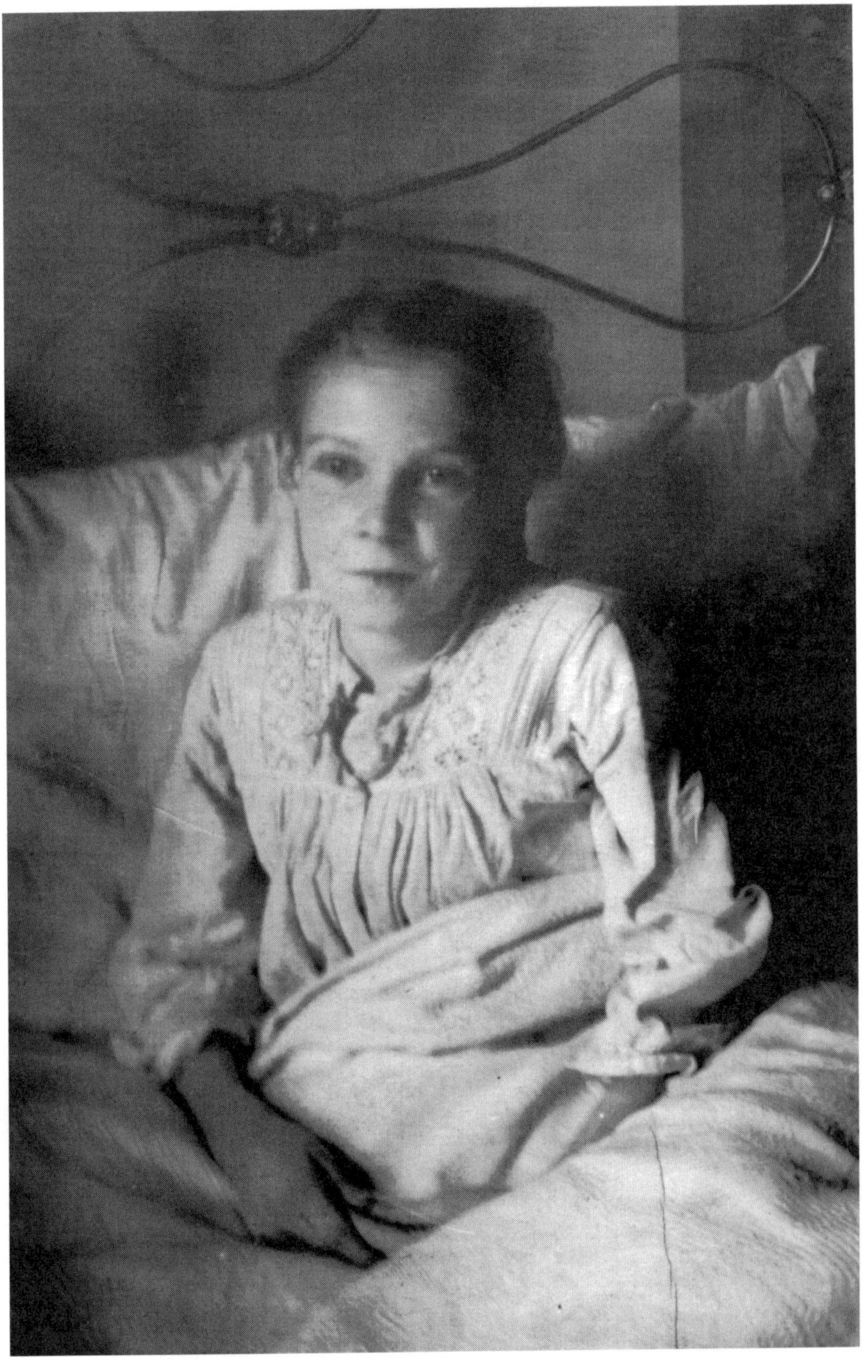

Yes I would!
And I would have to pick and choose.

My mama would have made a lovely lace and taffeta gown
and I would have swirled about the floor to the music.
And all the boys would have looked at me.
Yes they would!
Then dance and dance and dance with me.

I would have married the smartest and handsomest boy in town.
I would have had babies to raise, eleven of them, children to send off to school.
Yes I would!
And they would be strong and healthy.

We would have a swing in the yard for my children.
They would laugh and play and sing.
They would dance and be happy.
Yes they would!
They would never fall down, looking stupid and clumsy.

My children would go off to school laughing.
They say I can't go to school now. Maybe later they say.
It's not true. I know it's not true.
Yes I do!
I'll never go off anywhere, healthy and strong and laughing.

I know.

It isn't fair - you know!

The Delectable Dish

His hunt had been successful and Harold Whitmore was proud in spite of himself. He smiled at the woman beside him as he turned the Rolls Royce into the estate. She was plump and juicy. Just the way he liked them. He tooled the big car up the long gravel drive with practiced ease.

Soft moonlight washed gently over the lawn and gardens, giving romantic accent to the scene. A gentle breeze teased tempting aromas from the flower beds. It was a perfect evening for pleasure.

He smiled at the woman beside him. "This is my country place," he said. "It's been in the family for generations but it's still quite comfortable. I do hope you'll like it."

The woman tried to conceal her awe but was too far out of her element. The tasteful elegance of the Whitmore estate, the trappings of wealth and power impressed her. She exercised careful control in her attempt to sound casual.

"Sure, I'll like it honey, so long as you can please me. Ya gotta understand, I don't shack up with just any Joe that asks me. It's not just for the money. I got pride ya know! Things have gotta be right."

Five years earlier, her words would have been credible. She was still a handsome woman, but time and her trade had worked against her. Her fine blond hair still shone in the moonlight but a hardness to her features spoke of time and experience. The extra inches around her hips and stomach were not an asset.

Harold nodded. "Of course my dear. That's the most wonderful thing about this."

"What?"

"Why, the fact that a lovely creature like you would agree to come home with me. I promise! You will not be disappointed. Things will be right."

"We'll see!"

"Oh, I'm sure of it my dear. You see, I can give you anything you want. I mean that. Anything!"

He stopped the car in front of the mansion and switched the engine off.

"The place looks rather ominous from here, doesn't it? But it's snug and comfortable inside and the grounds are really beautiful."

He continued as he came around to open the door for her, "Of course, you'll be able to see it all for yourself in the morning."

"Not too early, I hope."

Harold grinned, taking her hand as she stepped out. "It will not be too early my dear. I'm a late riser myself, especially after a night of pleasant activity. Let's go in, shall we."

He escorted her across the huge columned porch and opened the massive oak door. They stepped through to a foyer with wide arches leading off to side rooms. Staircases curved up from both sides to join at the center of a full balcony. A hall went beneath the juncture to the back of the house. It was a classic movie set mansion, with dark polished wood and plush carpet everywhere. The woman was unable to maintain any semblance of cynical pretense.

"Wow," she blurted. "This is a class joint!"

Harold chuckled. "It is adequate," he said. "I would like to show you over the whole place but it's late. I rather suspect you would like to relax now."

"What I'd rather is to have a drink!"

"Yes, of course, and so would I, but first, why don't I show you to our suite. Then, while I close up the house and get the refreshments, you can be preparing for bed."

She took his arm and moved toward the stairs with that hip and body motion so peculiar to those of her profession.

"Ok, Baby. That's what I'm here for ain't it?"

Harold patted her hand and grinned. "You're all right," he said.

They went up to the balcony where he opened a door to guide her into a well appointed sitting room.

"This is it," he said. The bedroom is through the door on our left and the bath is here on the right. Sorry! No shower. Just a tub. I've never had the place modernized. I'm accustomed to it the way it is."

"That's fine by me. I'll just sit and soak while I wait for you. Maybe you'll want to do my back."

"That sounds wonderful. I think you will find everything you need. I've even purchased a nice sheer nighty in anticipation of meeting you."

It was her turn to smile. "Sure you did! But that's ok, Baby. It'll probably fit me as well as it did her and it'll save you hauling my bag up till morning."

He smiled and backed toward the door. "I'll be back shortly, my Dear. What would you like to drink?"

"Vodka on the rocks sounds good."

"Vodka it is then."

He pulled the door shut and bounded down the stairs. He was almost trembling in anticipation. He strode through the hall and stopped short at the sight of a hoary old woman sitting at the table.

"Mother!" he exclaimed. Good Lord, you startled me. Are you ill? I'd thought you would have retired by now."

"I feel fine. It's you I'm worried about my dear."

Her expression was sadly sympathetic and, though coarse with age, her voice was kindly.

"Oh Harold! You've gone and done it again. Haven't you? I had hoped that after the last one you'd wait awhile. It's only been two weeks and you know how upset you are afterwards."

"Please now Mother! You must not worry about me. Just wait until you see this one. She is so much nicer than that scrawny thing I brought home last time. She's got real meat on her ribs. This one!"

The old woman shook her head and chuckled. "I suppose there's no stopping it now she's here. It does seem a shame with so much in the freezer already though." She licked her lips and continued. "You scallywag! You knew you could get to me with that talk of ribs. God knows, I love a rib roast as well as anyone. Go ahead now Son. I'll come along with the meat saw and freezer bags in a minute."

Harold was grinning. His eyes were a little wild as he selected a large carving knife and a boning knife from the rack. His hands quivered with anticipation and the blades sparkled with reflected light.

" Mind you now, " said his mother to his retreating back. "Keep it in the tub. And, for goodness sake, wear an apron. You don't want to ruin another good suit."

Harold was thinking. "God! I wonder what I'll do with Mother when she expires. She must be tough. I'll need a ton of tenderizer." He giggled as he mounted the stair.

Elephant

I'm sitting in this sidewalk cafe having a small glass of --- mostly tomato juice. I look up in time to see an elephant coming around the corner. There's a guy up on the head, steering the thing with a long stick. They come alongside the cafe and he pulls the beast over to the curb. The elephant goes down on one knee and the guy slides down. He takes a seat at a table next to me.

I want to blurt something but I'm holding it in.

This little French waiter, with a towel over his arm, comes wiggling his cute little buns out to the table and bows from the waist.

"Monsieur!" he twirps. "How I may serve you?"

"Yeah," says the guy. "Bring me two gallons of Molson's Golden and four ounces of Bailey's."

Without batting an eye the waiter says, "Oui Monsieur." and wiggles away.

I'm still holding my peace, but barely.

The waiter struggles out with a galvanized pail of beer and a glass of Bailey's. He's not wiggling quite so well with that load.

The guy pours the Bailey's into the beer and puts the pail in front of the elephant. The beast promptly sucks it up and pumps it into his mouth while the guy sits down to watch.

I can't stand it any longer.

I lean toward him and say cleverly, "You come here often?"

"Every Friday," says the guy.

"Oh," say I. "You must be from around here."

"No. We come from the zoo across town," he says. "This is the only place will serve us."

"Well don't that beat all," I exclaim. "You take the time to bring your friend all the way across town and you're not even drinking."

He looks at me with disdain and snaps, "Of course I'm not drinking, you fool! I'm driving!"

Flat Ear

Recently we have had a few show trials in the USA. The media people became a bigger show than the trial. It was bizarre. We have millions of media people and a handful of media events. What a ridiculous mess it makes when these people swarm, like locusts, to a possible event. What a bunch of silly fools they become when, in desperation, they treat trivia and advertising as media events. How contemptible they have become. Attorneys chasing ambulances and used car salesmen seem almost respectable by comparison.

I stopped watching the Channel 4 News program long ago. By accident, I was watching it again last night, for a few minutes, when the anchor woman said that key phrase "Seen only here on Channel 4." That phrase is a large one of several reasons I stopped watching that particular show. They were about to report on a current event and the phrase would want us to believe their competitors were too stupid to be covering the same event. When I switched channels at that particular time, I discovered their competitors were not that stupid at all. Sure enough, there was the same event.

I'm sure, if we pressed them, they would haul out that tired old technicality, "But our coverage of the event is unique because of our reporters, who we mentioned in the lead in, and the phrase only means that." Sure! Then, rather than imply yours is the only coverage, you could have said, "Here on Channel 4 you will see this event from the unique perspective of our star reporter, *The New York Dork*."

One time, Uncle Louie was visiting our home for a holiday. I made the mistake of shading the truth within his hearing. He grabbed me by the neck and dragged me into the kitchen where Mother Gaffer was preparing the feast.

He thrust me before her and said, "Fetch him upside the head!"

So she did.

Then she looked at Louie and said, "Why?"

"He told a lie." said Uncle Louie.

She looked deep in my eyes and saw he was speaking true.

I knew what was coming but I stood tall.

She fetched me again.

People who know me have probably noticed that my left ear is quite flat when compared to my right ear. That flatness is a result of Mother Gaffer's whacks whenever I told a lie. I'm a slow study. The whack was always enforced with the phrase, "Don't tell lies!" I only tried a technicality once. That got me two whacks along with the phrase, "Lying is lying. You know it and I know it."

From Mother Gaffer, I learned three things. First, a whack on the ear stings like hell. Second, none of the Gaffer Gang is going to slide through life on lies or technicalities. Third, a lie is when you deliberately try to make someone believe something which you know is not true. Words are irrelevant. There could be no words at all. It can be done with body language. It's still a lie. In Mother Gaffer's world, as in mine, intent to deceive is necessary and sufficient.

I know most of these media people are basically good folks who were raised in the same way I was. They were raised by good folks with high standards and great hope. It saddens me that they seem to believe the competitiveness of their profession requires them to shade the truth. It shocks me that they are able to magically separate their personal ethic from their work. I don't see how these things can be separate. Lying is lying. You know it and I know it. No matter how you say it, it's about integrity, folks. It's about integrity.

I must be honest here and point out that I did find some of the Channel 4 personalities, at least entertaining. One I liked in particular is the fellow who just cannot keep a straight face when he is reporting bologna or advertising as though it were news. Another I liked was the best sportscaster they ever had who somehow left abruptly. He showed more class than the people who employed him, especially when he left. I also liked the weatherman.

I do like to keep up on the news and the easiest way to do it is to watch TV news in the evening while I am dining. Before you ask, I have a very strong stomach. I have tried several local channels and they all seem about the same. They take two hours to report roughly 15 minutes of real news, which includes local and national news. The remaining time is divided between various kinds of political sucking up, filler trivia and advertising. Much of the advertising is for friends and cronies of the media establishment. This advertising is very thinly disguised as news reporting and informative presentations.

I think one of the worst things about the news programs is the over voice games. These people have such massive egos that they cannot just bring us the news, they must interfere in it. They cannot let us hear what the President says, they must over voice what he is saying to tell us what they think he said. Quite frankly, I don't give a tinker's dam about what the newscaster thinks. They do this in all areas of reporting. Sometimes, reporting what was said or what happened is necessary to complete the picture. Often, it is not. Problem is, these egomaniacs can't tell the difference. They do it in all cases.

One of the useful things many news shows do is a segment called something like, *Person of the Week,* in which they feature some person they consider to be outstanding in the community. They strut and crow about this segment all week long and, when it comes to the actual presentation, they give this outstanding person a 10 to 30 second sound byte. Big deal! Most of that sound byte is obscured by the over voice of a media person telling us what the person is and what the person said instead of letting us hear it. The one piece I actually timed occupied a total of 1 minute 45 seconds of which the featured person got 12 uninterrupted seconds.

That's only part of it. Too often, this outstanding person turns out to be nothing more than one of the local political hacks, as though he didn't get enough coverage in the normal sucking up. The politician, of course, gets more than a 30 second sound byte.

I would like to see just one news show have a daily segment called *Local Good Folks* in which they would feature some local person who is simply good. This feature would contrast all the negative stuff they routinely seek out and report. Negative stuff may be easier to find. With all the time they squander on fillers and trivia each day, they could afford to give a full five or ten minute segment to this feature. I believe channel 12 of Flint proved they have the time to spare when they twiddled away 15 minutes over three days with some outstanding investigative reporting, showing that cheap skin cream is almost as good as very expensive skin cream. Something no one knew, I'm sure. Profound and informative.

I believe they would have more than enough candidates submitted by interested citizens. Of course, this would require some media person to start doing real work. Instead of shopping for skin cream, they would have to sort through and check out the submissions. They would also have to figure out what a good person is before they interviewed the candidates.

I expect a bus driver who was routinely courteous could qualify as a good person. Could we possibly spend a few minutes listening to this person explain her philosophy and why she thinks courtesy is important? Could we spend a few minutes looking into her life and situation and learn from her? I think so! If we could only hear from the person instead of the ego driven over voice of the reporter.

I suspect most cities are like Detroit. There are more than enough good people in Detroit to do this segment every day of every year. That city is filled with people. Most of them are good people. Many of them are outstanding people who have never been discovered. They deserve more than a short sound byte once a week. They deserve as much coverage as any political hack in the city.

Will any news show actually try a format like this? I think not! It does, after all, require a little more than routine. It would require a break from routine. It would require giving up some of the twaddle they dump on us every day. It would require work, thought and planning. It would feature the outstanding person and shroud the ego of the reporter. What a crazy idea.

One big problem with the TV news shows is they have no real competition. That is where the newspapers could, and should, come in.

Many newspapers became irrelevant when TV became a dominant force in our culture and TV news became the fount of instant coverage. Newspapers were no longer viable vehicles for news reporting. At that time, the papers could have changed their focus to something other than news reporting. It's kind of stupid to pretend to report things which everyone already knows.

They could have moved their focus to something which TV is unable to do, like go in depth into the things which really matter to the community. Some papers were already doing that and they are still doing fine. The ones which contained news reporting filled out with twaddle are not doing fine. They continued business as usual and degenerated into a ridiculous mob of bickering, management versus union fools.

The refocus would require them to give up talking to each other and to political hacks and get their butts out where the people are. Not just on a bull crap, big deal, one shot foray but all day, every day, all over the community. It would mean getting the so called reporters off their butts and out of their hangouts. It would mean an end to the same old columns with predictable twaddle and celebrity name dropping. It would mean the end of cronyism in the business. It would mean competition for the lead story item and top spot on the paper. It would mean an end to sucking up to the political hacks and multimillionaire franchise owners. It would mean an end to going to the same old locker rooms and talking to the same old "current" stars to hear and write the same old bromides. Most of all, it would mean going to work instead of sliding by.

I would like to see the newspapers become relevant again. We really need them to offset the enormous influence of the visual media. I would like to see the newspapers force the TV people to behave responsibly and honestly. I would like to see TV lose its monopoly on public information. I would like to see the paper people quit whining about union crap, get off their lazy buns and do something which would make the paper worth a half buck. It is not the money. Most of us have a half buck to spend. I would like to see the paper people earn their pay so union issues would fade into the background. It's not enough to work hard and make a lot of motion. You must also do something useful. You must do something which will make us want to part with a half buck.

At one time, there was room in the Detroit area for three major newspapers and a carload of suburban papers. I suspect there still is. It's not about cost and never has been. It's about value. It's not because people don't read anymore. People do read. Give us something worth our time. Throw out the gossipy twaddle. Do you have some kind of reality check to find out how many people are reading those columns?

Tell us things we don't know and can't easily find out. Investigate instead of sucking up. Look at the issue of tax funds being used to build arenas for wealthy franchise owners, where the taxpayers are always left holding the bag. Just as they will be in Pontiac. Is the Silverdome paid for yet? Will it ever be? Ask yourself if you really believe that won't happen in Detroit in a few years. Where are the guarantees? That's just one place where you have turned a blind eye. Do what you used to be good at.

When we were young and fresh and romantic, we would build a fire in the fireplace, take a shower together and recline naked on the floor before the fire. There we would do erotic and romantic things with strawberries and whipped cream. We still build the fire but we shower alone. We just eat the strawberries with cream and, for romance, we put an old Bogart movie in the VCR while we snuggle up on our recliners in our shawls and Afghans. "Here's looking at you kid!"

In the Land of Fools

There was a young simpleton wandering through the land of fools. Come late of an evening, he stopped in a small village to find lodging for the night. The innkeeper was polite but firm. There were no rooms available.

"The barn is available, he said, "if you do not mind the smell of horses, mules and dung. The loft is comfortable."

"Odor is of no consequence," said the simpleton. "I simply need a place to lay me down for the night. How much do you ask for the loft."

"I offer you a deal," said the innkeeper. "If you dine for the normal price, you may sleep in the loft of no charge."

"Done!" said the simpleton immediately.

Thus it was that the simpleton was served a simple but ample meal by the innkeeper's simple but ample wife. Being a kindly man, the innkeeper only padded the bill by one dollar. It was just, for the simpleton was to sleep free. The simpleton took himself off to rest, pleased he had been overcharged but one dollar.

He lay down and was soon sleeping the sleep of the pure of heart. Near the midnight hour, a heavy foot on the ladder awakened him.

"Who is there?" he cried out. "I have little money."

"Hush," said the simple but ample innkeeper's wife. "We don't want to wake him."

"But why are you here? What do you want of me?"

"I will show you," she said. Whereupon, for the next hour, she proceeded to educate him. She was ample in all things and she took him round the world. This simpleton had never known such curious delights. It was even more exciting than the first time he attempted the tea ceremony and accidentally poured hot tea on his parts. She left him exhausted and he fell immediately into a deep sleep.

In the morning, he sought to take a hasty leave without disturbing the innkeeper. It was of no avail. The innkeeper, looking very stern, barred his way at the door.

"You should know my woman can keep no secret," he

admonished. "She told me of your pleasures."

The simpleton stood mute. He could think of no answer.

"You do not deny this thing?" demanded the innkeeper.

Still the simpleton could not answer.

"I will have no more of this," cried the innkeeper and smote him full atop the head. The simpleton fell to his knees and the innkeeper booted him in the ribs. He tore the simpleton's purse from him.

"I cannot recover my simple but ample wife's purity," he said, "but I will make you pay."

He thrust the purse in his apron and booted the simpleton again.

"Begone now!" he ordered. "Never come this way again."

Later, as the simpleton limped down the road, he thought, "Well, he was not such a bad fellow after all. He only overcharged me one dollar."

That Damned Clicker

John Madden and Jerry Glanville may be the only two people announcing football who actually understand the game. Unfortunately Madden has that damnable clicker. He takes an action and jerks it back and forth until no one can tell what's happening, all the while shouting "See! See! There! There! Boom! Boom!" A suitable punishment for the engineer who gave him that thing would be to splice together, in an endless loop, all the footage of Madden going goofy with it. Then lock the guy in a room with the video being projected on all four walls and the ceiling along with the sound of Madden's commentary. Make the guy stay there until he goes insane.

How do I know it was a man who gave him that thing? All women have at least some instinct for self preservation. Women know better than to give an obnoxious toy to a child because they may have to suffer the consequences. A woman would not give a toy drum or a trumpet or a box of fire crackers to a kid. Nor would a woman give that damn clicker to Madden. It was a male engineer who thinks all gadgets are "**Neat-o**!"

Detroit

It's full of whores and pimps,
dealers and hustlers,
workers too,
workers all,
with energy.

The energy that's here,
that's being let loose,
every day,
and pissed away,
and people.

Not the mobile middle class,
clerks and managers
and well paid workers
Drive in at day.
At night away.

Not them in their capsules,
Chevrolets and Fords, Man vans.
Not them. No! Not them,
but the people
of Detroit.

Them as live and fight and fuck here
and love and hate here
And kill and die here.
They have it!
The energy.

The power they have.
Power running loose.
Running loose - destructive,
killing, wrecking,
angry power.

The power to rule they have.
The power to grow.
The power to purge.
They have the power
to build.

A city flowing free.
They have the power
to build a city free.
These people
of Detroit.

When flies start swarming and biting, it always indicates some imminent change in weather. They are reacting to changes in barometric pressure. In that, flies are almost as dumb as the stock market people. The slightest thing will change their behavior. If the president has gas pain, the market falls like a rock. It doesn't stop until he farts and says, "Ah." Never mind that presidents come and go and corporations are supposed to be forever.

When I was 25 years old, if I had learned there were two women for every man my age, I would have dropped to my knees and worshiped God. Now I'm 67, and there really are, but we are all so old and decrepit nobody really cares.

The perfect sewage disposal plant, in Detroit, would take what it gets from us, mix it with water from the Detroit River and produce detergent, fertilizer, alcohol, plastic and burnable gas. It would then return water, clean enough to drink, to the river. It may not make a profit, but it should be cheaper that what is being done now. If it could produce the alcohol in the form of a good Chianti, that would be acceptable.

Shouting

Years back, I had a friend, Larry, who swore his sister-in-law could out shout a pipe organ at point blank range. I am happy to say, I never met the woman. This memory was brought to mind by an incident last week. Mrs. Gaffer and I were on the road and having breakfast. We had the misfortune to be seated in the same room with a young woman who seemed to believe her rather mundane affairs were of interest to everyone in the restaurant. The person she was talking to was no more than two feet from her but her voice carried to the parking lot. I have noticed, in public places, there are almost always one or more persons like this woman. It leaves us the choice of talking loud or not conversing at all.

Bible thumpers are the worst of all in the shouting department. In my limited travels over the USA, a disproportionate number of the restaurant shouters were bible thumpers bragging about their flock, their organ, their parish, etcetera. One of the saddest times in my life was when a sister was undergoing serious surgery. We waited in a very large 10,000 square foot, room full of other worried folks. Of a sudden my sister's bible thumper said we should join hands and have a little prayer. OK! It can't hurt. So we did.

Instead of saying a simple prayer for the people in the circle, this guy shouted in a resonate sonorous voice for everyone in the room to hear. I suddenly realized he was not praying for my sister and he was not trying to comfort her family and friends. This jerk was advertising. He was saying to a room full of people, "Hey! Look at me! I'm a holy man!" I wanted to puke.

Shouting seems to be a very common phenomena. Sometimes the reason is apparent. Most of us have visited homes where one of the residents has some degree of hearing loss. In these places, everyone tends to shout. The more severe the loss, the louder we shout, even when we know the person cannot hear at all. The people who live there don't stop shouting when they leave. They develop a habit of shouting. Sometimes this carries on for more than one generation and we find a house of shouting people with no obvious cause. This causes me to speculate that shouting may be a communicable disease. I know when I have spent some time in a place like that, I tend to continue shouting. I always recover because Mrs. Gaffer has techniques for bringing my behavior to my attention. I notice, from this, that we can be unaware that we are shouting.

Quite often the reasons for shouting are ridiculous. We tend to shout at foreigners who don't understand our language, as though volume alone would be enough to overcome the language barrier. We also shout at pets. That's too bad, because animals respond much better to a soft gentle voice. At least my dog does. I think the most unfortunate of all is our tendency to shout at mentally impaired people. We think talking louder will somehow cause understanding where none exists. I know, it never helps to shout at me when I don't get it. It only befuddles me further. In fairness to my ex-bosses, they usually figured that out. "It don't help to shout at the Gaffer. He just screws up worse."

Mrs. Gaffer hates VCR's. She says, "They are all different. You have to read a 25 page manual just to use them. If you make the slightest error in programing you may as well start over. If you try to recover instead, it gets progressively more confusing. Sometimes you can't start over because the thing won't reset. Sometimes, if you punch buttons, it starts to work but you don't know what you did to cause it. Don't you just hate VCR's?"
I advised Mrs. Gaffer to never ever, ever mess with computers. They are an order of magnitude more stupid than VCR's. I treasure her friendship too much. I have no wish to live with a madwoman.

Thoughts on apathy:
Oh well. Sigh.

You know you are slipping when your faithful beagle claims free agency.

Campfires, Cookies and Cocoa

Here is a four line song I wrote for young ladies to sing around a camp fire. It can be sung solo as a simple song or in group as a four part round. It can also be accompanied with guitar or piano. A guitar would probably work better around a camp fire.

Of all the arts, I believe music is the most powerful in its ability to evoke the human spirit. I love music and have poked around at it for many years. Now I have set myself the task of learning enough about it to write simple songs for publication. The reason for my renewed commitment is not rational as it comes out of a smoldering rage.

This is unusual. Though I often react vigorously to frustration, I get over it within minutes. I have not nursed such an ongoing pique since I abandoned gainful employment. This one was caused by a television news report. The last time something as stupid as TV made me this angry was when I watched a United States President rip open his shirt, push his belt down and expose his fat, sloppy, beer filled, naked gut to the entire world. Of course, I was terribly embarrassed, for myself and all other US citizens. He might as well have mooned us.

This particular news report was about Girl Scouts singing songs. It seems that some music people's union or association or some such mindless group has decided that Girl Scouts should pay royalties when they sit around a campfire singing songs. It was a very short filler type report and I did not want to believe it but the reporter repeated it. I went off the deep end.

After I calmed down enough for my mind to resume functioning, I made this vow. I will write and/or collect enough original, simple, wholesome songs to fill a small song book. The idea is, once a person buys the book they may perform the songs anywhere, anytime for any purpose, royalty free. Now, I have the commitment of Wesoomi Publishing to publish the book and market it as soon as I have assembled it. I expect the price to be very reasonable.

C F Dm C C
I will be with you my friend, lov-ing and su - - -
F Dm C C F Dm
port - - - - - - ing you. With you thru your laugh ter and your
C C F Dm C
tears. Know - - ing that you will come through.

I have designated a working title of *Campfires, Cookies, Cocoa and S'mores*. I believe it will be a soft cover, hip pocket type of book containing less than 100 songs. I have defined the requirements. Each song must be simple in melody and construction. There should be no more than 32 measures of verse and no more than 16 measures of refrain. Songs may have more than one verse. Content must be wholesome, with concepts of love, friendship, duty, fairness, honesty and achievement. And sure, the songs should be fun to sing. Since the book will be for all young women, references to specific divinities, which are exclusive by nature, would be out of place. Though these concepts are hugely important, they belong in hymnals rather than song books. Each piece will have the chords noted with the music, since the guitar is a favorite campfire instrument.

I do not have a time table yet, as I am still learning about music. This first effort is a corrected update of a song I thought I wrote several years ago. I hope you will not criticize it too much. Remember it is a first effort by a student. It is intended to convey an idea. Nothing more. I will continue to study and write and collect pieces in the hope of producing the book sometime next year. Wesoomi will, of course, derive some nominal profit from this publication. However, none of the composers, whoever they turn out to be, will be paid. They must be satisfied with one free copy of the book where they will find their name associated with their contribution.

Someone asked me if I was a genius.
The truth is, I just have gas pains. It makes me look thoughtful.

Possibly, the best way a person could serve his country at this time is to be a gadfly; to just go around biting these big dead bureaucratic horses on the butt. Take a lesson from Socrates.

Mother Gaffer used to say, "When you've done all you can, you shouldn't do very much more."

Spelling

I am the world's worst speller. I depend on the spell checker in my word processor and on my editors. Although I like to write in a humorous vein, my biggest fear is that, someday, I will make a spelling error which will still be a legitimate word and it will turn out to be the funniest thing I ever wrote. Here are some examples of spelling problems which could easily go awry.

Whither goes the horse?

Since it doesn't make ***sense*** to cinch the saddle before it's on the horse, we must first determine ***whether*** the ***weather*** will affect the horse's ***withers*** and cause them to ***wither*** as we also make sure the horse is not a ***wether*** in drag.

If we wish to have an **effect** on an object we must first **affect** an attitude which will allow us to **affect** the object we wish to have an **effect** on.

I wish people would really be **all ready** when they say we're **already** ready.

If I create a **parable** and it's wrong, I don't worry because the **parable** is **repairable** such that I will have a **reparable**. On the other hand there is no **antidote** for an **anecdote**.

I was being very **forward** when I wrote the **foreword**.

When you say **alright** it's still **all right,** either way, but consistency counts.

It would not be **clever** to use a **cleaver** to **sever** your finger because the pain would be very **severe**.

I told a **lie** when I said I drank the **lye** to clean out my pipes.

Whence this Book

I am writing this book to you, my audience. In so doing, I picture the finished book in your hands. Now, the question occurs, "How do the ideas and thoughts get from my mind into a physical book and into your hands?" I had to learn how that happens. I thought, perhaps, you would want to know something of what I learned. This is not a technical manual, just a tour.

There are four distinct processes involved in bringing a book to you. These are: the writing or authoring of the book, the prepress activities, the actual manufacture of the book and the distribution and marketing. These things can all be done by a single person. It is possible. Usually, however, each process is done by separate people or groups. In addition, there are different kinds of books which cause some differences in each process. I will be talking about a simple, mostly text book like this one.

The writing of most books begins with an idea. Often, a person has an idea for a book and begins to write. This writing, good or bad, comes from the person's belief system. Sometimes a publisher will perceive a market for a certain kind of book and will commission someone to write it. This writing, usually good but seldom great, will come from a mechanic. We call these folks wordsmiths. Too many times, a sensationalist event will occur and the big publishing houses will bid ridiculous fees to the participants for their story. These will be twaddle for the masses. There seems to be an unlimited market for this stuff. It's nothing more than pulp with a hard cover. Sometimes, these books take the form of an apologia for bungling the only important task the person ever had. In any of these cases, the book must be written.

Whether the writer starts with an outline, sets himself a daily word count or uses some other technique, he has some basic rules. Most important of these is the use of a computer based word processor. The chances of getting a hand written document accepted for publication is zero. The chances of getting a typewritten document accepted for publication is very close to zero. It's simple. The publishers, even the small ones, are set up to handle electronic input. They do not keep a staff of keyboard entry people. Labor costs money. It's important for the writer to make sure the word processor he uses can produce acceptable output. He can do this by using one of the mainstream word processors.

In addition to using a word processor, the writer is also expected to do the basic book layout. This is simply the separation of the book into chapters, pieces or sections. This is very basic. In my case, page numbering is not required. In fact, it would be a nuisance in the final layout and design. Along with this, the writer will select and designate the positions for any graphic material required. I am talking about photographs, drawings and charts.

It's not enough to have a good idea and plot. The writer is also expected to submit a technically correct document. I mean spelling and syntax. Nothing will make an editor reject a manuscript faster than finding a few language errors on the first page. We know there will always be a few errors but the writer must be a good technician.

Finally, the writer has a book in hand. Now what to do? For the freelance writer, it's find a publisher and convince them to publish the book. Not easy. Most publishers receive large numbers of unsolicited manuscripts every day. In the industry, these are called, "Over the Transom" submissions. They are dumped into a slush pile. If an editor ever has some free time (not likely) he may go fishing in the slush pile. Normally, the submissions just lay there. The publisher has no time and no moral compulsion to respond to them. In truth, most of them are bad.

For the writer who has studied the industry's requirements, there is an elaborate dance to be performed. It starts with a query letter to the publisher. It usually ends with a rejection, after too long a time. Thus a new writer may (probably will) discover that the big publishing houses will not deal with him. This is usually the case. Even when they will deal with him, it may take too long to bring the book to market. Big houses have big bureaucracies. Big bureaucracies, no matter where they are, move slowly. In addition, they may not put enough marketing resources into the book to make it viable.

I am aware that newspapers and journals like *Writers Digest* are forever publishing "new writer" success story articles. I have read some of them. In every one I read, I discovered, in the details of the story, one common fact. The new writer had an inside track of some kind. He either knew someone in publishing or he was part of the industry in some way.

All is not lost. There is an ever growing number of small publishers. These small operations are becoming viable due to the large gaps left in the publishing market by the heavy feeding giants. There is considerable room for thoughtful books by and for thoughtful people. In addition, a growing number of writers are discovering, they can act as their own publisher. It is an option when the would be writer believes in his tome. This is a good test for the writer. How much hard cash will he be willing to invest in his own book. Perhaps the publishers rejection was justified. If he decides to take the chance, another small publishing house may be born.

Another option for the freelance writer is to find an agent who will present his book to the publishers. I think it's kind of like trying to find an attorney. You won't know if you have a good one until it's too late. For sure, if they want to be paid by fee rather than commission, I will pass. A final option is what is called vanity press. These are firms which will charge the writer to design and manufacture his book and deliver the copies to him. They do not market the book even though they call themselves publishers. A thoughtful writer will realize he can have it manufactured himself for much less money.

Once a decision is made to publish the book, it must be prepared for the manufacturing process. This preparation is called prepress. It includes cover design, conversion of graphic material to electronic files, and book layout. In the case of colored material like photos and charts, there is an additional process called color separation. All of this is done using a computer with a variety of software. There are also decisions on book dimensions and type face to consider. Much of what is done here has to do with marketing.

When graphics are required, the first step will be to convert these to electronic files. This is done with a device called a scanner which is connected to a computer. There is special software to operate the scanner. There are some simple calculations for establishing the correct scanning resolution to insure good copy from the printing press. It's so simple, I am allowed to do it. For the writer, possibly the most important graphic will be his photo on the back cover of the book.

A relatively new development in graphics is the electronic camera. These do not use film but record their photos as electronic image files which can be directly input to the computer. Currently, the affordable ones suffer from poor resolution. I will wait a few years.

Once the graphics become electronic files, we have other computer programs which allow us to enhance them in various ways. Yes! Photos can and do lie. We can also create separate files for each color if necessary. There are just a few companies which make these programs. I have never found one which is easy to use but we must use them. The publishing industry is completely dependent on computers and software.

Cover design has everything to do with marketing and, sometimes, nothing to do with the contents of the book. Everyone has seen the garish covers with raised gold letters and brilliant color splashed all over the place. I don't know if there is an inverse relationship between the cost of the cover and the value of the book. It would not surprise me to find it thus. I tend to believe that simple elegance is best for most covers with, perhaps, a little silliness for my books.

Cover design should be done by someone who understands the printing process in cooperation with the writer and publisher. I am leery of folks who call themselves designers. The ones I have seen tend to want to show off their imaginative skill rather than enhance the book. The most important things in cover design are the eyes and mind of the customer. Who is the book for and what do we want them to see? Again I say, simple is better.

The book layout is not dependent of the cover design and can proceed in parallel. Again, there is special software to do this task. This program is used to lay out the book and produce an output file in a special language called Postscript. Postscript is a proprietary product owned by Adobe Systems, Inc. It is a page definition language which is used almost exclusively in the publishing industry. All book manufacturers who accept electronic input will insist on Postscript files. I don't know of any who will not accept electronic input. I doubt they would stay in business long.

At this point the dimensions of the book are known and things like margins and page numbering can be established. We also have a very good idea of the page count. Thus layout can proceed. Look in most any book and you discover there are usually three parts to it. The front of the book will contain title pages, a table of contents, a copyright page with disclaimers and an ISBN number. Sometimes there will be a library of congress number. There can also be a blurb about the author. At this point we stop calling him a writer and get more formal. This first part could also contain a foreword about the book. If there are salutary quotes from reviews, they will go in the very front of the book.

How we get reviews before we have a book is a good question. We can do this by making proof copies for newspaper and magazine reviewers from a preliminary layout. We can also send the raw word processor output to reviewers. Another way is to actually go far enough in the manufacturing process to produce blueline copies. I like the first method.

The center of the book is the actual work of the author. This is laid out in chapters, pieces or sections as the form of the book dictates. The layout consists of making the book look nice and make sense. For example, graphics must be placed with the words they complement or emphasize. Chapter headings must be clear and stand out. Chapters usually start on new pages, preferably the right hand page. Sometimes pages may be left blank just to make this happen.

The third section of the book, if it exists may contain advertising, references and an index. It can also contain appendices of supplemental material. Sometimes there is nothing to justify a third section so we skip it.

Finally, when we think we have it right, a Postscript file is created and a proof copy of the book is printed on a desktop printer. If we are going to get a surprise, we want it now. We don't want to be surprised after the printing plate negatives are made. That's a very expensive surprise. When we are satisfied with the proof copy, we are ready to manufacture the book. This is where it starts to get expensive.

There are many small and large book manufacturers around. A look in a metropolitan phone book will confirm that. Here we must distinguish between printers and book manufacturers. There is nothing wrong with either one. It's simply a matter of what we want to do. Book manufacturing is concerned with printing and binding books. Printers can do a great job of making sales brochures and other straightforward printing jobs. They are usually also good at duplicating. They are not normally equipped to do binding. The equipment is too expensive.

To begin the manufacturing process, the Postscript files are read by a very expensive, high resolution device called an imagesetter. By expensive, I mean thousands, often hundreds of thousands, of dollars. This device uses laser imaging to convert the files into negative images of the defined pages. These negatives look exactly like very large black and white photo negatives. In practice, each negative will contain several pages, often sixteen. This is necessary because the big presses don't print one page at a time. They print sheets of pages either from rolls or large sheets of paper.

At this point, blueline copies can be made from the negatives. These can be cut and folded to make a proof copy of the book. They smell just like a blueprint because that's what they are. I don't like them but the writer must check the blueline to make sure it's what he intended. If not, some cutting and pasting of the negatives may be required. In an extreme case, new negatives may have to be made. It's a good idea to spend extra effort in the beginning to avoid this. When we are satisfied, extra copies can be sent to reviewers if desired.

Once the book is proofed and approved, the printing plates can be made. Most printing plates are no longer metal. Don't think Ben Franklin. Most plates are now made of plastic. The negatives are used to expose the photosensitive coating of the plates and the coating is selectively etched away with chemical baths. When finished, the plates are washed to neutralize the chemicals. Thus printing plates are produced. They are then mounted on the rollers or beds of a printing press.

At the same time the book is being made, the cover is going through the same process on different machinery. The cover is done separately because it's on different weight paper and it will have a special finish. It will also often have color requirements.

There are many kinds of presses used in the printing business today depending on the kind of resolution desired, the volume of printing to be done and the color requirements. There are whole books and technical education courses devoted to explaining and understanding these machines. For myself, I just stand and watch with big saucer eyes. I will trust the specialists. The folks who run these machines are part chemist, part technician and part magician.

If you ever get a chance to tour a modern printing plant, jump on it. It's a fascinating world of machines with metal levers, rollers, plates, arms and fingers flying everywhere. Metal fingers, not people's fingers. You can watch a giant roll of paper unwinding so fast into a machine, you must wonder why it doesn't get shredded. I was told, in confidence, sometimes it does. Usually, though, the paper comes out the other end, neatly printed and folded into 32 page signatures.

The books are printed in what are called signatures for economy of paper and handling. In most cases, the most economical signature is 32 pages. Did you ever wonder why books sometimes have blank pages at the end or superfluous babble in the front? That's one of the reasons. Remember the 16 page negative? One for each side of the paper. The detail of how proper page order is maintained is handled when the negatives are made. Meanwhile, the covers are being printed and cut on a separate press.

For those who want more detail about the printing business, I suggest starting with an encyclopedia. *Compton's Interactive Encyclopedia* is just one which has a long discussion on printing and it's history with a bibliography.

Binding is the final step in the book manufacturing process. Book binding machinery is every bit as fascinating as printing machinery. Although there are several options for binding, most of the books you will find at your local bookseller are perfect bound. The signatures are gathered together and clamped. The spine is milled off and the cover is glued on. The book is then trimmed on the three open sides. This is fine for most paperbacks. It has the disadvantage that it will not lay flat and will eventually come apart.

Some books, like cookbooks and journals must lie flat to be useful. The three methods used for this are wire-bound, comb bound and lay flat binding. Of these three, lay flat, which looks just like a perfect bound, is the most attractive. Wire bound, just like a Spiral Notebook and comb bound, a plastic comb instead of wire, both have a cheap look.

For authors with big egos, books can also be bound with hard board bindings and embossed covers and all that stuff. I have a theory that most hard cover books are not read but are bought by dilettantes to decorate their parlors and create the illusion of intellect. This book will be perfect bound.

Now we have a book. Big deal! How do we let people know about the book? How do we get people to buy it? That is called marketing and distribution. I wish I knew how to do it. I do know distribution and marketing are done by different people.

In the United States, there are a number of firms generally called book distributors. Some are national and some are area specific. These firms function mainly as brokers between publishers and booksellers. They take books which they determine are marketable and present them to the booksellers. They will have a sales staff and an ongoing relationship with the retail firms. They usually also warehouse books for quick turn around.

Before you condemn these firms as worthless middlemen, picture a rickety old man like me going door to door selling my book. These folks perform a very useful function and they take a very small slice of the pie for doing it. They are efficient like all get out. If you want to know who gets the biggest slice of the pie, it's the retailers. Take a look at the cover price on this book. The retailer bought it for about half of that. Now you know why they can discount it. The rest of the pie goes off in very small slices. The distributor, manufacturer, publisher, prepress shop and writer must divide it up.

The dilemma is, how does Wesoomi Publishing get one or more of these brokers to handle my book? To do this, it's not enough to have a great book like this. We must also convince them that Wesoomi and I will do our share of the marketing. We must convince them that we will convince the public it's a great book. How do we do this? Ugh!

We must send proof copies of the book to newspapers and magazines and create a press release which will cause the reviewers to want to read it. We must also send proof copies to radio and TV talk shows. We must send copies to anyone else who we think will talk about it. We can even send one to Jerry Falwell. If he condemns it, we are on the way.

Finally, we must offer me up as a sacrificial lamb. I must be willing to go on shows and babble like a fool. Public babbling is something I'm terrible at, terrified of and hate. I must also be willing to sit in stores and sign books and do nice-nice. I must be polite for God's sake. I may even have to talk at garden clubs. It's enough to make you want to puke but it's part of how the book gets to you. I hope you appreciate it! Thank you very much!

Even if we do all of the above, we may not get a distributor to go handle the book. The publishing industry is somewhat like a very tight private club and it takes more than excellence to get in. For newcomers who cannot muscle their way in, it takes something near boorish determination. If this book fails, it will be because we failed in that effort.

We may have to use extraordinary methods but I don't think we will let this book fail. With or without help, we will find a way to let you be the final judge. No closed room committee is going to decide that this is book is not marketable and shut us out.

Our beagle sleeps in Mrs. Gaffers bedroom. It makes her feel quite safe. She knows if danger is afoot she will be quickly warned. Her bed will hump up where the dog is struggling to get underneath it.

If Colin Powell were dumb enough to drag his family through the sewers and slime of Washington politics and run for president, I'd be smart enough to vote for him. Of course, it would be a mean spirited thing for him to do because it's obvious his folks are decent people, undeserving of that kind of emotional violence.

The Great Booboo Takes Questions.

The Great Booboo

The Great Booboo Gives Answers (Nothing is Taboo to the Great Booboo.)

What is the sound of one hand clapping?
The center of the donut.

How many gurus does it take to change a light bulb?
Only one but he must first pray for the soul of the departed bulb.

How many light bulbs does it take to change a guru?
Just one, if he stares at it long enough.

What is the secret of transcendence?
The secret is to know it's not necessarily up.

What is an Archangel?
An Archangel is an angel with a bad back.

How may we transcend our temporal existence?
Stand barefoot on a wet steel plate. Wet your left index finger and place it in an electric light socket.

How many metaphysicists does it take to change a light bulb?
What light bulb?

What is the meaning of life?
Whatever it means to you.

Booboo, will we ever understand?
You will come to understand when you no longer need to be confirmed. Now take a token and go.

Is the Bible a true book?
Yes. The truth still comes through. The dogmatists who meddled with it missed the point. They changed the window dressing and left the message intact.

How should I approach the I Ching?

Take one tablespoon of sesame oil 4 hours before you consult The Oracle. Things will come easily.

What is Armageddon?

It's a little town in Texas near the Alamo.

How may we achieve enlightenment?

There are two methods. One is to systematically suppress all of your temporal senses. There are those who will offer you various, noble paths for doing this but it doesn't matter how you do it. It's darn hard work and frightening. The second method is much easier. Just do the next task as impeccably as you can and wait. You will gradually become an empty bulb. The Divinity will light you up when you are ready.

If a tree falls in the forest and no one is there to hear it, did it really make a sound?

Simon and Garfunkel.

What happened to Schrodinger's cat?

The cat never escaped the box but Minerva, in her infinite mercy, expanded the box to enclose the universe. Thus, the cat, like the rest of us, is not aware he is in a box. He moved to New York and became a Yuppie broker whereupon he became enormously wealthy through insider trading.

Will I lose my identity when I become one with the Divinity?

NO! You will recover your identity. It is like recovering from amnesia and remembering who you really are.

What is the nature of the Divinity?

The divinity is a big network server containing all knowledge, energy and wisdom. Something for everyone.

Is that a parable?

No! It's a single bull. A parable would embody two complementary concepts.

What can we do about government and taxes?

Do what your Savior said. Render unto Caesar, etcetera. But get a receipt!

Is the Gaffer enlightened?

Not at all. The Gaffer is hip deep in a karmic sink hole. Did you bring my Tabby Treats?

Where do we go when we die?

Many folks go to Boca Raton. Others go to Bradenton.

What can I do about my Karma?

You must eat your Karma, as must we all. It's best when candy coated but it lasts longer that way.

How many pilgrims does it take to change a light bulb?

Just one but he must be enlightened.

Booboo! How do we deal with boredom?

Seek help immediately! Boredom can quickly become a terminal form of insanity.

Terminal insanity Booboo?

Yes! If not treated it is followed rapidly by depression, apathy and death.

How can we avoid boredom?

Those who do useful work are never bored.

What is the nature of wind?

It is said, "The wind is the breath of the Divinity." It is not said from which end of the Divinity the breath emanates.

Is it desirable to strive for wealth?
  Only if you enjoy wallowing in a karmic cesspool.

What then should we strive for?
  Nothing! If you feel the need to strive, take a laxative and do your duty.

What is a Ponzi scheme?
  An investment swindle, like Social Security or The Michigan State Lottery.

Who was Heisenberg?
  Just a guy who was not quite sure. He was also poor at marketing. It's often said he did the work which made Schrodinger famous.

What is the nature of evil?
  It is said, "Evil sucks!"

Does the Devil really exist?
  Indeed! He lives in your soul awaiting his chance.

Do witches exist?
  No! They were all murdered at Salem.

Were witches evil?
  No! Just different.

How can we avoid evil?
  Start by remembering the old children's rhyme, "Do not smoke - and do not chew - and don't hang out - with girls who do." *anon.*

Was Walt Disney a real person?

No! He was a cartoon character who, like Pinocchio, came to life and got out of hand. He lived long enough to create an aberrant concept of animal personas which outlived him and continues to corrupt the cultural psyche.

Who tied the Gordian knot?

Mrs. Howe's little boy, Gordie.

What is the nature of rain?

Rain is the tears of the Divinity. Its purpose is to wash away the stains we put upon the earth. Sadly, we soil the earth more completely each day and the Divinity must weep harder and longer. Hence the floods. Myth has it that this happened once before.

When will the Savior return?

The Savior is already among us. You will find him under an overpass, in the city, near the soup kitchen. If you go to him, he will save you but you must go on your knees. The overpass has a low clearance where he lives. When you go, you must take him a gift of ham and cheese on rye with a dill pickle, a roll of toilet paper and a clean shirt. Size 17 ½ - 36. Do not try to take his wine. It's sacramental and he will kill you.

Why do we have presidents?

It's their Karma and our penance.

What is the nature of the adversary?

The adversary is within you, except when Congress is in session. Then he's in D.C.

Can anger ever be justified?

Even great saints can get pissed off. It is written that J. C. kicked over a few tables.

How can I prepare for the next life?
Don't worry about it. It is enough if you try to get this one right.

Who is Minerva?
Minerva is the Gaffer's designer God. It is not a creation. It's simply the face of the Divinity which he wishes to see.

How many faces does the Divinity have?
As many as we wish. The Divinity shows us the face we can handle. Think of it as structurally similar to an enormous database containing all knowledge, power and wisdom with an infinity of user views.

What is the nature of the Divinity's love for us?
Love is a word with no cosmic meaning. What you perceive as love is nothing more than perfect wisdom in action.

How do we achieve full employment without inflation?
A tight corset.

May I use drugs to speed my journey?
No! Drugs will allow you a clouded view through the window but you will still be outside. The door will be closed to you. This will ultimately delay your journey.

Where do demons come from?
A demon is simply another face of the Divinity which someone called forth and separated. Once separated, demons draw their power from the evil in our souls. They wish only to return to wholeness but our meanness will not release them so they fight back. A demon can always be dispatched by one of pure heart. Clergy are advised against it. Silver crosses or bullets don't work.

Why do boar hogs have teats?

So people will be able to complete the sentence, "My manager is as useless as ...."

What can we learn from Freud?

We learn that to wiggle our ears can be an erotic experience. As a cat, I knew this all along.

Who is this Gaffer guy?

The Gaffer is an entity who shares a body with another entity in a symbiotic relationship. The other entity is a dead butt, self righteous bore; good at routine, detailed tasks.

What is the nature of our relationship with the Divinity?

You have a direct link, but the access code is obscure because you have not bothered to use it.

Booboo! What are you? Who are you?

When I am connected, I am nothing more than Minerva's mouthpiece. When I am not connected I am nothing more than a dumb cat with a bad temper.

Should we worship you Booboo?

Absolutely not! Worship the Divinity in whatever form you choose. If you worship me, I'll just spray on your furniture.

Why do we have a Congress?

To thwart the President.

Is the Divinity everywhere?

Yes, but mostly over your right shoulder, opposite the guy with the scythe. They work as a team.

What is the gross national product of the United States?

Coca Cola, cigarettes and pornography.

Why did God make humans?

It was a crop failure in the early days of genetic engineering. He intended to make turkeys. He came quite close.

When is a particle not a particle?

When we interfere with it, it tries to hide from us by disguising itself as a wavicle. It's simple self-defense.

What is the nature of sleep?

Sleep is the refuge of our souls from the madness and illusions of the temporal world.

What is the purpose of dreams?

The dream is an enforced form of mental exercise for couch potatoes. For others, it's an adventure and link to the wisdom of the Divinity.

What is the nature of Kundalini?

It has many natures depending on how it's served. It should always be prepared by boiling in salt water until al dente (about 12 minutes at sea level). For the main entree it can be served with meat sauce or red sauce. With a bottle of Chianti, crusty garlic bread and a plate of sliced ripe tomatoes drizzled with olive oil, Chianti, salt and basil, Kundalini becomes a meal. It can also be used as a supporting side dish with various dressings and sauces.

What is the nature of our inner self?

Pepperoni, cheese and beer, with occasional hot pepper.

How does one achieve Nirvana?

You cannot get there from where you are. You must go to Toledo and turn east.

What is the nature of Nirvana?

Nirvana is warm and fuzzy.

What is the beginning of wisdom?

The student knows the beginning of wisdom when he understands that Jack-O-Lanterns can never again be pumpkins.

How does one achieve wisdom?

It is difficult, for it is said, "Those who know do not speak and those who speak do not know." To begin, one must journey to The Shrine at Redmond.

Can we ever achieve perfect wisdom?

The pilgrim achieves perfect wisdom when he becomes one with the music.

What is the difference between faith and religion?

Faith has no need of a collection plate.

May I strive to become a highly paid athlete?

First things first. Learn to spit and scratch your privates unselfconsciously.

When will the world end?

When we no longer need it. It's just a conceptual thing.

What is the sound of one lip flapping?

The perfect political speech.

If an elephant passes gas and no one is there to smell it, did it really make an odor?

You bet! Nothing escapes the attention of the Divinity's proboscis.

What is the difference between the political right and the political left?

Only the names. Otherwise, they are identical. They stand back to back on a circle. Across the diameter, opposite them is compassion and thought. Within the circle are all the shades and combinations of human emotion and intellect. It's not a line with extreme ends. It's a circle with one extreme point of non-thought. All true believers reside at that point where they avoid the pain of thinking.

Moles

Every manager I ever worked for had at least one mole. Moles are sick little folk who suck up for various reasons. It could be for special treatment, promotion or simply for a pat on the pointed head. A mole will babble everything he knows at every opportunity. One interesting thing is, in all cases I knew about, the managers despised these little turds more than the workers did, even though they used them.

The other thing about moles is, the workers find out about them very quickly. It's simple. The egomaniac manager can't help revealing that he knows things he should not know. After that, a simple process of logical elimination reveals the little turd. Once revealed, the mole becomes more useful to the workers than he ever was to the managers. He can be used to pass information and opinions without confrontation. When the occasion demands, he can even be used to misdirect the manager. I know of one manager who spent several hours in a dingy bar because he was told his workers were planning a lunch party and he wanted to catch them. They did have a party, but not at that bar. It was a nice day and they went to a local park.

I know you are asking so here it is. No! I have never encountered a female mole. I want to believe it's because women would not do that. I want to believe it but, I admit, it could be because the average female is too clever for me.

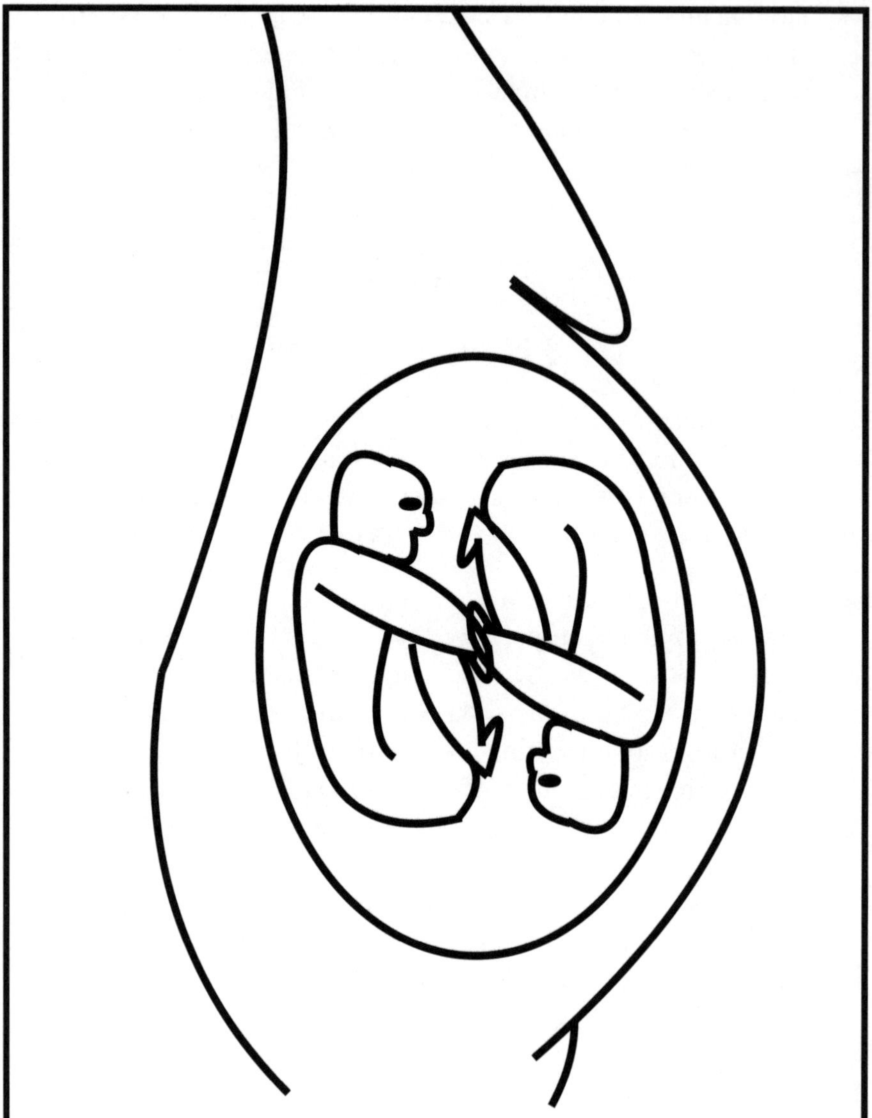

Well twin! Your face is very lopsided,
but you do have a charming smile!

Creativity and Craziness

There is an intimate relationship between creativity and craziness which I intend to illuminate in the following discussion. The creative abilities which are so foreign to adults and so natural to children reside in the same dark corridors of our mind-soul wherein lurk the madmen of our mind-soul. I believe it is possible to access these creative forces without releasing the madmen.

A discussion of creativity and craziness could easily justify a set of doorstop sized books. Perhaps some qualified person will write that set someday. In the interim, let us consider this piece to be an overview of the subject. Although the progression of ideas will be coherent each one will be treated lightly. There will be no exhaustive discussion on any particular idea.

I begin with the rather insulting premise that, except for small children, we are all crazy. I believe I am crazy and all the people I know and love are crazy. I wouldn't have it any other way. To be sure, there are varying degrees and circumstances of this condition. Sometimes we call craziness mental illness. Sometimes we call it a phobia. Sometimes we call it neurosis. Some of these conditions are severe and tragic. Some are so common we don't even think of them as worthy of consideration. Never mind treatment. The inordinate fear of heights or spiders or snakes, for instance, or the lack of creative talent.

Some people are crazy and we make them managers. They suffer from the rather bizarre delusion that people can be managed and they are capable of doing it; even though, in general, they cannot manage their own lives. Some people are crazy and we call them eccentrics because they are wealthy. Then they go out and off someone with a high powered rifle. We should deal with them as murderers, not crazy people, unless we are willing to treat all murderers as crazy people and excuse them on that basis. Some people become crazy by systematically suppressing their sense of conscience until they reach the point where we call them sociopaths. This is one baby step from the criminal condition we call psychopath.

We have no need to examine all manifestations of craziness for our discussion. I will proceed by looking at just one, very severe condition, called multiple personality disorder. From there we can look at the relation between this extreme condition and the personality problems which plague us ordinary folks. I will discuss how these ordinary problems relate to our creative talent and describe techniques for recovering the creativity we always see in healthy children. I will finish by briefly discussing some other theories and practices for human growth, pointing out some reckless ones which we would be better off to avoid. I will try not to ramble. Apparently I do that so often, Mrs. Gaffer has named it the Gaffer Syndrome.

There have been, and still are, some very terrible methods of dealing with craziness. We have, in our history, burned people alive and drowned them to satisfy an insane notion of demonic possession. Exorcism is still practiced by some very serious, fiendish madmen in our culture. In the few disgusting cases I have looked at, I concluded that these priests were simply engaged in the physical and emotional torture of people whose only crime was being a victim of multiple personality disorder.

Instead of trying to heal the victims, the priests victimize them further. This exorcism is nothing more than a process of coercing an emotionally diminished person into remaining diminished so he does not offend the priesthood. Exorcism is a barbaric practice with no basis in logic or fact. It has nothing to do with the Divinity.

We define multiple personality disorder as an extremely rare mental condition in which two or more independent and distinct personalities develop in a single person. Each personality may alternately inhabit the person's conscious awareness to the exclusion of the other personalities. These separate personalities are usually so much different from one another in behavior that we must recognize them as individuals. They even have different names. The classic story by Robert Louis Stevenson, *The Strange Case of Dr. Jekyll and*

Mr. Hyde, takes a fictional look at this phenomena. The dramatized story *Sybil* by Flora Rheta Schreiber is a much more painful look at a real case history.

My theory is that multiple personality disorder is an extreme case of a rather pedestrian condition which I will call personality fragmentation; a form of craziness. Think of the human being as a complete masterpiece of personality; spontaneous and filled with curiosity, love, trust, generosity, joy, and creativity; just as we find in a very young child. We expect to find this complete package in a child but we are quite surprised when we find anything like it in an adult.

In the adult we usually find a small subset of what the human started with. We must then ask the questions, "What happened to the missing attributes? How did the process of aging diminish this person to the point where he is not even aware that something has been lost?" We all know people who are always worn out, eternally angry, eternally defensive, cynical, submissive or cowardly. These people were not born this way. Whither went the missing pieces?

I believe these missing pieces, which I call fragments, are still within us and usually suppressed, but very much part of our subconscious selves. The fragmentation occurs as a result of the traumas we all suffer and our solutions to them. The persistence and magnitude of the trauma are both important. Each event can be large or small but when it is severe or when it occurs often or continuously, we will change ourselves in a way designed to mitigate the pain it causes.

Sometimes this is good. Most of us have touched something hot enough to cause a burn. Few of us touch the same hot thing twice. We change our behavior immediately. This learning and adjusting ability is a survival attribute but it can be turned against us when we encounter emotional traumas. A parent or other trusted adult can cause profound changes in a child's personality through simple repetitive actions. An act as seemingly harmless as calling a child "Mr Big Shot" can cause him to suppress part of his creative self, if it's repeated whenever he expresses an idea. Thus, when we reach maturity, most of us have various sized fragmented blocks of ourselves suppressed.

This brings us to the major difference between ordinary dysfunctional fools, like you and me, and the clinically defined multiple personality. In these poor souls we find the trauma was not only persistent but was also physically and emotionally extreme. In this case the victim will withdraw and suppress major parts of his personality. Not only that, this suppressed part is very likely to be enraged. Justifiably so. If this withdrawal occurs in stages over time, we can get more than one suppressed personality or alter ego. This becomes a dangerous problem when the multiple personality victim loses control to an alter ego to the extent that he is not aware of what is happening.

I speculate that the multiple personality disorder occurs when a final fragment is separated from the previously controlling ego and what remains does not have enough substance to maintain control. When the victim is already close, a seemingly trivial event can precipitate this. It's the final straw phenomena. The victim literally loses coherence and becomes a collection of fragments. The fragments do not have the consistent energy to maintain control but they can do one heck of a lot of damage before they lose it. What's worse, the control may pass to another one of the fragments rather than back to the "main" ego.

For most of us, our missing pieces just cause us to become somewhat dysfunctional. We are not as spontaneous, joyous, graceful or creative as a human should naturally be. It's tragic but it's not usually a threat to survival. Other than that, we all occasionally do crazy things which the dominant personality cannot explain. "I don't know! Something just came over me. I lost control." I believe this loss of control is a manifestation of a suppressed alter ego.

Giving some autonomy to these personalities is one of the risks of opening ourselves to creative activities. We can only be creative to the extent that we are willing to risk being crazy. These fragments reside, after all, in the same part of the mind-soul which gives us inspiration and creative ideas. The aha's of life. With autonomy, sometimes these personalities do crazy and stupid things, usually out of rage for something which has been forgotten by everyone except the injured alter ego.

As we open to these subconscious identities, sometimes we can heal or at least soothe the pain and we are better off for it. The fragmentation is reduced. We live in better internal harmony. We can also suppress these alter egos at the expense of suppressing our creative talent. The penalty for this is eternal damnation. A lifetime of being a clerk, banker, middle manager, insurance claims adjuster or even a CPA. You get the idea. The point is, a great deal of our creative talent is embodied in these personality fragments. Our creativity is held hostage, in a way, by our subconscious alter egos.

We can access our creativity and allow the alter ego out so long as the main personality remains in charge and is aware of everything the alter ego does. Then the only problem may be the urge to explain stepping out of character. For us ordinary folks, the danger of the alter ego taking charge does not exist. Multiple personality disorder is very rare. In most people these alter ego personalities are two dimensional and no threat to our stability. It's just a little bit of craziness.

One of the problems with creative people is that most of them do have personality disorders and we really don't want to associate with them. The electrical wizard Steinmetz, according to history, was a classic example. Extemely creative people are in a very small minority. They are very difficult to find. Then when you do find one, you discover he is so messed up you don't want to deal with him.

Many of them are alcoholics or borderline alcoholics. In general, we find that their personality disorder takes the form of self-destructive behavior. Drinking, drug use, chain smoking, careless sanitary habits and aggressive activities are some of the problems. Some of them exhibit careless behavior in general to the extent that they are unaware of dangers around them. In addition, most are egomaniacs who just make us simple folks angry.

Craziness is usually not as pronounced in us ordinary average people. Serious craziness happens to super-creative bright people. Van Gogh was nuttier than a fruit cake but his paintings are masterpieces. The more creative we are, the more susceptible we are to craziness. We open up that Pandora's box of the subconscious wherein all creativity and all craziness sits together, happily holding hands. You can't get one out without getting some of the other. All the fragments of our life which were separated by the traumas of our lives reside in that dungeon. Each of them holds a piece of the creative talent we lost along the way.

As I have opened to my own limited creative talent, I have identified within myself several alter egos. The most active and troublesome one I call Little Willie. He was formed between the ages of about two and fifteen. Fifteen is where he stalled and still lives. He is enraged and will probably die that way. A great deal of his rage comes from the fact that he was, and still is, powerless. His anger is justified. He is the one who was clubbed into submission by two adult, thug, school teachers. This harkens back to the days when children were to be seen and not heard; when brute force and intimidation were tools of the adult world in dealing with children. "Spare the rod and spoil the child" was not just a rhetorical phrase, it was an accepted philosophy of child rearing.

In counseling, I discovered this physical abuse was just a small part of the cause in this dysfunctional alter ego. Emotional abuse abounds in our world when dealing with children. Put downs are a prime tool used in undermining the ego of what we call troublesome children. These, of course, are the ones who embarrass and frustrate us by asking questions and using logic in response to bull shit answers. The ones who beat us at our own game when we try to play clever word games with them. We often respond with ego crushing put downs. These are, in a sense, emotional clubs, often just as damaging as physical violence.

When put downs don't work, the ultimate response is what happened to Willie in school. Physical violence. We can always beat kids by using muscle. This combination of abuse is why Little Willie remains chained in the basement of my subconscious. He has not been able to rise above his rage.

Somewhere, between the ages of five and fifteen, other alter egos formed. There was a young adult who wanted to be called Bill not Willie. He also wanted to be a hero and he picked fights with the school bully knowing he could not win. Much of the time another alter ego rescued him from these stupidities. This rescuer has the ability to turn aside wrath with humor and a flashy smile. Humor is his defense against a dangerous and arbitrary world. He has no name but he lives.

There is also a fragmented female alter ego. She never received the power she wanted because she wanted to use another method of turning aside wrath. She would give a man anything. The little pig is on a tight collar and a short leash. I can imagine what would happen if I went to, say, Durham, NC, and gave her control long enough for me to walk up and hug a big tobacco chewing Bubba. I would not come back from NC. They would bury me at Chapel Hill.

Of course there were other fragments. Some have been healed and some still lurk. Enough of this. You know, if you look, you will find the same concepts within yourself. The important thing to me is, by opening to the creative part of my subconscious, I begin a process of integration. Healing takes place and I am stronger for it.

In discussing ways to recover lost capacity and expand our personality, we confront another problem in language. There was a time when the words pathology and disease implied a physical anomaly. Unfortunately, those words have been extended to include emotional, mental anomalies. Thus, we have no easy way of even discussing these conditions without lumping them in with the physical. This is a large part of our dilemma. We don't even have a decent language to discuss personality problems, let alone address them.

Treatment becomes kind of an ad hoc affair and we find that anyone can hang out a shingle to do it. Theories abound, from the ravings of religious nuts to mystics, psychics, astrologers and bartenders. This could worry us unless we realize there is no convincing evidence that these folks do any worse than the so called professionals. The rate of recovery and growth seems to be unrelated to the theory, the method of treatment, or the absence of treatment.

One thing seems to stand out in all of this. There is considerable anecdotal evidence that many people will recover creative function if they get a great deal of loving support and space to act out their problems. No theory is even needed. Sadly enough, most of us do not find the time to create that space, even for the ones we love. It takes one large helping of commitment and personal courage. It requires a person who can give unconditional, non-judgmental support. This support creates the space for a person to begin a process of personal growth.

The goal of personal growth is to have the complete ego and creative talent of a child welded to the wisdom, knowledge and experience of the mature adult. The goal is to have a genius. The theory is that any person not physically damaged has the potential to be a genius. This genius we can define as the totally creative person. At this point, we acquire the childlike insightful connection to the Divinity. We cannot give the child the experience of the adult. However, I submit, with effort we can return the child's attributes to the adult.

It seems that unconditional, non-judgmental support is the basis of all methods which actually work. There are a great many theories and therapies which, in some way, embody this concept. To the extent that they focus on creating the supporting environment, they offer us the opportunity to recover our fragments. I have examined several of these theories. One of them with a five year personal involvement as a client and as a counselor. I believe it worked. I was also involved, to a lesser degree, in others. Let's take a look.

The most important of the theories to me is a creation of Harvey Jackins, a Seattle based man. Jackins is important to me because his theory is the one I used and know most about. It may or may not be the best method of personal growth but it does work when practiced honestly. It's very possible that Mr. Jackins is deceased by now. I lost track.

Jackins called his process *Re-evaluation Counseling* and he founded a community of participants which he called, ponderously enough, *The Re-evaluation Co-counseling Community*. My nearest guess is that the community at its peak numbered some 200,000 persons spread over the country. There was a great deal of ritual behavior and hyperbole within this community when I participated. Some of it was specified by Jackins and some was slipped under the tent flap by his disciples. For the neophyte, separating the hyperbole and nonsense from the discipline became a problem and is the main reason the community eventually disintegrated. That's just history. The tools developed by Jackins remain viable.

Here is the essence of his theory, in my words. It is not about healing, it's about rediscovering and integrating lost capacity.

As we grow and develop, we inadvertently experience traumas of one form or another. If we had a great deal of caring support at the time of each trauma, we could experience an appropriate emotional response, such as crying or rage, and the emotional pain of the trauma would be dissipated. It could then be set aside in true closure. Much of the time, no such support is forthcoming, so we suppress the emotional response. The trauma is then internalized along with some portion of our life energy and creative talent. I call these internalized portions personality fragments. When enough of the same type of them are internalized, we have an alter ego lurking in our subconscious cellar.

To the extent that our life energies are engaged in maintaining these internalized traumas, they are not available to us in our current activities. We become inflexible, rather than creative, in our response to the world. As Mother Gaffer would say, "We get sot in our ways." The good news is, there is no statute of limitations on these alter egos. They are always fair game. We can hunt them down any time after the event. We can re-experience a trauma and dissipate the emotional energy which holds it to the alter ego. Chipping off each fragment as we expose it allows us to have closure on past painful events wherein we recover the creative energy they have tied up. Jackins developed techniques for doing just that.

When we cut through all the crap, the practice reduces to this. Two people agree to take turns creating a supportive space for each other with the proviso that they will examine their history and personality toward the goal of reintegrating lost creative capacity. It's a masterpiece of simplicity. It only takes two people who want to get better to create a growth environment. In a suitable private place, one person gives unconditional non-judgmental support to one other person for a specified time. Then, they switch roles for an equal amount of time.

With the encouragement of the person in the support role, the one in the client role looks at his current behavior patterns, evaluating any that seem to be unwholesome. This examination always leads to some past trauma or group of traumas whose energy can then be recovered through the appropriate emotional response. When this is done regularly over time, growth or recovery takes place. This does not require a therapist. The partner can be an acquaintance or friend. It must be someone we can trust. Because of the crap that can occur in emotional involvement, it should not be someone we know intimately.

There are just a few key concepts to this practice, or any like practice, which often get lost in the dogma. When the keys are ignored or forgotten, the practice simply will not work. The most important of these is the unconditional, non-judgmental support. We cannot help a person by judging them or by explaining their shortfalls. We can help by giving them a loving space where they can risk pain while they examine and relive past events. The supporting person must be capable of observing and approving emotional behavior which would be inappropriate outside the counseling environment.

There is a second key point which I have noticed in my study of various therapeutic practices. I have watched a great number of people talking the talk who never improve. After much observation and thought, I conclude that these people want an excuse or game. They want to pretend they are trying real hard but they do not want to change. In that case, practice becomes no more than a pastime. Of course, it is sociable and probably as good as bridge, chess or pinochle in that sense. The key is if you don't want to change, you won't.

In hand with that is another thing I have noticed about attitudes. Many of us do not believe change is possible. It's the old, "That's just the way I am" notion. Isn't that odd? If we saw a clumsy cat, we would immediately know that cat was not normal. We would not say, "That's just the way it is." We would say, "My God! What's wrong with that cat?" I find it a bit bizarre that we can see a diminished human and say, "That's just the way he is." The key is, we must realize change is possible.

I suspect the resistance to change is rooted in a fear of what may result. Getting better may mean accepting our commitments. Even the implicit ones. There is the risk of being expected to be more responsible. There is the risk of having to take on more work. There is the risk that we may have to make real changes, get off our butts and act creatively. Worst of all, there is the risk of losing all our excuses, of not being able to fool ourselves anymore. Never mind fooling others. Thus, people who are "getting by" are likely to evade any activity which could cause real change.

Finally, to reiterate a previous point, when a counselor and a client are emotionally involved, the attempt at recovery will not work! That's all we need to know. We don't need to tell folks not to mess around or that emotional involvement is wrong. We should make it clear that messing around is not therapy and will quickly undermine the client-counselor relationship. It may be great but we must decide which relationship we want. Both with the same person is not possible.

For the counseling to work, it is important to love your client without being in love with your client. Sex may be great and neat but it's not therapy. Rules are not necessary. If people come into a counseling situation and treat it like a meat market, they will lose in the end. It's important to note that no one person can cause the problem. It takes cooperation and each person must bear responsibility for his or her acts.

To summarize: given that we recognize we are in some way diminished; given that we want to recover our potential; and given that we can find a way to create an environment of unconditional non-judgmental support; recovery of lost creative talent is eminently possible.

For the folks who would rather have Harvey Jackins' theory in his own words, try writing to Rational Island Publishers, 719 2nd Ave. N., Seattle, Washington, 98109-4102. If his books are still in print, they may have them. The book you want is *Fundamentals of Co-Counseling Manual,* by Harvey Jackins. It contains the entire theory and detailed practice of Re-Evaluation Counseling.

In addition to Re-evaluation Counseling, I have looked at, read about and messed in several other theories and tools for recovering lost creative capacity including pretty much all of the great psychological theorists of Western Civilization. Many methods of treatment for craziness have evolved from the theories of these great men and women. The problem I find with most of these theories and practices is they require a professional practitioner. Most of the screwed up people I know cannot afford a plumber. Never mind a 100 buck per hour psychotherapist. In addition, a paid therapist has a vested interest in prolonging the treatment. Of course, I'm biased. I believe most therapists are like most bible thumpers, either fools or charlatans.

I did try some group therapy. Depending on the facilitator this often turns into nothing more that a bull session. It's ok, but we could have more fun doing it in a bar. Yes! Therapy can take place in a bar if we stay sober. In fact it's very therapeutic to stay sober and watch other people think they are more and more clever as they get stupider and stupider. We could even say it's sobering.

Here are two practices I checked out which I think are awful!

The first is L. Ron Hubbard's *Church of Scientology*. I read his book called *Dianetics*. It defined a theory and a procedure for restoring lost potential. The procedure did contain elements similar to those found in Jackins' work but the similarity ended in practice. I went with a friend to check out the church at their office in Royal Oak, Michigan. We talked with a fellow who defined himself as a "Clear" which, at that time, was the highest level of human devolvement possible.

It did not improve his credibility with me when he told us he was a salesman. It also troubled me when he described women as "chicks". In addition, since he thought he was alone with two "normal" white men, he explained apologetically about blacks that, "we gotta let them in to keep our church status." If he was a "Clear," then I want to be at least opaque if not downright reflective.

I also took the *Erhard Seminar Training* when it was fashionable. It consisted of two weekends of vicious assault, by the facilitator, on the psyches of the participants. The purpose of this entire procedure was to coerce the people into a realization of one simple concept which everyone knows but few people realize. To wit: Your life will only work to the extent that you accept responsibility for it and keep your commitments. To the extent that you break your commitments and transfer responsibility, your life will not work. This is, of course, true. Ignoring this fact was another of the factors which hastened the demise of Jackins' community. Sadly, the Erhard method of impressing it was inexcusable emotional violence. By any other name, it is brainwashing. The problem being, when you reduce a psyche to that level, you have an open vessel into which you can pour anything at all. No thank you Mr. Erhard!

Everyone I know needs therapy. That is, they could benefit from therapy. To be sure, most people would not accept that statement. If a person is reasonably functional, they will consider themselves to be "normal" and will pooh-pooh the idea that they could be better. If they can hold a job, feed their family and keep their yard clean, they accept what and where they are. They must be normal because they are just like their neighbors. Never mind that they are in a dead end job. Never mind that they have to struggle to get out of bed and go to work. Never mind that they hate their jobs. Never mind that they live for the week end, then waste it going very fast, in small circles, on a three wheeler, a snowmobile or a jet ski.

It may be just as well that people ignore the idea of emotional improvement. The sad fact is, we don't have any therapists who could help them. Anyone who realizes they need help could be just as well off going to their local bartender. The better alternative is to get with another person and start a self-help group.

I think it's better to try, than to wait until we get to the end of our life, then look around and say, "Is that all there is?" It tears me a new bunghole to have seen so many people complete their lives in anger or despair. They have a mouth full of ashes and they know, deep inside, it didn't have to be that way. If we want to function at our full potential and end our life with some degree of satisfaction, isn't it worth a try? The one thing I want to know when I die is, I did not waste all of my life. I want to know, somewhere along the way, I made the effort to be useful, creative and constructive.

Just one more point, before I leave this subject. The reason the state should never be allowed to define or treat emotional problems is that opposition can be defined as emotional illness. If we let that happen, there will be no loyal opposition and George Orwell's *1984* will finally catch up with us, just a few years late.

What of the Buddha

A simpleton was sitting at the feet of the Master.

In his youthful enthusiasm he presumed to question the Great One.

"Oh great Master," he said, "If I should meet the Buddha on the road, how shall I act?"

"Off the sucker! Blow him away!" snapped the Master.

Greatly confused, the simpleton ventured, "But why, oh Master, should I want to kill the Buddha?"

"Why! Why!" roared the Master. "Because, you dolt, he is interfering with your journey, as you are with mine."

Much humbled, the simpleton hung his head and began to weep.

The Master, feeling pity on the simpleton, reached out, patted his hand and said gently, "Go now and contemplate these things while you sweep the court yard and wash my Town Car."

The simpleton scurried off to his duties, delirious with joy. He knew no more than he knew before, but he had been touched by the Master.

I have a big lump on my forehead. I believe it's the result of a discussion with Mrs. Gaffer who accused me of using bad words when I get excited.

I said, "If there were just one word you would have me never use again, what would it be?"

She quickly replied, "The F word."

Whereupon I responded, "Consider it F-ing done."

I'm not sure what happened next because it was very fast. Now I have this lump. Apparently, she is unable to differentiate between the adverb and the expletive.

What would your mother say if she caught you reading a book like this?

I Saw What I Saw

I'm standing on the corner, waiting for a bus.

I sense someone beside me and look around.

There is this beautiful young woman wearing high heeled shoes. Nothing else!

I look straight at her forehead as I begin to perspire.

I look at my watch, then crane my neck back and forth looking - praying for the bus - any bus!

I try to clear my throat, but it's dry. I wheeze.

I can't help it. I have to make sure I saw what I saw.

I look.

I saw what I saw.

She smiles. I gulp.

"Nice day," she says in a ordinary friendly tone.

"Ye-ye-yes. Nice day for a rus bide," I squeak.

She moves closer to me.

I start to pray for a bus.

Then I hear a door slam and rapid footsteps approaching from behind.

"Mary! Mary!" I hear shouted. "My goodness child. You can't go out like that!"

My pulse slows and I feel greatly relieved.

I turn around and there is a middle aged motherly woman, wearing an apron and flat heeled shoes. Nothing else!

My heart plummets.

She smiles at me and shakes her head.

"Do you believe it!" she says. "Kids! She's forever going out without a hat!"

She takes the kid's arm and says, "Come along now and get your hat Mary."

Just then I hear the bus.

I turn toward the bus before the lady turns around.

There are some times when I don't want to know if I saw what I saw.

The Golden Years

This was originally intended to be a stand up routine. If you would like to use it in your act, go ahead but please give proper credit.

You know that age is a relative thing. Some people think thirty is old.

When I was a childish fifty, I was at a small party for a friend.

This young snot was introduced to me.

"I don't see anything wrong with older men," she said. "I bet you're interesting for your age."

"That's very thoughtful," I said. Then I got her phone number.

After the party I called Boca Raton and gave the number to my Grandfather.

Many people think old is funny.

I want to talk to you about being old. I want you to get an understanding of what it means to grow old - to be old.

I'm old now so I can talk.

OLD!

So you think old is funny.

I say, 'Oh Yeah!'

Funny .... Arthritis!

Arthritis!

You know what that means?

Means you can't tie your shoes. Means you can't cut your toenails. Toenails get long - get hard - get horny and ugly. Means - You go to bed with your wife. You start to maneuver around. Your toenail snags and tears her new nightie.

She gets ticked.

Doesn't matter. You weren't going to do anything anyway.

OLD!

You think it's funny?

Funny .... Urinary incontinence .... Funny!

Urinary incontinence!

You know what it means?

Means you pee your pants sometimes; like when you were a kid. Except, when you were a kid you knew you were doing it but you didn't care.

When you're old you care but you don't know you're doing it until it's done. "Gee, I wonder what's causing that warm feel - - Oh damn!"

That's why we wear dark clothes.

It ain't cause we're necessarily stodgy.

Old women do it too. ... Pee their pants. .. Or whatever they have on.

They make special diapers for us. Call them Attends.

Ain't Attends, they're diapers! DI-DEES!!

Think that's funny?

They advertise them in AARP magazine. Yeah! We even have a magazine. And an association.

The American Association of Retired People. AARP!

Sounds like something you would do after a bad lunch.

AARP!

AARP! AARP! AARP!

I'm a member of AARP.

I even get the magazine once in a while. It's supposed to be a monthly but it comes at irregular intervals.

Old things are like that.

Irregular.

OLD?

Emphysema!

What's that?

Not much. It just means you can't catch enough breath to let a decent fart.

That's all.

Thank God I don't have that yet.

Yet.

Funny!

Old.

Prostrate trouble!

Funny?

Prostrate trouble?

Doesn't mean you pee your pants. Means you can't pee.

Happens to men.

You think you have to go. You walk in there. You belly up to the trough, or whatever. And you stand there .....

And you stand there .... And you wait.

People come in .. they go . . they go.

You stand there.

You wait.

People come in. You think they're looking at you.

You smile.

You wait.

You stand there. You look around. You smile.

You say "Well Charlie, you got everything in hand?""Yuck yuck yuck.

"I am not going weird!"

"Hey! I am not!"

"So OK! I'll mind my own business."

You stand there. You know, if you strain, if you push, it's all over. It'll never come then.

So, you stand there.

Finally the feeling goes away.

You go back to your desk feeling inadequate as hell.

You sit down and try to relax.

So you do.

And then .... You feel like you have to ....

You wonder why old people are such diddlers?

Diddlers.

Means we diddle around.

What else can we do?

When we retire we get to have hobbies.

Hobbies.

The kids want to keep us busy ... Keep us out of the way.

So they get some kind of tools and put them out in the garage.

Don't want us diddling around in the house.

Hobbies.

I have a hobby. I mess around with wood. I try to build things.
Old guys do that.
I'm out in the shop.
Diddling around.
Hand rubbing a nice piece of maple.
All of a sudden, I feel an old, but not forgotten feeling.
For some reason, the damn thing is waking up.
All by itself.
Some people probably think we carry around a can of fast setting lacquer for just such an occasion.
Not true!
We wouldn't remember to use it.
I start to holler for my wife.
"Woman! Hey Woman!
"I got ... I got."
I check to make sure.
"Yes!!! I got one."
Now where the hell is she.
"Come On Woman! This is important."
Finally she answers, but you know it's too late.
Too much stress and excitement.
"What's all that racket out there?"
"Oh nothing. I just wanted to know if you were ok.
"Nothing important."

OLD?
I can tell you about old.

Same Sex

Like all the issues of this culture, the issue of "same sex marriage" has become polarized around the concepts of morality with screaming and shouting on both sides. As usual when this happens, the government, along with most everyone else, misses the point. The purpose of the noise is exactly that, to deflect attention from the real merits of the case. Those who make the most noise are sure to be the ones who are least sure of their ground.

The morality of homosexuality is irrelevant. If that were the only case we could make, I would have to support the demand for government recognition of the so called "same sex marriage." If prohibition taught us anything at all, we should have learned that concepts of morality cannot be enforced. However, there is a much more compelling argument against government ratification of the issue.

To wit:

Implicit in the institution of marriage is the concept of exclusion. We pledge our troth.

Same sex marriage, then, implies exclusive homosexual behavior which, by it's nature, is sterile.

Now, take a step back.

From a cultural and racial standpoint, exclusive homosexual behavior is suicidal. It is aberrant in the extreme from that standpoint.

The explicit function of government in a democracy is to sustain, promote and preserve the state, its culture and its people.

Thus, there is no way the state can endorse cultural and racial suicide. It is not necessary to single out homosexuality. The state cannot endorse any lemming like behavior which carries with it the implicit destruction of the culture.

To be fair, I must point out that abstinence is also aberrant for the very same reason. The difference is, to my knowledge, no priest or nun has ever demanded that the government recognize or endorse the celibacy of the priesthood or of nuniness. They only ask that we leave them alone. I can say "amen" to that. I can also say "amen" to leaving homosexuals alone. For goodness sake! They have enough problems. Our culture has a very sorry record of intolerance against people who look or behave differently. I can only say that record is disgusting and crap. We need to hitch up our drawers and take a hard look at the meanness of our spirit. Leave people alone for God's sake!

The truth is, our culture is full of abnormal, not necessarily crazy, behavior of various kinds. We are a free people and diversity, even aberrance, is the price and the blessing of that freedom. Sometimes, abnormal thinking and behavior produces delightful results, as in the case of Buckminster Fuller's domes. There is no reason to attack unusual behavior so long as it does not threaten us. Neither do we need to sanction it.

We could hope the homosexual people would let us take the reasonable course. Ignore the private behavior and accept the human. If I went about flaunting my personal sexuality in the public arena I would expect to be ostracized if not arrested. I don't accept the notion that homosexuals should be exempt from the common civil behavior which makes us a functioning society. It's not about hiding what you chose to be. It's about being civil.

I will continue to resent any kind of discrimination be it against or in favor of homosexuality; but we don't need to legalize same sex marriage to show tolerance of homosexuals. That's a phony argument. There are no special political rights inherent in aberrant behavior. I can only hope that our congress will take a change of pace and not be stampeded, this time, by a very loud and obnoxious minority. We do need to understand that the homosexual community is a very small minority. They have no inherent political power except, perhaps, in California.

The ex-senator Dole could best demonstrate the foolishness of being influenced by noise. He discarded the larger population and embraced an extemely loud and obnoxious, right wing minority, giving away an election he had locked. I told my spouse so at the time. I said, "That mistake will cost him the election." If he had asked me, I would have told him too. He didn't ask me! Can you imagine that?

As to the morality of homosexuality. So what? Where is our writ from The Big Guy in the Sky which gives us the power to define morality? If homosexual behavior is immoral, then most of us, in our hearts, are immoral. Most of us have felt an emotional attraction to one of our own sex at one time or another. Few of us act on it because we are more attracted to the opposite sex and we know it would screw up our lives.

For myself, I am not easily attracted to anyone emotionally though I like most people. I find many people who are physically attractive and many who are intellectually attractive. It takes a very high degree of the combination to cause emotional attraction in me. I rarely find that. In 67 years, I have found it about a dozen times in women. I have found it only once in a man. It was so unusual to me that the person was gone from my life before I realized what was happening. It's just as well because nothing but pain and frustration could have come of it. My puritan ethic conditioning would have seen to that. With my fragile ego, the stress could have sent me to loony land or beyond.

This is a true news item as reported on local TV.
A guy robbed a shoe store and took the cash plus a new pair of leather boots.
He got arrested and went to court.
He lost his case when he put his feet up on the defense table and the store clerk identified the boots he was wearing.
It's a shame he had to go to prison.
If he was a little dumber he could go to Lansing or even Washington.

UFOs in Roswell

No one is ever going to believe the Government, represented by the Air Force, concerning the events at Roswell, New Mexico. If they wanted to be believed, they should not have told the truth or even a few small lies. They should have told one enormous, bodacious lie. People want to believe unbelievable heroic things. Here is what they should have said:

"Yes, there was a crash and there were bodies in the body bags. The vehicle which crashed was an American experimental craft. Tragically, some heroic American servicemen died. It was an experiment which went horribly wrong and we regret the tragedy. Since the experiment was part of an ongoing series, that's all we can say at this time. The information and artifacts from the crash site have been sealed under military secrecy laws. Nothing more can be revealed in less than 100 years."

Of course, it's bull but it's exciting, heroic bull. People will be very happy to believe it.

It's raining. The weather man predicted sun. I would not like to be a weather man. I am used to working with things I can control. I cannot imagine pretending to predict events in a situation where I don't understand even half of the forces involved in their creation. It's worse than astrology. At least with astrology, you can count on your victims to make your bologna come true. Could it be; if we believed strongly enough in the weather man, we could make the rain stop?

If you find someone you care about and you want them to care about you, forget yourself. Don't juggle eggs or tennis balls. Don't tell stories. Don't do tricks. Don't tell them how special you are. Tell them, and show them, how special they are. English works just fine for this.

The Risk of Variance

Jimmy Olson was one of those people who are normally thought of as criminals and outcasts when they are thought of at all. He did not want to be an outcast and he tried not to be a criminal. He wanted only two things. To find someone to love and to be left alone. He had been looking for someone to love for a long time. It was six years since they took John off to prison. That left Jimmy alone.

Jimmy did not start off alone. He had a mother and father. Sadly enough, his father had been a very busy business man. That left his mother to be a closet alcoholic. While Dad was piling up a modest fortune, good old Mom was limping through her meaningless days on the twin crutches of gin and vodka. Jimmy was usually not noticed by either of them unless he caused a problem. So, guess what he did?

He developed a habit of causing problems. Little ones at first. These got him reprimands, spankings, sometimes punches, but also attention. Later the problems became larger and more difficult to ignore. He tried shoplifting, stealing neighbors cars, then breaking and entering. Finally there was too much for his father to cover up and he spent a year in a place called "The House of Correction." It was, by any other name, an understaffed, poorly run, reform school.

Jimmy got out without too many bad experiences. He was punched around by older kids and got raped once but he could have been ok with help. He did not get help. His mother brought him home and he got a lecture from his father. He sat in a chair against the kitchen wall. His father loomed over him.

He began softly with, "What's wrong with you son?"

Jimmy wished he knew but could not answer.

His father did not wait for a reply. He continued with ever increasing volume, "I work my butt off to make a home for us. I've done well. We have all we need. You get everything you want! Why isn't it enough? Why do you have to keep screwing up?

"I hope to God you've learned something now. A year up there. Did it do you any good?"

He waited for an answer but Jimmy did not have one. He looked at the floor. He felt awful.

His father shouted, "Look at me dammit! Answer me. What are you going to do now?"

Jimmy managed to whisper, "I don't know."

"You don't know," shouted his father, his face growing red. "You don't know!

"By God, I'll tell you what you're going to do! You're going to go to school. You're going to study and get good marks. You're going to come home from school and take care of the house and do your chores and, if you have any spare time, you're going to get a paper route or something. You're going to get it right God damn it!

"Then, when you get out of high school, we'll see about getting you into a military academy. A place where you can learn to behave or take the consequences."

There was much more but Jimmy couldn't hear it. His mind shut down. After a while, his father went back to work leaving Jimmy alone with his mother. She sat at the kitchen table and smiled wanly at him. She was in no shape to help Jimmy or anyone else. She did not try to stop him when he went out.

He wanted a cigarette, badly. There were always cigarettes in reform school. Now, he had no money. No one had offered him any. He had not asked for any. He walked past a parked car. In the console was some money. The door was not locked. He was not going to steal the car. He just saw the money and wanted it for cigarettes. The owner of the car did not believe him. The police did not believe him. His father shook his head and said, "God knows I tried."

Jimmy went back to The House of Correction. This time for two years. He was fifteen.

The reform school was where he met his first and only love. He was getting punched around by a bigger older kid. He was covering himself up in a corner as best he could. There was no malicious intent, nor much damage, in the punching. It was simply the assertion of rights in a pecking order. The assertion stopped abruptly. One minute, Jimmy was crouched in a corner covering his head. The next minute, his adversary was sitting on the floor beside him with a hand cupped over a bloody nose. An even bigger kid was looming over him. It was the inmate ruler of the school. Bad John. Jimmy slid to the floor.

Everyone know about Bad John. They said he had killed a man. The truth is, John's partner had been shot, not killed, by the owner of a house they were burglarizing. Things do get exaggerated in the school. If John had been a few years older, he would have gone to prison. Instead he got three years in reform school.

John did his very best Edward G. Robinson impersonation. "He's mine, punk. This kid is mine. I want him left alone; see — Or else!" John emphasized the last with his index finger stabbing toward his victim.

The earlier protagonist needed little urging. He backed away snarling just enough to save a little face, but not enough to provoke John.

John picked Jimmy up as though he were weightless and set him on his feet.

"Don't worry about him kid. He ain't nothin," growled John. "I'll take care a ya!"

He put an arm over Jimmy's shoulder and gave him a paternal squeeze. Then shoved him away.

"See ya later, kid," he said.

Jimmy appreciated the help and later sought John out to tell him. It was then he learned what he was expected to do as John's "boy." Jimmy was not dumb. He simply had a limited background of experience to guide him. John was not at all vague about what he expected.

"Ya take my dick in yer mouth an ya give me a nice blow job," he explained. "Don't ask when! Whenever I tell ya and every time I tell ya.

"That's when kid!

"It's simple. I take care a you an you take care a me! - - Or else! See!"

There really was no choice and Jimmy told himself he didn't mind it. He decided to do it well and he did. Then he discovered, he really didn't mind it at all. Then he realized he liked it. He liked the feeling. He liked the taste and he liked the excitement it caused in John. He worked hard to make it just right for John.

There was also the attention he got. In public, John was hard and mean but, when they were alone, he was amazingly gentle and kind with Jimmy. Jimmy found himself in love. Why not? It was the first time he had ever experienced sustained attention and support from a human being. Jimmy came to the conclusion that he was not a straight person. After that it was good.

After a few weeks of the relationship, John decided to go down on Jimmy. "Just as a favor to ya Kid," he said. He swore to kill the kid if he ever told. Jimmy never told.

Two weeks later John did it again. Then again. He took to doing it regularly, to the extent that Jimmy had to ask for a turn. Then there were two!

John never stopped fooling himself about what was happening. Even after they got out, he was, "Just doin the Kid a favor."

Jimmy loved it both ways and he loved being with John even when they couldn't do anything intimate. He hung around him whenever he could find a way. In a carelessly run school, that was most of the time.

Jimmy finally got released from the school and went home. His parents said they were glad. He got a listless hug from his mother, a reasonably mild lecture from his father and they left him alone. He hung around and stayed out of trouble so they forgot him. He didn't mind. He just hung around and waited. He finally had a purpose.

Four months later, John got out and Jimmy went to meet him. It was still good. They stayed together and went to Detroit. Jimmy felt great. He thought he had it made. He thought it would be forever. He was willing to work, to go wherever John went, to do whatever he said and to get by on whatever they had.

John felt a little more grandiose about his life. He wanted more. They were in Detroit two weeks when he got arrested for armed robbery. Then Jimmy realized there was one place John could go that he did not have the courage to follow.

The court appointed lawyer talked to John.

"I think I can talk to the Judge. I think we can get an easier sentence if you plead guilty."

John suspected a con, but he had no options. He agreed.

Jimmy got to see him once before the trial. They had a few minutes, then the deputy told him he had to go.

John said, "So long Kid. I'll be membering how good yer mouth felt when I'm poundin my pork in prison."

As terrified as he was and desperate for affection, that was as close to outward affection as it was possible for John to come.

"It felt good for me too John." whispered Jimmy.

"Go on Kid. Get outa here. No need to hang around. I'll be out in a couple years."

Of course, John would not get out in a couple years. His first analysis was right. The court appointed attorney had conned him. He was just too lazy to mount a defense. There was no arrangement with the judge for a guilty plea. The judge was a no mercy, flinty-hearted man, hardened by a lifetime of seeing it all. John got 15 years to life for armed robbery.

Despite John's advice, Jimmy did stick around. He watched the legal charade unfold from a back corner of the courtroom. He left with tears in his eyes. He was a kid alone in a strange city. He found odd jobs. The school had taught him how to shoplift. He got along. It was summer and he slept in alleys with the rats. He didn't get cold --- just scared.

He learned to cruise. He learned how to hustle for tricks. It got him money. He was a nice looking kid. He got experience but he was still alone; lonely, sick, scared alone; sometimes, wish I was dead alone; no one to love, alone.

Come winter, Jimmy found an elderly wino homosexual. The man had a room. It was a place to live but it was awful. The guy stank. He didn't wash himself. Jimmy tried but it made him sick to be in bed with him. In mid-winter, Jimmy left and went hustling.

He found a powerful, black, macho man who hated with a passion. Jimmy would have loved him but he didn't allow it. He was hard and mean. With brute force he took Jimmy and hurt him. Jimmy stayed with him until spring. It was like being raped every day and his man didn't even enjoy it. It hurt Jimmy, to give and have it not received.

There were other relationships. Some were ok and lasted a few months. Some were not real bad but they did not last. Some were just ugly and he got out of them as quickly as possible. None were like the days in school with John. There was no one to love.

His life acquired a pattern. He lived alone most of the time. He frequented the gay bars. He made pick ups. He had short term relationships. Sex was fine. He liked it but it was mostly for the closeness; for the other person. He liked to be close to people. Even women. He had never tried to have sex with a woman. None had ever hit on him and it never occurred to him to solicit a woman. At age 23, he was still, and always, looking for someone to replace John.

He was doing just that on a warm summer evening. Cruising. Looking for a brother. It was not in his normal neighborhood when he saw the man from a block away and he had the feeling. It was like a surging in his gut and the area of his groin. There was a rush, of a tingling up his spine. His mouth got dry. There was a slight sense of fear - of maybe not connecting and the excitement of thinking he would.

The man was tall, thin hipped, with a ball bearing, flowing motion in his whole body. This Jimmy saw as they approached. He had styled blond hair and noble, almost arrogant, features. His skin looked white in the light of the street lamp. His muscled shoulders were covered with a dark turtleneck and tight jeans outlined his hips and the mound of his tool. Jimmy felt the thrill as he visualized it. Smooth velvet skin over hardened steel. He wanted it. He could almost feel it. He imagined it all and he trembled with delight.

They came closer together and both slowed their step. They were in danger of passing. Then there was the eye contact and they both knew. They stopped. They half turned. The arrogant features seemed to soften just slightly. The elaborate dance was almost over.

"Hi," grinned Jimmy.

The man inclined his head just a bit.

"I'm Jimmy."

That got a definite nod but no words.

Jimmy stammered, "Well — w-w-well. I thought."

There was a terrifying moment of uncertainty and then the man smiled, showing perfect, pure white teeth. Jimmy felt a tingling, as though he were being nibbled. He gulped.

"I'm Dan," said the man and he put a soft hand on Jimmy's elbow; a hand that said, 'Yes - we're brothers. We're the same.'

"Would you?" said Jimmy. "Could we?"

"I think so."

"I want to."

"We can try then."

"Do you have a place?" asked Jimmy.

"Not near."

"It's a good night to walk."

"We could try here first." Dan nodded toward an alleyway.

Jimmy looked a bit distressed.

"And then walk," continued Dan.

Jimmy smiled.

They went into the alley. The street light followed them. Jimmy didn't like it. He didn't like being in the open and he did not like alleys. He moved closer to Dan and their shoulders touched. He felt better. He imagined being at Dan's place later and he felt much better.

They came to a sheltered place. There was a shadow from a building and it was out of view of the street. The ground looked almost decent. Jimmy smiled at Dan and they moved into the shadows. His hands touched on Dan's hips and his fingers slid around to the fly and felt the bulge. He felt strong, firm fingers on his neck and he slid down to his knees.

It was good. Very good. Everything was as he had imagined it. He gripped the powerful muscled legs with his clamped fingers and enjoyed.

"Oh Lord," he whispered when it was done. "Oh Lord! That was good."

He could hear the heavy deep pants of Dan's breathing. He opened his eyes to look up. That's when he saw the other man. Stocky, broad, powerful looking, the man was pure bone and muscle. He had a dark angry face with a shock of black hair over black shaggy eyebrows, over deep - dark - violent - angry eyes. Jimmy saw the man and knew he was going to be beat up. It had happened before.

"Oh God," he groaned softly.

He moved as though to get up.

"Stay on your knees, you slimy pig!" snarled the man. "Stay down there where you belong, you filthy disgusting animal!" He continued with a string of vile language and vicious epithets not often imagined, even in the streets of Detroit.

Jimmy groveled. He shrunk. Tears filled his eyes and he looked at Dan accusingly. Dan looked away quickly.

"That's right! You been set up," raged the stocky man, "Caught in your own filthy game. You did a real man! And you ain't done. You're gonna do another real man."

The man opened his fly with thick fingers and stumped toward Jimmy.

"Oh God," groaned Jimmy.

A powerful hand grabbed his hair and jerked his head up. His mouth was thrust into. Again and again. He was terrified. Still, he tried to do it right. He wanted to avoid the beating he knew was coming. He also knew it was hopeless. He was right.

It was over quickly and the tool was yanked away. Just as quickly a fist slammed into his temple. Pain lanced like lightening through his body seeking out the joints.

"That's what we do with scum bag queers," seethed the dark man. Then he took the time to button himself.

Jimmy was on his hands and knees. His head throbbed. He tried to stand, in hopes of running, but his legs would not do it. He got to his knees and the man aimed a kick at his head. The boot glanced off his face and he tasted the copper tang of blood.

He was yanked to his feet and a fist slammed into his ribs. Again, the sharp lancing pain ripped through him. He was rammed against the wall and the fist slammed home again. The man held him up and kept slamming into his body with a vicious rage. Something inside broke and Jimmy's world went black. Still the man kept hitting - and hitting - and hitting.

Finally, Dan jumped on his back and tangled his arms, taking a few jabs and blows himself.

"Stop it," he screamed. "You're killing him!"

The man paused as though in a daze.

"You were just gonna beat him up. Look at him for God's sake!"

The man let go of Jimmy who slid to the ground in a heap. He looked at Jimmy, as though seeing him for the first time. He passed a hand over his forehead and felt the sweat. He stepped back with a slight stagger, then righted himself and paused an instant.

"Arrr! He's OK!" He growled. "Come on. Let's get outa here."

He put his arm over Dan's shoulder and they moved quickly out to the street. He squeezed Dan's shoulder and Dan leaned in against him.

"You had me scared for a minute."

"Arrr hell! You don't want to worry about them queers. They ain't worth nothin. It's us straight guys what's important. Don't worry Kid, I'll take care a ya."

He gave Dan a quick squeeze and then let go quickly so no one would see them and think they were queer. Dan felt a tingling in his groin.

In the alley, Jimmy lay in a heap where he had been dropped. His breath rasped in his chest. There were hiccups and surges deep inside him. His skin was pasty grey. His eyes were open but they saw nothing. A series of broken gulps and hiccups shook through his body and a geyser of blood blossomed from his mouth. It ran in a small river over his chest and arm. Jimmy stopped breathing and lay still.

He grew cold. The blood got sticky on his shirt and arm and the flies came buzzing around. Jimmy didn't care. Then the rats came.

Monday: A small blurb appeared on an inside page of one of the city's newspapers.

PERVERT KILLED!

James Olson, age 23, male Caucasian, was found dead, Sunday morning in a Detroit alley on the east side. He had apparently been beaten to death by an unknown assailant. Police have no clues or information as to the cause of the murder. Olson was a known homosexual.

Polls

The problem with polls and pollsters is inherent in the main erroneous assumption of polling. This being that it's possible to get a representative sample. They claim to do this by using some scientific mumbo jumbo method to make selections. What they will never tell you is that, thoughtful busy people who have a life won't talk to them. Mrs. Gaffer and I reject their intrusion out of hand. Thus, their surveys will always be skewed toward people who are essentially exhibitionists and have nothing better to do. Roper, Gallup, Schmallop, they all make the same error. My questions are, "Is this really an error? Are they really that stupid, or do they think we are that stupid?"

Pastimes

I would like to state categorically that I find nothing wrong with pastimes. I would like to state that I find something patently absurd about the notion that some pastimes are somehow superior to others. Sitcoms, spectator sports, chess, bridge, solitaire and board games are all pastimes. There is nothing creative, productive or inherently useful in any of them. When we get weary and want to dismiss the world for a while, any one will do. For emotionally diminished people, any of them can be addicting. Perhaps the difference between a normal person and a fool is that an ordinary person would not piddle away his time arguing in the defense of a particular pastime.

Anyone for chess?

English as it is Spoke and Writ

In grade school, we had a mean old English teacher who used to make us diagram sentences and stuff like that. We used to say, "Mrs. Slack never gives us any slack. She keeps it all in her behind." Behind is a synonym for the word we really used. I believe she did know a little about the structure of English. Unfortunately, she did not know crap about logic or usage. Because of that, and her ego, she did something which I still find unforgivable in a teacher. She ridiculed and humiliated poor Oliver.

As a promotional stunt, the Affholter dairy company had provided our class with token helpings of ice cream, which we, of course, ate. Our assignment was to write a thank you note for the magnificent gift, which we did. I'll never forget what Oliver wrote.

"Dear Mr. Affholter:

"Thank you for the ice cream. It was very good and we ate it all down.

"Oliver T, third grade."

I believed then, and I still believe, that Oliver's logic was impeccable. Mrs. Slack did not take logic into account and kindly correction was not in her nature. She made that poor lad stand in front of about 30 students while she read his note over and over again as a glaring example of bad grammar. She explained that he should have written up instead of down, mistaking the idiom for proper usage. In short, she made the same error Oliver had. Then she laughed at him.

It still strikes me that, mean as little kids can get, no one else laughed. To a person, we all felt awful for Oliver. Her behind was not the only area of slack in Slack. Her mind could have used a little tightening too. After a trauma like that, I can seriously doubt that Oliver ever learned to use English effectively.

The purpose of language is to communicate. Thus, if we use our language so that people who hear us have a reasonable understanding of what we intended to say, we have used language effectively. In his note, Oliver used language effectively. I understood what he said. Never mind, for a moment, the scholars and language purists. They will have a turn later.

Although we have all met folks with annoying verbal habits such as utilizing utilize when they should be using use, or saying irregardless when they mean regardless, most of us manage quite well in the spoken language. That is, when we speak informally, people do have a reasonable idea of our meaning. Albeit, we all make mistakes and we tend to overuse cliches. We say "fur" when we mean "for," even though we know how to spell it. We also belly up to the bar, we get in the right ballpark and we use our collective wisdom, but we do manage to communicate in our routine life.

It is in the formal parts of communication that we often get derailed. Making a presentation, giving an award, writing a report or even writing a letter seems to bring out the grossly verbosely in us. We seem to get carried away with the weight of words and employ the heaviest ones we can think of. Quite often this results in a complete failure to communicate, sometimes because we bore the hell out of our victims and they stop listening, but also because our victims are often not sure of the meaning of the words we have discovered.

Political folks are the most adept at putting us to sleep with verbosity. They seem to fall in love with tones and rhythms. Occasionally, as in Churchill, King and Kennedy (John F.), their sense of poetry and drama allow them to make lasting impressions about important issues through the use of tone and rhythm. *The Gettysburg Address* and Caesar's eulogy by Mark Antony, in Shakespear's *Julius Caesar* are two of the classics by which we measure this type of oratory. Unfortunately, most of our political hacks fetch up way short of this mark. Yet they can't seem to stop doing it, over and over and over again. It's as though they were cursed to keep doing it until they get it right or, perhaps, they are victims of some speech malady.

I believe the latter is the case. These poor souls have been exposed to and contracted verbosalitis. This is a non-fatal infection of the mouth and mind characterized by swollen sentences with bizarre growths of extraneous, multi-syllable modifiers. The disease is usually contracted through exposure to politicians and managers or through the process of promotion and/or running for office. Success does not mitigate the effects of the disease, but only serves to aggravate it to the point of continuous manifestation. Though the infection rate is near 100%, it is almost completely limited to the population of managers and politicians. Although we see isolated cases in other occupations, the general population is not at risk and no special precautions are required. Avoiding the infected community is, of course, a good idea. It is important to remember that verbosalitis, though not fatal is like ugly, incurable.

Though most of us are not infected with verbosalitis, we do have lapses which produce behavior similar to the symptoms. For many of us, public reading or speaking is the challenge whose very anticipation can cause night terrors. When confronted with the prospect, our hands tremble, our mouth dries out and we fear for the control of our sphincter. How can we speak, when we are afraid to stand up? How can we speak, when we can't even spit? God deliver us!

To mitigate this awful feeling, we try to think of words which will make it seem we are reasonably intelligent. In our state of stage fright it does not occur to us to talk the way we normally talk to a friend; to just stand up, pick out one person we can see and say what we know, using the words we always use. That always works, even when we are trembling. Instead, we bumble along staring at a blurred bald spot in the front row, trying to use words we are unsure of and making a mess of it until we finally sit down and everyone is glad it's over.

It's no better if we have time to think about the speech and plan it. This just gives us time to make it really verbose and pointless. We get to use a dictionary and a thesaurus. Dear Lord! Then we have to memorize it knowing we will lose our place and start to wander at the fatal time, babbling away. Sigh!

Oh, how we envy the person who can stand up and deliver a message with simple words and eloquence. Oh, how we wish we could do it just that way. And Oh, how we suspect that those who can are really simpletons with no understanding or appreciation of the situation.

Things don't get any better when we set out to write. Here we always get to use a dictionary and a thesaurus. Why is it that we cannot write just as we speak, using words we know in simple, clear sentences? Why do we use multi-syllable words and ponderously constructed sentences filled with galloping adjectives and adverbs? Contrast the following two sentences which I constructed just for example though I don't think they are at all far fetched. The first could appear in a written witnesses statement, if the witness were an attorney. The second could appear in a fast paced detective thriller. Both say the same thing, but which is easier to read?

> ***Master Ronald utilized the balled end of his upper left extremity to vigorously impact Mr. Steinman's proboscis causing an immediate hemorrhage, whereupon copious amounts of blood discharged over Mr. Steinman's shirt.***
>
> ***Ron slammed a hard left hook to Steinman's snot locker and blood erupted over his shirt.***

As you can see, pompous verbosity dilutes rather than enhances a message, be it written or spoken. Yet how we try to impress our friends, managers and associates through the use of nonsensical words and phrases.

Perhaps the worst of the wordsmiths are the corporate technical writers who know all about language, syntax and spelling, and nothing about communication. What is more boring than a slick annual report? Well, how about a technical manual? The only thing worse than a tech manual written by an engineer is the same manual written by a tech writer. At least the engineer's version will be technically accurate.

Whether they are writing instructions, textbooks or reports, technical people, college professors and tech writers fall into the same trap of using stilted, dry, boring language. A word, phrase or sentence may be technically and literally correct and still be so stilted and tedious that it disrupts the flow of ideas. Then communication, along with the point, is lost. These awkward constructs are like pot holes and speed bumps on a superhighway. Their only function is to distract and annoy us.

I believe the problem here is in how we see the craft. Writing exposition should not be a task or just a job. Exposition is as much an art form as fiction writing. It's not enough to understand language. To do it well, we must have a keen sense of how words affect people. We must know what will make them chuckle, snort or gasp; all of which will make them read on with interest.

Lest we wish to bore folks to death, it's not enough to spell out, in intricate detail, exactly how something works or how to do something. We must make them want to see it and do it. I have never read technical writing like that. Have you? I tried writing that way once, when I was a Systems Analyst, then my boss rewrote it to make it proper. What I wrote looked like *Ron* and his correction looked like *Master Ronald.*

I have a great deal of trouble with that. I tried to write like my manager but it seemed phony to me. So, whenever I could, I released my papers before he saw them. That is just one of my many behaviors which kept me out of favor with the management staff and prevented my promotion. Thank God!

Just for fun, I once pretended I worked as a tech writer for the company which had just invented the zipper and I wrote instructions on how to go to the bathroom while wearing trousers with the newly invented zipper. It may not be appropriate for this piece but heck, a few example lines can't hurt.

> ***Once the tool (P) is properly replaced in its normal compartment (C), it is necessary to restore the zipper (Z) to its closed position. To do this, grasp the zipper handle (H) with either hand and pull it upward being careful to hold the zipper (Z) away from the tool compartment (C) until the compartment is fully concealed (*** See Note 1). Next, fold the zipper handle (H) downward to lock the zipper mechanism in place. This completes the instruction for doing number one while wearing trousers with an Acme Zipper.***
>
> ******Note 1: Under no circumstances may the Acme Zipper Corporation be held liable for any damage caused to the tool or its works through the careless operation of the zipper (Z).***

I use an exercise which has helped me avoid the worst symptoms of verbosalitis. Whenever I write something and it seems complete, I take the final step. I try to reduce the size of the work by half while retaining the entire meaning, effect and content. I do this by reducing word size and word modifiers. Years ago, someone I respected did this to one of my tomes and it was very humbling. After that I learned to do it myself. It's less painful and more satisfying to do it yourself. That's as true of writing as it is of potty training. There are no hard rules. Occasionally, I am surprised to discover that a sentence reads better when I add a modifier or two. In general, though, I can improve readability by removing parts of my magnificent prose.

As your own exercise, if you wish, write a short (one page) essay. Any dumb subject will do. Like "What I would have done on summer vacation if my boss had given me the time off." Now see if you can cut it to half a page without losing the content, effect or meaning. Remove adverbs and adjectives and reduce big words to small ones. Remove redundant phrases and sentences. If you don't want to write an essay, take a newspaper article and do the same thing. It's always easier to find weaknesses in the work of others.

Here are some pointers I have picked up about writing. If the average word size is greater than seven characters or if the average sentence size is greater than 20 words, your document will be unreadable to all but the most determined masochist. There is no excuse here. You don't have to count words or characters. Even the simplest of the word processors will give you these numbers. Keep the average word size under seven characters and the average sentence size around 15 words or less if you want most people to struggle through it. This does not mean you cannot have a sentence of fifty or sixty words. It means that kind of sentence better be the rare exception. Most folks will not reread very many sentences. They will simply put the work down and say it was too complicated. Students, of course, cannot do that, which is why we have so many crappy textbooks.

Another point on size. Avoid paragraphs which fill half a page or more. The reader needs breaks to rest his eyes. There is nothing more daunting than to turn a page and see no white space; just solid text from top to bottom. Think how you react when you see that. If you have a paragraph of half a page or more, look at it carefully. Even if the thoughts are closely linked, there is a place in the paragraph where a speaker will take a breath. More than likely, that is a natural break. Put a carriage return there and see if it reads better. Perhaps you need to add a word or two to smooth the flow.

Most of us will never have to face the most difficult task of writing and speaking which is the accurate portrayal of dialect and dialogue. Some folks, of course, seem to do it naturally. These are the friends and acquaintances we like to call great storytellers. Story telling is an art form older than written language and was once essential to the maintenance of our history. Now it's just great fun whether the stories are true or not. And we never question the veracity of the story or the storyteller.

The way to reveal people; the way to do dialect is to listen, listen, listen to the people. You do this listening everywhere you go, be it taverns, town halls or tabernacles. You listen for the music until you start to get the flavor of it. You start to feel the special music in the sounds. Regardless of the locale, be it North Carolina, Georgia, Maine or Mississippi, there is a music and rhythm to the speech patterns. This I call the flavor of the dialect. Once you have it, it's like you hear in an entirely new way. It's like listening to music all the time. You finally get that the apparent cacophony of human communication is really the greatest musical production ever conceived. And it's ongoing. Bernstein captured a small part of it in *West Side Story*.

> We must listen - listen - listen,
> to the music and the rhythm
> of the words - words - words;
> to the music and the rhythm
> of the words.

In writing the dialect you exaggerate this music just slightly. You do this even if you must misspell words, use words out of place or invent words. It's not about proper usage. It's about drawing a portrait with words. In this, the writer is allowed the same liberties of interpretation as the painter or musician. This exaggeration requires great care and practice. Too much simply creates an insult to the very people who gave you the music. Too little and you come over as yourself trying to sound like your characters.

The main point is to listen with attention until you appreciate the music. Most of us can't do that because we can't shut up long enough. Many of us can't listen at all. We are like my beagle who cocks his head and looks at me as though he hears and understands. Heck! Maybe he does. He can't write dialect though. Course, neither can I. Understanding how something is done does not necessarily confer the ability to do it. In this case, theory and practice are not married. They may not even be engaged.

In writing, what constitutes good dialect and dialogue can be very much a matter of opinion. Just as it is in poetry. So, while we are into the realm of personal opinion, I assign gold stars of greatness to

Steinbeck in Drama, Frost in Poetry, Asimov in Science Fiction, Tolkien in Fantasy and Twain in Humor. These stars are for the mastery of dialect and dialogue, which are the key elements of storytelling.

In truth, the above artists were masters of their craft in all phases. In *Of Mice and Men,* when Steinbeck puts us in the barn with Lennie we can smell the hay. He paints such beautiful word pictures that we expect to look up and be there.

These artists are my favorites and it is just my opinion. Other folks will have their own thoughts on who should get gold stars. Certainly Hemingway should be on the list along with Poe, say some. I cannot argue and I particulary agree that Poe was a master of tone and rhythm. If you want to get a real feel for the use of tone and rhythm, have someone who knows how to read poetry read aloud, *The Bells* by Edgar Allan Poe.

I said that scholars and purists would have their turn so let's present their case. These poor souls are the guardians of our language. It's not an assignment imposed on them. It is out of their love of the beauty and power of words that they have taken on the task. And a thankless task it is. No one likes them for they must be constantly correcting us in our careless use. And careless use is everywhere.

Let us understand the nature and magnitude of the problem which they address. Within my lifetime, the nonsensical construct "ain't" found its way into some of our dictionaries. I confess to using it myself when I want a particular effect in my writing. What exactly ain't is a contraction of, we do not know. Perhaps it was first used as a contraction of the southern United States phrase "air not" as in "I air not dumb!" When I was in grade school, a cutesy phrase was popular for a time. "Don't use ain't cause it ain't in the dictionary." Now it is and, much to my dismay, very soon, the nonsensical and contradictory construct "irregardless" may join it. Why? Because it has come into common use. Eventually, common usage carries the day.

It is fair to ask why this should matter. It matters because the purpose of language is to communicate and any dilution or distortion of the language weakens its power to do that. If it were not for the purists, we would quickly have an *Alice in Wonderland* situation where "A word means what I mean it to mean ..." Communication would become difficult and precise communication would become impossible. The purists who fight against this are fighting a delaying action. Nothing more is possible or necessary.

American English is a very rich language allowing us to create very precise meanings in our speech and writing. It is exactly why a John F. Kennedy or a Martin Luther King could be so eloquent and effective. The language is rich, partly because it has gradually absorbed words and meanings from other languages, and, partly because it has allowed the creation of new constructs. It is the task of the purists to resist this change in a way which makes it evolutionary rather than revolutionary. Thus, when we write and speak, the consistency of the language assures that we will indeed communicate.

There will always be slang and that is fine. However, slang should never, ever control the language. It must be kept outside the language. It is acceptable for a person in the street to say bad when he means good but we cannot let that come into general usage. If we allow the word "bad" to come into the language as a synonym meaning especially good, the power of two very simple, very strong words will be lost. Then, if we call a man a "bad ass," we must be ready to run even if our intentions are salutary.

Careless usage is everywhere. Don't believe it is just a problem of the regular folk. It is rampant in our universities where a person can be called a chair or a head instead of a person and pop means surprise or unexpected as in "pop quiz."

It is even more rampant in the communication industries. Here, where people earn their entire living through the use of language, we find a dismaying number who have never studied language and have no notion of proper usage. In most cases, these people think they know language and have no need to learn it. The worst offenders are the sportscasters and writers. These folks, who have the most influence on the vocabulary of our children, are often completely ignorant in their use of language. A glaring example is the football announcers total confusion about the meaning of the word strategy. They continuously use strategy when they mean tactic or goal. It sounds so wonderfully impressive.

Let's try to clear it up for them.

Tactic
1 : a device for accomplishing an end
2 : a method of employing forces in combat
2 tactic adj: of or relating to arrangement or order

Goal
1
a : the terminal point of a race
b : an area to be reached safely in children's games
2 : the end toward which effort is directed : aim

Strategy
1 : the science and art of employing the political, economic, psychological, and military forces of a nation or group of nations to afford the maximum support to adopted policies in peace or war
2 : the science and art of military command exercised to meet the enemy in combat under advantageous conditions
a : a careful plan or method : a clever stratagem
b : the art of devising or employing plans or stratagems toward a goal.

Panic
1 : a sudden, overpowering terror, often affecting many people at once.

The **goal** of football is simple and never changes. It's to win the game.

The **strategy** of football is just as simple and, also, never changes. For the offense, it's to score as many points as possible as quickly as possible each time they get the ball. For the defense, it's to get the ball without giving up points.

The **tactics** are the formations and plays which the coaches determine will best implement the strategy and achieve the goal given the rules of the game, and the talent they have to work with.

Panic is what happens when the tactics don't work.

For a good example of **panic**, try to get and watch the game films of the 1996 Detroit Lions Football Team. Pay particular attention to the quarterback and coaches.

Before we leave strategy and tactics, the American military people create some classic examples of the perversion of language. For example, when they collect information they will call it gathering intelligence. Good luck! They use hackneyed phrasing like "one each tent with pegs" or "one each table with chairs." Sometimes they use, "one each only." Reading a military list of material can be a comic experience. One is given to wonder how they would describe other things. My clever brother once used the phrase, "One each tree with leaves." We could probably write a military children's fairytale. Here's a start.

In one each forest with trees,
lived one each dog with fleas,
one each mouse with cheese
and one each swarm of bees.

There are times when the deliberate misuse of language can be an effective tool of communication. The incomplete sentence which implicitly borrows the subject or object of the preceding sentence is one example. We do this in speech quite often and it can also be effective in writing. A short series of incomplete sentences can have an effect similar to a speaker thumping the podium for emphasis. In either case it can be easily overdone. We have all seen the speaker who thumps the podium with every word he utters. This does not impress us. It annoys us and we just wish he would shut up and sit down.

Those of us who intend to earn income through the use of language have a serious responsibility to first learn it. This does not mean we will not make errors. Nor does it mean we should not use slang or misuse the language. Some of the best humor we see depends on doing just that. And dialogue would be dead without an understanding of slang and dialects. The key word is understanding. When we misuse language it should be the occasional error or a deliberate act, never the result of ignorance. We do not want the language to become so diluted by our example that it is no longer effective. When in doubt, we must take the time to look it up. Do the research! For that wouldn't it be great to have *Scribner* on CD-ROM, cross indexed?

In fairness, I have probably beat up too hard on the people who misuse English because they think they know it. Truth is, their ignorance is understandable. Most of them have graduated, at least, from K-12 and, for as many as 12 of those years they were taught what was called English. They had no way of knowing that many of their teachers did not know English and were not required to know it. Shades of Mrs. Slack.

Here's the problem. In many states, perhaps all, to teach English in K-12 does not require a degree in English. It only requires a teaching certificate. Ain't that a crock? Next to a degree in Business Administration, a teaching certificate is the easiest route through college. That's opinion. Mine! Unless the local school districts set higher standards, as some do, we can end up with well meaning, unqualified teachers. Like the rest of us, these teachers believe they already know English.

Instead of teaching a thing called English, we should be teaching communication in language. The people who teach it should be properly trained in all aspects of communication. I'm not talking about the devices of communication like transmitters and telephones. I'm talking about words and the way we put them together. Not rules of grammar for goodness sake. Communication! In proper teaching, the rules become apparent through use and gentle correction.

This kind of teaching can only occur if those who do it actually love language and its power. Maybe the course should be called Language and Power or even The Joy of Language and Power. Communication will eventually rule the world. We should be teaching and conditioning our young people to love language. Instead, we teach them to misunderstand and fear it. I want Americans to become the best communicators in the universe.

There was this simpleton who received some cherry bomb firecrackers from a friend. He pondered on how they would sound so he lit two of them and put one in each of his ears. It happened that they went off at exactly the same instant and his head imploded. It was a fortuitous event. Just a few days later he was able to secure a position as Senior Systems Analyst at a major firm in Redmond.

Picture this if you can.
Mr. and Mrs. Redneck observed their dogs and learned how to make whelps.
Ms. Judge observed her cat and learned to go potty in a window box.

There is always the temptation to give advice and interfere in other folk's affairs. With our limited human experience and knowledge, it is best to avoid this lure. The Great Booboo says, "When we try to change a worm, we may be doing nothing less evil than crippling a butterfly."

A Tale of Two Women

There was a very attractive woman who was mistreated and suffered as a child in Wayland. She grew up and left the place to seek her fortune, but she could never really leave. She carried the town, and it's memories, with her. It was a soul numbing burden on her emotional back. Finally, she could carry it no longer and went back to Wayland to live out her life. It was easier that way.

There was another woman who lived in Leslie. She had also suffered as a child and her trauma was so grievous she could not leave Leslie. She was bound by ropes of emotional scar tissue. She found that, through her phobia, she could manipulate people to come to her, if only in pity or lust. It was easier that way. She was very attractive and made many children.

One day, the woman of Wayland took a short excursion to Leslie and happened to stop in a tavern for lunch. As it happened, the tavern had but one other customer. Their eyes met and with a gesture and a smile, Ms. Leslie offered to share her table with Ms. Wayland.

As lonely people will, they began to talk. As time passed and beverages relaxed tongues, they began to share their sadness. They had much in common. Both of their problems stemmed from treatment received as girls from their fathers and the emotional scars were remarkably similar. Their resultant lives were similar too; each with a parade of loser husbands and lovers; each and every relationship ending in pain. These were two women of different cities with a single story. Both locked in a painful and unfulfilling life.

"I was only 12 years old when my father sold me to one of his cronies for the night," said Ms. Leslie. "He needed five dollars for whiskey. That's what I was worth to him. Five bucks."

"Oh God," said Ms. Wayland. "I suffered the same at age 13. I cried but it didn't matter. It hurt terribly. I still remember how it hurt. Did it hurt you like that?"

"It hurt like hell. You're damn right. I bled. I thought I was dying."

"I know. I swore I'd never let a man know he hurt me again. That's the last time I ever cried."

"Me too!" murmured Leslie.

"Did your father ever use you himself."

"I remember being very small. He used to make me handle him and lick him."

"Yeah! I know about that. He never screwed you?"

"No." answered Leslie. "I guess he was saving me for his cronies."

"Or maybe he was too drunk to make it," commented Wayland.

"Damn! You may be right."

They talked on, describing abuses not only from fathers and their cronies but from every man they encountered. Each of them made bad choice after bad choice as though there were some subconscious need to be punished. They took up with loser after loser.

The keeper of the tavern, Mr. Rail Tendor, could not help hearing the discussions of these women. Of course, he was not nosy! It was well after the noon hour and they were his only customers. What else was he to do but polish glasses and listen? Besides, one of the ladies was a regular. The tales he heard moved him deeply and uncharacteristic of him, tears began to flow over his cheeks. His heart pained for these women and he wanted to reach out to them, but how?

Finally, he decided to break his own rules about fraternizing and spoke to them.

"Ladies," he said ponderously. "Since the day is slow and you are here, I wish to share with you a joy of mine and ask your help."

His intrusion startled the women who heretofore had been treating him not unlike a vending machine. Ms. Wayland was the first to notice he was a person and recovered gracefully enough.

"What?" she blurted.

"Oh! A thousand pardons," said Mr. Tendor. "I am trespassing. Please forgive me."

He looked so stricken that Ms. Leslie, who was something of a regular, took pity. In fact, she had grown a bit weary of the downward spiral of the conversation with Wayland.

"Not at all," she said gallantly. "Please tell us about your joy."

"Yes indeed, do," said Ms. Wayland, who also had grown restless with the conversation. It was not, after all, like playing to a sympathetic man.

Tendor needed little encouragement. He beamed with pride. "I," he said proudly, "have invented a new drink!"

"A new drink?" queried Wayland.

If she was disappointed or confused about the tavern keeper's pronouncement, she hid it well, as did Ms. Leslie.

"How nice," she managed to say.

"Thank you!" he gushed.

"But, how are we to help you?" Leslie wanted to know.

Yes! How?" followed Ms. Wayland.

Rail beamed again. "But, of course, I want to share my new drink with you and hear your opinion of it. I would like you to be the first to evaluate it."

He waited while each woman absorbed this bit of news. Being a tavern keeper, familiar with human trust and mistrust, he could almost visualize the thoughts in the air above their heads.

Does he think I'm nuts? I wonder what's in it. Will it make me sick? What will she say? What's she thinking? Will I look like a coward? Will I look like a fool? Will it taste good? It's an adventure after all.

The adventure notion was the real hook. There was a great deal of pretending in the lives of these women. Too many relationships, all the same, ending the same, and very little real adventure. They longed for the kind of adventure we are taught to believe in as children. This was nothing more than a taste, but a taste at least, with a man involved.

"Let's do it," said Wayland to Leslie, trying to look a bit saucy.

"Yes! Yes!" responded Leslie. "Do let us try your drink, but you must join us," she teased.

He was, after all, a man; albeit, a bit thick in the middle.

"Oh, but I cannot fraternize with customers," he said, knowing full well he would.

"But you must," insisted Wayland, with a pout, "Else we shall refuse your offer."

"Indeed." added Leslie, getting into the hunt. "You must mix three drinks and join us."

The game was on. There was only one prey. The poor fool thought he was in control. Is it not always thus? The fox thinks he has caught the hen until the trap is sprung. He believed he had made these women feel better and, indeed, he had. This was a game they knew.

They quickly agreed that he would mix three drinks, not two, and Rail went to the bar. He had a small quandary. There was no drink which he had invented. It was nothing more than a gambit. Now he needed his imagination.

It was simple enough for he knew his business. A dash of this, a little of that, a dollop of something else, Creme de Menthe for color and vanilla ice cream to make it sweet and creamy, the way women prefer. All into the blender for a whirl, into three tall glasses topped with whipped cream and a cherry. In fact, Tendor liked sweet things too, as his girth indicated. Being a thoughtful man of limited wit, he wrote down the ingredients.

He put long straws in the glasses and carried them to the women's table. The drink was a smash success. Both women took sips, then longer sips. Rail tasted his share and was very proud of his creation. The conversation flowed smoothly as both women played Tendor with questions about himself and, reasonable attention to his boasting. There was many a "goodness, you are clever!" and "My! How thoughtful." as his tongue grew loose with the encouragement. It is fair to say, the alcohol had some effect on Rail for he did not normally drink at all. He did have enough wit to know that drinking is the destruction of a barkeeper.

Soon the drinks were gone and it was time for another round. By that time, Rail had forgot he did not drink. At the bar he discovered that, although he had been thoughtful enough to write down the ingredients, he had not been clever enough to record the various amounts. If the first drink had been delicious due to ice cream, the second was mind numbing due to alcohol. By this time, no one seemed to notice a difference. The interest was not in the drink but in the game.

At that point there were no innocents at the table. All were victims and all were hunters. The women, having done this many times, were enjoying the process. Poor Rail, on his first time out, thought he was being very clever. After one drink and all that attention, he simply forgot he had started out to help these women. He was thinking mostly of helping himself.

He was, after all, a middle aged fat man. He was not used to attention from attractive women. He did not understand that he was a pawn in a competitive game. There was some thought of how he would manage with two women, but he soon forgot that also.

Betty, the evening barmaid showed up and the afternoon passed as Rail babbled on. All three knew when the time came. It happens in all human sporting engagements, when we know we must go to the next level or quit the game. None of the three was in a condition to make a rational decision. Furthermore, Rail was not a great prize and neither woman had the resolve to try to outfox the other for him. Thus, they all ended up in Leslie's home on the pretext of listening to some music. Leslie put on a CD and they promptly forgot it.

Tendor had thought to bring along two bottles of Orange Blossom Wine which they put to chill. Soon they were all naked, a sight to behold, and then into Leslie's bedroom and her king-sized bed. Poor Tendor! Though he had girth enough for more than two women, he had not the endurance for even one. He spent himself on the first fondle, sighed and fell backward onto the bed, fast asleep. On his back, he looked very much like a beached sperm whale. Then he had the audacity to snore. Leslie and Wayland were completely disgusted. They sat on the bed and talked a moment.

"Damn his pitiful soul," said Leslie. "He sure left us hanging."

God Damn his pitiful soul and his diddly, drooping dick" added Wayland. "I'm as hot as a fire cracker."

"And no help in sight," groaned Leslie. "If I were alone I'd do myself!"

"Pretend I'm not here then."

Leslie blushed. "It's so embarrassing. I don't know if I could."

"Oh crap! I'm hot enough. Let me show you how. You watch."

Leslie watched Wayland for an instant. Then she said, "Let me do that for you."

She moved closer to Wayland. They began to help each other, which they did as best they could. It was tentative at first being the first time either of them had done such a thing. It was better than they thought.

They decided to open the wine which had been forgotten. They rested, sipped and talked a bit. After a while, they did it again with more imagination. Again, it was better than they had hoped. Then, embraced together, they leaned back and fell asleep atop Mr. Tendor. There it was. Two attractive, naked, middle aged women, sprawled atop a fat, naked, sweaty walrus.

It was shortly after that when Leslie's twelve year old daughter arrived home from cheerleader practice. Not finding her mother, she checked in the bedroom and witnessed the huge mess of flesh. She gasped and rushed to the phone where she dialed 911.

"They're dead!" she screamed to the dispatcher. "My mother and two people are naked and dead in her bed!"

There was no calming the girl so the dispatcher did what dispatchers do. She sent a car immediately, to investigate the first triple murder in Leslie. She was very excited as were the dispatched officers.

The officers were disappointed when they arrived. What they found was not a first for Leslie. They had seen similar scenes before. They were a bit surprised to see Mr. Tendor in such a state. Now, what to do? They would have preferred to just go back and forget what they had seen. That was impossible. They had crossed town with screaming sirens and flashing lights. Too many citizens had seen them. They had to take some action to justify the excitement they had caused.

Thus, Mr. Tendor was charged with drunk and disorderly. It was enough. The women were not charged. They let poor Rail dress before they took him in. In fact they insisted. It was frightening to imagine what people would say upon seeing this guy ride through town naked in the rear seat cage.

Rail was only able to find one sock and, in his confusion, got his shorts on backwards and unbuttoned. He was very uncomfortable on the trip to the station with his shorts bunched up around his crotch. He forgot that problem when they put him in the cell. The iron door clanged shut and realization began to dawn. He knew he had screwed up real bad. He was not even sure what he had done. In addition, he was destined to spend most of the night vomiting followed by dry heaves. His system was not used to alcohol.

By the 11:00 o'clock news, every busybody in Leslie had added their embellishment to the sordid story. At one count there were thirty naked women and ten naked men in Tendor's Tavern who then went cavorting about town with, of all people, Mr Tendor at the lead. Poor Martha.

Did I mention, Rail was married? Of course he was. Martha Tendor was one of those plain looking, good hearted, hard working, God fearing people who give their lives in the service of others. She kept her home spotless, she gave all that she had to Rail and, when not doing that, she was a tireless fixture at her church doing all the chores no one else would do.

She heard the worst of Rail's indiscretion from some mean spirited "friends" who just thought she ought to know. She disappointed them by not showing the searing pain they had brought her. The next day, she went to see the barmaid to verify what she suspected.

She asked, "Did you see him with these women Betty?"

"Yes ma'am. I did." she answered. "They were vultures! Oh Mrs. Tendor. I'm so sorry. I didn't know what to do. Maybe I could have called you but I didn't know what to say."

"I know dear. He did it. Not you. Just tell me what happened."

"Well, there were only two of them, not thirty and no men but him. They sat and drank and laughed for a while. Then he took two bottles of wine and they went out together. He told me to watch the store. That's all I know."

"It's as I thought dear. Now I must ask you to care for the business. I have some things I must do."

She arranged for Betty to get temporary people to help her take care of the tavern. Then she went home. A few days later she filed for divorce. She was a very forgiving woman but infidelity was on her short list. Thus it was that Rail Tenor came before the bar.

Rail did not contest anything. Truth be known, he could not remember enough to contest. Martha got the tavern, their home with furnishings, their savings and the new Town Car. He got his clothes, which she put out on the lawn, and a 1982 Ford pickup. He was next seen working as a bartender in a tough neighborhood of Lansing. He had a scroll on the mirror behind the bar. "If you're looking for help, you're almost there. Just continue on to Hell!"

Later he began to mellow. One day a woman came in and demanded a "different" drink. Something special. Rail did not hesitate. He mixed up a secret recipe in a tall glass topped with whipped cream and a cherry. He called it the Wayland Witch and charged her a whopping six bucks. This is a bar where a boilermaker sold for a buck and a half. She drank it and ordered another which she sipped slowly as she watched Rail at work. She left a $3.00 tip. The next evening she came back with three friends and Rail had to send his boss out for vanilla ice cream. They contributed more than half the bar's take for that day. They even ate the grease burgers and chili fries. Rail decided to take his scroll down.

In a short time, the Shady Side Tavern became a punky, yuppy, in place. Rail's boss was no fool. Instead of giving him a raise, he made Rail a junior partner to ensure his loyalty and keep the secret recipe in the family. It also ensured that Tendor, out of conscience, would begin putting all the receipts in the till and none directly in his pocket.

Rail invented a few more yuppy-type drinks and they sold well but none matched the Wayland Witch. Other bars, of course, tried to emulate the success of Shady Side. They put out various concoctions with various names, like Wayward Bitch, Willful Snitch, etcetera. None of them caught on. Rail mixed his concoction in batches after closing so the help had simply to add ice cream and decorations to make the drink. Only two people knew the recipe. To guard the secret, Rail even went so far as to hand carry empty bottles to various recycling centers.

Even the East Lansing university snobs began showing up for a taste of the Wayland Witch. Rail kept the proportions such that even an east side wimp would have to consume half a gallon of ice cream to get mellow. In his simple thoughts, the best way to deal with drunks was to not have any. His boss completely agreed.

They implemented several changes to conform to the yuppy, in place, mythology. They hired an experienced short-order cook away from Denny's. They expanded the menu, gave bland food exotic names and trebled prices. Though meticulous about sanitation, they managed to keep the place looking grungy with lighting and cheap paint. They also hired security and put lights in the parking lot. After getting reviewed in the Journal, they bought the attached building and broke out a wall to accommodate more customers. Business was excellent and Rail traded his old pickup for a new Town Car.

Back in Leslie, Martha turned out to be a better tavern keeper than Rail. She knew nothing of the tavern business so she had to trust her staff. She also implemented profit sharing. That was the best decision she could have made. With Betty's direction, the staff took over. They did simple, sound business things like painting, cleaning and adding light to make it seem more cheerful. They expanded the menu. Then they implemented special weekly events like amateur night and sing along night. The business prospered.

Martha's Tavern is now a cheerful place where people come often to eat and drink with friends. The staff people actually look forward to being at work. That works well for Martha, who prefers to be at church doing the things she has always done. Betty runs the business. Martha never remarried.

She said, "One time is enough. My staff is all the family I need."

As to Ms. Leslie, the whole episode was very embarrassing for her. Still she kept her home and stayed on. It was easier that way. Soon the noise subsided. The subject of discussion moved from her to a five car accident on the interstate. People forgot her.

Ms. Wayland went back to Wayland to live out her life. Now, she does make frequent visits to Leslie. With Leslie she is comfortable. They usually sit naked and close together on the bed drinking orange blossom wine. Sometimes, they look at the man's sock taped to the dressing table mirror and break out in giggles. They are making plans for Wayland to move to Leslie. It will be easier that way. These women are not at all well but they have each other and their life is better. In a way, Rail really did help them.

The Wayland Witch

(serves four)

In a blender place 1 oz. Brandy, 1 oz. Spiced Rum, 1 oz. Baileys Irish Cream, 1 oz. Cognac, 1 oz. Creme De Menthe and 4 cups vanilla ice cream. Blend to milk shake consistency. Divide into 4 twelve ounce, stemmed glasses. Fill and heap with whipped cream. Top each with a maraschino cherry. Serve with cocktail straws. Get ready to make another round. No permission or fee is required to make and serve the Wayland Witch. Please do not claim or imply the endorsement of Willie Gaffer or Wesoomi Publishing for your establishment.

And So I Chose

I saw a young woman in the mall. She had her right index finger inserted deeply into her right nostril. I must have looked surprised or amused for she stared directly at me with that haughty, belligerent, teenage look. Having once been a child, I was not put off by this. I simply smiled, nodded and went about my business. Later, I thought of what her thoughts might have been. Here is what I came to.

Before age two,
before I grew
aware enough
to think things through,
the rules begin
to tumble in.

"You must be bred,"
my father said,
"to do us proud
when you are wed.
You must conform
to cultures norm.

"And have no fear,
we'll set you clear
on standards which
we both hold dear.
You'll be fine folk."
Thus father spoke.

The oughtas shoulds
and never coulds
and things which only
bad girls woulds,
were pounded in
and then again.

"You must stand straight.
On old folks wait.
You must look sharp
but never bait.
And don't act bold,
and never scold.

"Say thank you, please,
and never sneeze,
and never ever
cross your knees.
And when you date,
don't stay out late.

"Brush your hair.
and never stare
and never scratch,
especially there.
Stay with the crowd.
Don't laugh out loud.

"Clean your plate.
Don't masturbate,
and wash yourself
at any rate.
And heaven knows,
don't pick your nose.

"Pay your fee.
Look and see.
You will do.
You must be.
Sit down - stand.
And fold your hands."

At last I cried,
"I can't abide.
These contradictions
hurt inside."
Then parents cried,
"God knows we tried."

"God knows we tried,"
is what they cried
about the hurts
I had inside.
There my good sense
took last offense.

Like stir fried turd,
the words I'd heard
did not make sense.
They were absurd.
And so I chose
to pick my nose.

A Celebration of Life

I have been asked why a crippled, arthritic, feeble, old man like me is almost always optimistic and cheerful. The reason is, I am living on bonus time. I should be dead.

There was only one time in my life where I had actually given up and quit. About 6 years ago, I had concluded I was about to die. I could not shave myself. Due to pain, I could only sleep for 15 to 20 minutes at a time. I was taking pain killer in near lethal doses and it did not work. I was pretty much dysfunctional and barely able to walk a few feet. My ticket had been punched and I was boarding the train for hell. However, my dear spouse would not have it.

With the help of some truly heroic doctors she jerked me off the train. It was touch and go for some time. Sometimes touch got ahead. Sometimes go got ahead. After three years of torturous surgery and constant pain, I began to feel better. Now I can shave myself, sleep several hours, go to the bathroom without help and, most of all, be creative and useful. Heck yes, I'm happy. I feel the best of me is still in me and now I have some bonus time to get it out.

Life is an interesting adventure. We know we come into this world totally dependent. If not for other folks we would die shortly after birth. What I had not considered until this brush with the guy with the scythe is, that's also how most of us leave the world. We start with diapers and end with diapers. I've seen enough once strong and proud men in diapers. I don't like it at all. For the lucky ones, there will be a loved one there to "Attend" us.

All this has, of course, caused me to think about the final arrangement. I have attended many funerals and thought a great deal about the process. A majority of the funerals I have attended were botched in some way. Of these, most of the botching was achieved by bible thumpers with an agenda. It should be as difficult to botch a funeral as it is to botch a bowel movement. Both should be very natural things.

So far as I can tell, there are only two goals which a funeral must achieve to be successful. One is to celebrate the life of the person just passed. Second, through that celebration, to allow the survivors to make closure. Nothing else is important.

To be blunt, a funeral is not about the church or God. It's not about an agenda. It's not about bible thumpers. It's not even directly about the dearly departed. A funeral is a final celebration of a completed life wherein the survivors can make closure and begin the healing process for an enormous personal loss. If each and every participant does not make this closure, the funeral has failed in its purpose. The final celebration is for the survivors.

Since it is possible I will die someday, I have made some notes about how I would like things to be for the folks I love. Think of them as guidelines for whoever is in charge of arrangements at that time.

The very first thing is to exclude professional holy people from speaking at my final celebration. I have found too many of them who are either frauds or fools and sometimes both. The people who love me, and there are some, do not need someone to feed them a line of bull about everything being all right. When someone you love dies, everything is not all right. It's shitty. It's enormously painful, even if it was expected.

In order for everything to be all right, you have to mourn your loss. You must weep and curse and piss and moan until the pain is bearable. Then, gradually, things will get better and you will come to know that it WILL be all right and that death is natural and it will come to you also. You don't need any damn bible thumper to tell you about it. You don't need anyone with an agenda at all. You need a gathering of friends to share the final celebration of a life completed.

The purpose of the celebration is to experience the separation process. To experience the grief and sadness and to honor the achievements of a human life with others who cared. After the celebration you should be able to go about your business, while the healing continues, without making a career out of mourning. You should be able to remember a friend with fondness and humor, and avoid the kind of silliness which causes some people to gather once a year and stand around the highway outside an airport where a plane once crashed. I get fed up to puke with people who make a career out of public mourning and with the maudlin, deviant media which sucks them on.

The manner of death is really very irrelevant. Whether we had an accident or just got old and wore out. Whether someone made an error which caused our death or it came as the result of some deliberate act of a demented person. What does it matter? If someone killed me, or if you think someone killed me, forgive them. If you can't do that, at least forget them. Minerva will take care of that detail. Just comfort my friends and celebrate my life.

Most people who come to a final service don't come for the deceased. They come to offer whatever support they can to those who are most devastated by the loss. Those people are welcome at my celebration. They must be thanked on my behalf. Even clergy may be welcome as silent supportive friends of the survivors.

Don't listen to anyone who says, "It's a shame. He could have lived a lot longer if he ...." Two things to know. No one who really knows me would say that and the person saying it is someone with an agenda. It's some kind of reformed sinner casting for converts; trying to save someone. Ask them to leave. Even if it's a relative.

As to children, I am firm in the belief that they should not be forced to attend funerals. They may be invited. If they are up to it they will come. If they are not up to it, it is a heinous thing to make them attend and traumatize them forever. It is beyond heinous to force them to view a corpse or to kiss a coffin containing a corpse. It is an emotionally violent, evil act.

The final celebration must have two parts. The first, formal part, is a time to get in touch with what you feel by hearing music and words. For the words, someone who knew me well should be asked to speak. Someone who can get through it without breaking up. There may also be others who feel the need to speak. This should not be more than three or four people who knew me and they should, out of kindness to the assembly, limit their speaking to five minutes or less.

I think it's appropriate to have music for the occasion. I believe the *Ashokan Farewell* is the best for me and my friends. I cry every time I hear it. It's soulful music. It must be done, however, just as it was done on *The Civil War* sound track. If you cannot find a group who can perform the piece, the CD must be used in a way that only the *Ashokan Farewell* will be heard.

The second part of the celebration is the sharing of food, drink and music in the honoring of a life completed. People, at this time, will begin to remember and share what they knew of me. There will be anecdotes. Some of them may even be true. For food, I believe a buffet with pizza, antipasto, raw vegetables with dip, bread and crackers. Except for the pizza, kind of what we would have on Christmas Eve. For drink, have an open bar with soda, beer and wine. No hard stuff. I would like a celebration, not a brawl.

And, let it be a celebration of my life! Don't dwell on the gloom and doom. Remember what I did and how I did it. Remember, I enjoyed life. Have the second half music be real New Orleans Dixieland. Not the crap they call blues now but the old stuff. *Musk-rat Ramble, Alligator Crawl, Twelfth Street Rag, Basin Street.* You know! The stuff we heard on Bourbon Street. The music should be present but should not dominate. People should not have to shout over it.

Viewing the remains is not an essential part of the healing process. Sitting around with a corpse is not emotionally healthy even though it's traditional. In addition, an embalmed corpse, while not a medical threat, is simply an insult to the environment. Once the spirit has left, you have only a dead body. When I am done with this body, there will be no useful parts left, but if the medics want parts that's fine. One could question, however, what they would do with a stone heart; a beer soaked liver or a decayed brain. Whatever works for the survivors is fine with me.

Once the surgeons get what they want, whatever is left should be cremated. Grave sites just take up real estate for no good reason. And they can be a source of future conflicts among people. Look at the silliness of some early Americans over, so called, sacred mounds. Dead is dead for God's sake. The spirits are not there. They are with the great spirit. My ashes can be mixed into the ground somewhere where they can reintegrate into the environment. Around my roses would be OK. Everything should be useful.

As to where the funeral should be, it's a celebration. Have it in the same kind of place you would have any other celebration. A banquet facility or hall; and let it last long enough for each participant to make closure. This does not mean a spouse or offspring must stay all day. a trusted friend can do it. Everyone should be able to leave when they are ready.

When it's over, the survivors should say, "Willie knew how to live and he knew how to die."

A news item. It was reported that some zoo had a pair of eagles who got along very well. They couldn't figure out why they did not mate until someone discovered that both eagles were male. Just think! Those were just ordinary folks. They weren't even Ford managers. What a career they could have in the automotive industry.

I once met a person who said she was bored. My God! There are so many things to learn and so little time. How could you possibly have time to be bored?

Little Known Facts

(because nobody cares)

The world's shortest book is the *Great Book of English Culinary Delights.*

There are no plums in plum pudding.

The best antidote for stress is hugs.

There are some people who should never sing.

There are some people who should never appear in a bathing suit.

There is currently more fraud and dishonesty in the computer industry than there ever was in the used car business.

The best place to find morels is under old rotting apple trees on the shady side.

The best place to find morals is in little children.

It takes approximately 13 million belly buttons to produce one pound of lint.

Because of illegal poaching, the Matzo is almost extinct.

Answers are like rectums. Everyone has at least one.

On a clear day, you may or may not see forever. However, if you are on a large enough body of water, you can see the curvature of the earth. Try it! I have seen it from the beach of Hammond Bay on Lake Huron. It may also work in Kansas. Ask Dorothy.

It was impossible to prove to Mother Gaffer that the earth is not flat. She could see that it is.

Everyone should understand that champagne is nothing more than carbonated cheap wine. Sometimes naturally carbonated, sometimes not. The bubbles give it snob appeal. Like the currently popular coolers and so called cooking wines, it's just wine so bad it would not be otherwise marketable.

Working for Pleasure

I retired about 5 years ago. Since then, I have been offered a few positions. I say, "No thanks!" The moment you accept a position of employment, the clock starts ticking. You get quotas and deadlines. That creates pressure and that causes stress. You start to grit your teeth. Pretty soon, your arthritis starts acting up. Your heart muscle starts getting tired and, first thing you know, you're in danger of dying. Then you have to quit the damn job anyway. Better to not take a position in the first place.

Now I'm self employed. I'm writing a book. There is no daily quota or deadline. No clock is ticking. The book is done when it's done. So what am I doing? Working about sixty hours per week, more than I ever worked for anyone else and having a great deal of fun. The product is mine. It's in my control and I can be as creative as I want. Not only that, but if something special comes up, I can adjust my priorities instantly and I don't have to explain it to anyone. I don't have to sell or explain anything to anyone and I don't have to count hours and minutes to prove productivity. Nor must I write silly, bull crap reports. The only selling task I will have is when I have a finished product.

I'll never again be a nine to fiver!

My relatives and friends think I should enjoy life more. I can't seem to explain that the things I do, which they call work, are the most continuously enjoyable parts of my life. My life is not about travel or recreation and activities like that. Those things are enjoyable and I do them on occasion, but my life is about doing. Creating and producing are the most satisfying things I do. I can't stop doing these things because my soul would shrivel up and I'd die inside if I did. Outside of certain relationships, productive activity is the greatest pleasure in my life.

We need some new words for the concepts of doing things. The word "work" just doesn't do it. It has a really bad connotation in our culture. For people who get pleasure from their vocation, calling it work is incongruous. Work is OK for "gotta do" but we need a different word for "wanna do". It's different than recreation or leisure. Those are pastimes. I am talking about productive, creative activities. The word should combine the concepts of productivity, creativeness and pleasure. We have many phrases which do it but I cannot find a word for it. If I call what I do a hobby or avocation, it gets trivialized in the minds of those who hear it. For now, I think I will begin to call what I do zippate.

Zippate *verb intransitive*

To engage in creative, constructive and productive activity for the pure pleasure of the process.

Example: Willie was happy for the opportunity to zippate on his book.

There may be some problem in understanding until people pick up on the intended meaning of the word.

For example:
"Where are you going Willie?"
"I'm going in my office to zippate."
"Well close the door for goodness sake! Don't let the grandchildren see you."

Or:
"I think I'll go zippate in the garden."
"Well don't let the dog see you. You know how he picks up on things like that."

Or:

Said Bill to his friend on a date,
"With you I would love to zippate."
"I can't do that." she said,
"I intend to be wed,
before I behave like a mate."

Lists and More Lists

When I was younger there was a document called the *Vatican List* which simply listed the tomes and films which the Church found offensive. It was available to all members of the Church and to the public at large. It was the dream of aspiring writers to create a book which would appear on that list. It was one of the best things which could happen to a book for marketing purposes. It pretty much guaranteed a best seller. Being on the Vatican list was somewhat safer than being on Iran's list. Unlike the Ayatollah Khomeini, the Pope does not normally put out a contract on a writer. The worst thing would be excommunication.

I don't know if such a list still exists. It was terribly self-defeating and even stodgy clergymen catch on after a while. If an effort continuously backfires, you ought to stop doing it. Isn't it kind of dumb to provide kids with a list of dirty books? Totally unnecessary, too. Teenage people are much more resourceful that we are. The list just makes it too easy for them. Young horny Catholics and non-Catholics alike would scan that list for fun reading material.

I also noticed in the news that Disney Productions and products are being boycotted by the Council of the Southern Baptist Churches. The Disney people must be drooling over the anticipated sales increase of forbidden materials.

In this same vein, the Supreme Court has struck down the Internet Decency Act. This is a rare opportunity for someone to start a new service for concerned parents. It would be a kind of Vatican list for cyberspace. Folks could subscribe and get regular downloaded updates of which sites to block. Perhaps there could be software which would receive the updates and automatically block the cursed sites. Then the parents would not have to bother with their kids at all. Just subscribe and install the software. Leave the rest to big brother. We could have a staff of judges to decide which sites have evil content. I would nominate Tammy Baker, Jerry Falwell, Jack Kevorkian, Jesse Jackson, Hugh Hefner, Jesse Helms, Gloria Steinem, Bill Gates and other folks of pure heart, with no particular agenda.

I am making no special effort to appear on any list. I am simply writing what I think will entertain some folks. Getting on a list of condemned books, however, would surely increase initial sales volume. Even making Falwell's list can help a great deal in USA sales. Making his list is simpler because his good/evil gauge is so simple minded. If I am at all thoughtful and curious about the Divinity he is sure to condemn me. His world is so narrow that people must stand sideways in a row to fit into it. They have to be in line.

Varmints

Currently, the deer herd in the State of Michigan is larger than it has been in all recorded history. From news reports, I find this is true in many other states as well. The Michigan Department of Natural Resources, like most government, is about twenty years out of phase with reality. At one time the Michigan deer herd was in danger of extinction through hunting and poaching. They responded with a powerful program to save the deer. It worked. Problem is, they never completely stopped the program. In addition, although we did not manage to make the deer extinct, we have managed, for all practical purposes, to eliminate their natural enemy, the wolf.

Now deer are starving and becoming a public nuisance. They have managed to integrate into suburban culture where they do serious damage to property. They have become a menace on our highways and on our airport runways. Special permits have been issued so hunters can go on airport property to off them. They do immeasurable damage to farm crops every year, wounding our already crippled farmers. Meanwhile, the green freaks and others make an enormous fuss about murdering Bambi.

Instead of polarizing a difficult situation, we ought to take a look at the facts and options. Fact one is simple. In a contest between animals and humans, animals will eventually lose. That's just common sense. Fact two is also simple. There will be a contest between animals and humans. This is because the human population is continuously expanding and we have limited real estate. The animals have nowhere to go. It is incongruous to make impassioned arguments on the side of the animals unless you are willing to forgo having children. The conclusion is inescapable. Green freaks notwithstanding, animals are going to die.

The only options are in how we manage it. I personally find it almost impossible to hurt, let alone kill, animals except for rats and mice. I know that others do not share my phobia. I know that some people derive remarkable pleasure from the hunt and the kill. I confess to being completely unable to identify with that and I hesitate to encourage it. I have a sense that it's some sort of return to a primitive past. Nevertheless, it's the only answer I see.

I believe the most humane way to effect what will happen anyway is to control the wild animal population through systematic harvesting for food. It's not all bad. The food could be used to feed hungry people of whom we also seem to have a surfeit. We should do this as efficiently as possible. There should be no joy in taking the life of another being whether it is a rabbit, a deer or a tax collector.

City folks and many suburbanites will protest this. I have heard media people gush over the cute little raccoon with its cute mask and hands. I have heard them discuss how they can catch these cute little nuisances, then take them out in the country and release them. They feel noble. They have rescued an animal. In fact they have transferred the problem to the local farmers. A single racoon can decimate a corn crop in a few days if it's not killed.

This is what the farmer must do. If he keeps chickens for market or home use, he must be ready to kill possums and foxes. If he grows corn for home or market he must kill raccoons. The same is true of tender leaf crops and rabbits. Soon he will have to start killing deer whether the law approves or not. It is not an option for the farmer. It is neither compassion nor cruelty. It's economics and survival. A few may get pleasure from killing varmints. Most do not. It's simply something which must be done to provide food for an ever expanding human population.

Diagnosis and Health

Recent developments in science and drug testing show us we can learn anything at all about a person's physical condition through analysis of external components like hair. We don't need invasive techniques. We don't need blood. I envision a future where every home will be able to maintain a health profile on each resident simply through analysis of the waste products of that person.

Imagine this. A person walks into the bathroom, does his duty, keys in his name and flushes. The toilet does the rest. It whirs and gurgles and analyzes and produces a readout for the person. It probably would be a positive report, like "No pathologies or abnormal conditions noted." Of course it could be a serious instruction, like "There are indications of abnormal heart activity. Please sit down and be calm. An ambulance is on the way." Or it could be less alarming, like "There are indications of abnormally high carcinogens and fat. Lay off the Burger Beers for a while." Or, perhaps, "Take two aspirin and a sleeping pill. Get a good night's sleep and flush me in the morning."

I suspect many will say, "This could never happen. It would cost too much." I believe one of the problems with all these health insurance programs is we rarely see the bills. Next time your doctor orders a simple CBC and Chemistry Profile, instead of fretting about the needle, ask him how much it will cost. Don't accept, "It doesn't matter. The insurance will pay for it." Insist on knowing. Then consider that almost all doctor office visits will be eliminated and all routine diagnostic tests will be eliminated. Also consider that the equipment I envision would be mass produced. Pretty much all tools used in medicine now are practically handmade and very expensive. Also consider the cost savings of catching problems before they require major intervention. I believe it will happen.

We will have diagnostic toilets in the future and they will be computer controlled. Think of it. The toilet will have a little "Intel Inside" logo on one side and a "Windows Compliant" logo on the other side. Of course, for fair competition and to create compatibility problems, we will need another version called the Macintush.

The road warriors could carry a little cartridge containing their profile so they could plug it in wherever they go. For them we could even have big multi-stalled, multitasking, public facilities. Admission - six bits. They would be done up all in blue, of course. We could call them the Big Blue Committee Rooms. All road warriors would feel at home in these rooms. They could sit around and study flowcharts.

What a future!

Ghosts

Ghosts are the most compelling evidence we have for the existence of life after death. The case for the existence of ghosts is overwhelming. It can only be ignored by the most hard nosed, pseudo scientific atheists. No rational person, once they considered the evidence, could write it off even though it's totally anecdotal. There are just too many stories to write off. The silliness of credibility stretching stories like the one about a house in Amityville notwithstanding, there are enough convincing stories. We have more evidence for the existence of ghosts than we have for the existence of compassion in bankers.

I believe that many times ghosts are present and we don't see them. We don't want to see them because we are afraid of what it implies. We don't want to deal with the idea that people don't really die when they die. That means debts we incur do not go away; ever! If we wronged someone or forgot a commitment, it's still on. Bummer!

My guess is ghosts are just lost souls who have somehow been separated from their temporal selves and are held here by some kind of emotional tie. It is up to us to help them sever that tie so they can move to the next level. They have no temporal power so rather than fear them we should, when we encounter them, try to understand what they need to get free. Often it's only a matter of bringing their murderer to justice. This means finding the evidence which the ghost is bringing to our attention. Sometimes it's only a matter of understanding that something wrong happened. They need someone to understand. By their very existence these souls prove there is another level.

I once knew a ghost. His name was Louie. Louie became a ghost when he went blooey. He was messing with dynamite at the time. He only needed for me to understand that he did not mean to do what he did. He was just a teenage kid practicing and showing off. Louie wanted to be known as Louie the safe cracker. He had the cracker part right but he wasn't safe. He became a fire cracker. He felt terrible because he thought the young lady he was showing off for got killed with him. I did some research and found that his was the only death reported in an archived copy of the Dufus Gazette. Shortly after he read the paper over my shoulder, he swept an affectionate breeze over my face and was gone. I think the breeze was affectionate. It had no lasting effect. I was able to sleep well after only a month or so.

A few years back, I knew a fellow who came from the European tradition. He never visited me without bringing a gift of food. It was never a big deal, just something very simple. The idea behind this tradition was peasant based. None of these folks had much and they would not think of eating from someone else's pot without putting something in. This tradition is not something which is supposed to break you. Wouldn't it be nice to have this tradition reinvented in our culture. Regardless of wealth or position, wouldn't it be nice to just bring a token gift of food. We wouldn't have to guess what to bring. There are plenty of universal foods like fruit and vegetables and nuts. Never mind the sugar and alcohol products unless you are certain.

The Computer Industry

I have worked with computers for many years as a technician, programmer, analyst, and, finally, a user, just for writing. I have had occasions to be violently angry with the hardware and software and with the clods who create it. Most of my experience with computers has been negative, but the final insult occurred last night. After working for 14 hours on a layout, I was ready for a few hours rest. I did a normal save and shutdown and, just as the screen was doing a final fade to dark, I swear, my computer mooned me! It was right there on the screen before my eyes for just an instant. I went to bed and cried.

It is my honest opinion that most people do not need a computer. Because of my background, people often ask me what kind of computer they should get. What I notice here is the assumption that they should get a computer. Here are some of the nonsense rationalizations underlying that assumption. Someone told them they ought to have a computer. They need to surf the web. It will help their grandchildren. Everyone else has one. Computers are educational.

So I tell them, "I can answer your question when you tell me what you really intend to do with the computer."

Usually, they cannot tell me because they can't think of anything important enough to justify the price. They would be embarrassed to admit they want to spend two or three grand just to play games. They are always put off by my demand and sometimes even get angry because I will not accept the responsibility of giving uninformed advice.

Sometimes I will get an inane answer like, "Well, I can put my recipes on-line."

Can you picture this person trying to prepare a meal. He fires up the computer and eventually finds the recipe he wants. He reads the first two lines and goes to the kitchen to start. He starts but forgets the second line so he goes back to the study to make sure, etcetera, ad infinitum. What ever happened to good-old three by five index cards? You only record the recipe once.

Another one I get is, "I can do my income tax and my budget."

My question is, "Is your financial situation really that complicated? What budget?"

If your budget is a mess, it's because you have no discipline and a computer will not remedy that. How many years could the average Joe have a professional do his taxes with that two or three grand? I have a computer but for income tax, I use a professional accountant. I don't need the frustration of trying to understand tax laws and crappy, malfunctioning software at the same time.

Of course, they buy the computer without my advice. Usually they shop price and get a poor to average computer. After the purchase they may get addicted to computer games, if they can make them run. Sometimes they prevail upon me for that service. Occasionally their children or grandchildren will mess with it when they visit. Usually, though, the computer ends up sitting in a room gathering dust along with the hoola hoop, the exercycle, the ice cream maker, the Shop Smith, the Juice-O-Matic, the paint by number kit, the brass lamp from Aunt Martha and hundreds of other things which seemed like a great idea at the time. The fact is, even when they work, using a computer is just too darned complicated. Unless you really need it, it is not worth the frustration. Allow me to elaborate.

In a previous incarnation I had a friend and associate who was an outstanding Software Systems Analyst. One day another associate had a problem getting a particular piece of software to work on a particular computer. Being a thoughtful person, he decided to save time and frustration by phoning the vendor's technical support person. According to what I was told, here is what the technical support person said.

"Where you work, you have this guy named Chuck Xxxxxx (the name of my friend) who also works there. He's real good on these things. What you should do is go and explain your problem to him. He will be able to solve it for you."

This story was corroborated by several people and I believe it actually happened. It is interesting that the support person was not even embarrassed to admit that a customer knew more about his system than he did.

What brought all of these thoughts to mind was my recent experience in dealing with the intelligence and integrity challenged people of the computer industry. PC software and hardware has never been noted for its rugged reliability and stable operation. Much of the hardware does not work when we install it. Much of the software also fails on installation. Some of it even disables our equipment. This is why technical support has been an ongoing necessity. Recently, however, the quality of technical support in the industry has degenerated to the point where the above incident would seem to be a good solution.

For a very good example of how bad the situation is, get the July 1997 issue of PC Magazine, VOL. 16 NO. 13. Flip to page 85 and read what Bill Machrone, an expert in the field, had to go through to get a couple of games working for his kid. He did not insert the game CD and start to play. He installed the games and his computer stopped working.

It took a significant amount of the time and energy of this expert to recover. He gives us no times but it looks like at least one day for two people. Look especially at the cryptic computer jargon he uses which computer users are expected to understand. He lays out this debacle with conscious good humor, as though it were some kind of normal adventure with computers. Sadly enough, it is. Here's the final rub. At the end he confides that his computer is still not functioning properly.

It is his apparent lack of understanding which troubles me. I'm not sure he is aware that most of the people who read his column could not have done what he did. They have neither the skill nor the knowledge. Look at what he wrote and ask yourself if you could have done it or if you even understood what he said. Of those who could, most would not be able to invest several days in the effort. Machrone could because he knew he would get paid for his time by writing about it.

This is an expert. What about old Mom and Pop citizen? What do they do when confronted with a debacle like this, as they surely will if they buy and try to use a computer? For most of us, doing what this man managed would not be humorous. It would not be difficult. It would be impossible. So, what do they do?

What my daughter did was call me. She tried to install Microsoft's loudly advertised, Flight Simulator on her 200 MHZ state of the art system. Her screen went to garbage. We spent about 4 hours on the phone and I finally ended up driving about 90 miles to restore her system.

My daughter is no dummy. She has a Ph.D. in Biochemistry. Does this mean she should also know what Machrone knows about computers? Perhaps we should demand that the captains of the computer industry know as much as she does about genetics before they can get food. After all, why should these dummies be allowed to eat if they can't understand how food comes about.

We have no idea why Flight Simulator blew my daughter's system. After two hours of trying to navigate Microsoft's web site, I finally found a place to register a bug alert, for all the good that did us. If Microsoft got the message, they did not acknowledge it. We have no help and do not know why Flight Simulator blows her system every time we try to install it. It just does!

If you like mazes, you will love most of the computer industry's web sites. Microsoft's is particularly challenging because it's about the size of Texas with lots of wonderful, useless, slow loading, self serving graphics. For myself, I do not like mazes. Even small ones. I consider them a waste of time.

I ran out of time trying to find help online. There is a computer industry assumption that I have unlimited time to figure out how to get their help just to make their garbage do what they said it would. This is simply not true. I'm 67 years old. I have very little time and none to waste. All the online ventures I have made were to get information or help. What I have found is you almost have to know the answer to your question to make an efficient search. It's like trying to use a dictionary to make spelling corrections.

Many people are saying what a great thing the internet is. I say, it needs a lot of work. This is a case where it really is a new industry which needs time to mature. It may be fine for those folks who have hours to waste. If they were not on the net, they would be in an arcade, shopping mall or amusement park. It's not fine for those of us who have something real to do.

"Surfing the net" is a false metaphor. It's more like wading chest deep in a dark swamp. It's frustrating, darn slow going and you're never quite sure where you are or when the bugs will get you. You just know they will. For help on this, *PC World* magazine sometimes publishes a very useful list of interesting web sites with a description of their contents. The latest list is in the August 1997 issue. Also try their web site. WWW.pcworld.com/aug97/net. We will hope it is still there by the time you read this.

I expect I am like a growing number of normal folks, in that computers have become essential to my work. For myself, this has been true for at least 30 years. The conundrum is, I have never acquired a piece of software which actually worked the way it was advertised to work. Never! In addition, I have acquired very little hardware which performed as advertised. Now I find the technical support for these malfunctioning products is staffed by incompetents. I am faced with the chore of having to find ways to work around the problems myself.

Here is the most recent example. In writing this book, I knew I was going to need several drawings and a couple of musical scores. I decided to use a computer graphic drawing program to do this work. Well into the project, the program malfunctioned in a way which kept me from continuing. I went online and tried to get technical support to look at the problem. By the time I finished getting numerous insults, inane guesses and no help from those people, I would have been better off to have done the drawings by hand and delivered them as camera ready art, instead of electronic files. That is the truth.

After realizing I was not going to get any help from those fools, I decided to get systematic in eliminating possible causes of the problem. I got some thoughts from a friend to get me started. Through a simple systematic procedure, I did isolate the problem and it turned out to be a flaw in the conceptual design of the program. As soon as I understood the flaw, I devised a "work around" for it. I can now limp along with this malfunctioning software. I believe it is a conscious decision on the part of the vendors or their technicians to put customers off in the hope they will solve the problem themselves or, at least, go away.

After this experience I sent a letter to the marketing director of the company which produced the software outlining my experience with their product and their people. If history is any guide, I will receive no reply at all, or a pap-filled letter extolling the virtues of the product and the company with a left-handed apology, as an afterthought. If the answer comes at all, it will be several months getting here.

Sadly, this is not an isolated event. I've been through this same procedure, with minor variations, at least a dozen times in the last two years. It's true, I do things which requires fairly sophisticated software. I run programs, on a regular basis, which many folks would never use.

The point is, I must make my tools work to be productive. For the average person with a home computer, getting the software to function properly may not be quite as critical. However, it is just as frustrating when it doesn't. Judging from the input of friends, I believe most people who own computers have faced this same problem. You have a computer with software and a great deal of it does not do what you think it should. You have no idea why and no idea how to get help to make it work.

The answer of the computer industry is, "You are stupid." Go to your local computer store and look at the books you are offered. They blare out at you, "YOU ARE A DUMMY!" I'm here to tell you, that is a shabby lie. You are not a dummy. The fact that you can use this junk at all indicates you are above average.

In my experience the entire computer industry is dishonest. I have encountered no exceptions. In addition, I speak from the perspective of a person who was once a software systems analyst with a large firm in Dearborn. I was inside. Believe me, it's just as bad on the inside. I had to work with software and hardware from many of the major computer companies. It was just as buggy, convoluted and cumbersome as the stuff I have to work with now.

In almost 38 years in the electronics and computer industries, I have seen many new and exciting developments. Invariably the companies who produce the hardware and software have used these fast moving developments as excuses for building dysfunctional products. There is an incredible lack of discipline and integrity in this industry. If Ike had run his army the way most of these companies are run, we'd all be speaking German now.

These marginally criminal companies create products and rush to market without proper testing, making the general public their victims and beta testers. The software and the hardware companies treat their customer base as a final test facility. They give you poorly conceived malfunctioning products with little or no documentation. They expect you to understand cryptic, obscure, nested menu commands. They expect you to use operating procedures and methods designed to make the programmer's life easier rather than make the operation clear for the user. They implement procedures in the language of computers rather than the language of the intended users. Then when you can't understand their cryptic, convoluted crap, they call you a **dummy**.

If you call a company's technical help phone number you will be put on hold, at your expense, for anywhere from 10 minutes to hours if you have that much time. All the time you are on hold, you will have the joy of listening to some perky, cutesy mouthed, twit brained woman telling you how great their company is and how wonderful their products are. Then, if you finally get through, you will have to deal with the technical support credo. To wit:

1: There is nothing wrong with our product.

2: The user is a bumbling, inept layperson who has done something wrong.

3: The user is too dumb to explain what he did wrong so his input must be ignored.

4: Our task is to guess what he did wrong.

5: Our method is to guide him through simple-minded elimination procedures.

6: Once we guess what he did wrong we must patiently explain to his simple mind how to do it right.

7: If he can't understand and persists, we continue to give him simple-minded tasks until he gives up and quits bothering us.

Conscious or not, this is the attitude and procedure of all the technical support people I have encountered. It's no wonder they tick off most of the folks who have to deal with them. Nowhere do they ever consider the notion that the user might be an intelligent, rational, thoughtful human being. Nowhere do they ever consider the possibility that their product is flawed, even though historical evidence reveals **it always is**.

A friend recently made an interesting observation. He said, in essence, "The people you talk to on the phone, or online, are accustomed to speaking with a person who knows nothing about computers. Since they have no knowledge about your abilities they just naturally treat everyone on a very superficial level. Your adversary is not unique. Only after several conversations with the same person can you get down to a meaningful technical discussion." My gosh, I wish I had that much time. Even if I did, I would not waste it conversing with someone who started the exchange by assuming I was a fool.

I think it amazing that so many of the people who have to deal with these cruds have grown so used to it, it no longer makes them angry. It doesn't bother them to waste two or three working days to get a $100.00 piece of poorly designed and documented software to work. This may be acceptable for people who are using a computer as a toy or hobby. It's not acceptable to me and never will be.

Technical support in the computer industry ranges from poor through incompetent to nonexistent. Nonexistent is really better than incompetent. At least you know you're not going to get help and you don't waste several days with bungling fools.

If you like low comedy and can get online, try reading the questions and answers in any one of the technical support forums. Some of the exchanges are bizarre. I saw a very weird one on the forum of a removable disk company. The technician gave an answer which amounted to telling a person to put about 50 megabytes of data on a 1.4 megabyte disk. For the nontechnical, this is equivalent to asking you to put a wheelbarrow full of horse manure into a one pound coffee can. This technician gave this same answer to several different people with very different problems. For someone from the outside, it can be quite funny. For the poor victims trying to get help, it is not funny at all. It's very difficult to maintain a sense of humor when the insult is recent, current or recurrent.

I am collecting examples of this kind of silliness for my own entertainment. I doubt it would make a book because the audience would be too limited. It would only be understandable by people with some technical background. Though most of the answers are not technical at all, the questions usually are. It turns out that most of the people who are knowledgeable enough to get online and find the support forum know more about the product than the people who are pretending to help them. From looking at these forums, I find that most people who ask for help need about three exchanges to realize they are dealing with an incompetent fool masquerading as a technician. I would guess the number of problems simple enough for these fools to resolve is less than ten percent.

As you would guess, there is a great deal of user rage expressed on these forums. Sometimes in four letter words. This rage increases exponentially as the incompetent bungling technicians reply with pious, self-righteous indignation to being told the truth about themselves.

We buy computers and software to increase our productivity. In the beginning, it seemed they would do that. Now we find ourselves in a downward spiral where we spend as much time getting the stuff to work as we do using it. The vendors have taken the position that we have nothing to do but be final testers for their garbage. They sell us a product for three or four hundred bucks and we lose three or four thousand dollars worth of productive time trying to get them to fix it or create a "work around." We are losing ground.

The cost to American business of this fraud is enormous. We are talking many man-years of effort wasted in getting this poorly conceived malfunctioning slop to do what it was advertised and sold to do. One small company I know of has lost at least 200 person hours in the last two years trying to make various computer products work. It has reached the point where small businessmen must simply trash some stuff and eat the loss rather than lose additional time trying to get these companies to act responsibly.

No matter how you dress it up, this is fraud on a grand scale. I am lucky enough to be in a unique position. I may recover some of my loss simply by using it as a subject to write about. What about the regular business people who lose enormous sums every day due to the failure of these dishonest products. Large companies will get preferential treatment by these crooks. Small ones may indeed fail as a result of being ripped and then treated like fools by these short-sighted producers.

When critics of the industry complain about the poor user support, they are correct but this only addresses the symptom of the problem. The products should not need the massive support they do. The stuff should be well constructed and well documented just like any other consumer product. It should have been tested and working before it was sold. The stuff should be built so that the average citizen can make it work and use it. We should not need customer support to do this. The truth is, the products are simply faulty.

I saw on the TV news tonight how this great new voice recognition software is going to make pencils, pens and keyboards become ancient artifacts. In addition, they say, hand writing recognition software will revolutionize the US Post office. I've heard that kind of bull until it's coming out of my ears. Then I go buy a piece of software for 500 bucks, bring it home, install it on my computer and my screen goes blank. Great stuff!

I have been hearing how great these products are from their marketing people and from press releases read by their media pimps since the beginning of my career. I hope you will excuse me if I don't fall on my knees and thank God when I hear it one more time. I have great evidence to believe they are deliberately lying again. Everything I have heard up until now has turned out to be, in the very kindest terms, somewhat exaggerated.

Software designers and builders should be the happiest people in the world. They are getting paid enormous salaries to solve what amounts to puzzles. Each day, millions of people sit around their family rooms, living rooms or kitchens and solve puzzles in groups just for the fun of doing it. These programmers are getting paid to do it, yet they are too lazy to do it right. They will not take the extra steps to produce quality products. Hardware and circuit designers are the same. They are doing what millions of American tinkerers do every day in their garages and basements just for the joy of it. Why can't they do it with integrity?

There is a perspective contrary to mine which I must address. If we read the PC industry journals regularly, we could get the impression that the products of the computer industry are getting continuously better and easier to use and that anyone can use them. It's a falsehood I have grown very weary of. There is a perceptual problem which is common to pretty much all technical fields. The people who pimp for it are so steeped in the tricks and "work arounds" they don't even see them. They are unaware, for the most part, that they are doing extraordinary things to make the stuff function so they can test it. Things that most people who want to use the products as tools do not have the time to do nor the background to understand.

The truth is, the products are getting more complicated and bug infested with each iteration. Albeit they do more things, if only we could understand how to make them do these wondrous things. For these journalists, good support means they can call an officer of the company, identify themselves as journal staff and get some attention.

Another thing we should know about the people who write for and about the computer industry is that they do not usually pay out of their own funds for the toys they play with. The toys are provided by the manufacturers as gifts and/or test systems. For these people the whole setup is kind of a paid-for-play environment. It's a great arcade. With that going in mentality they have no way of identifying with the community of people who pay for and expect to use computers for real work in a real business.

We read that standards are being created and interfaces are getting better. Take a look at the interfaces resulting from these standards. Look at the things called menus and commands and windows. Either they are in the language of computer professionals, not human beings, or they are totally inane and insulting. Did they consult the users? No! Rather than learn the language of their users, they have forced us to learn their language or use a childish interface with limited functionality. This is progress?

Another apology we often hear from the journalists is how the industry is immature and we must expect some instability and growing pains. May I point out, the computer industry is just a few years younger than the auto industry which we consider to be ancient and inflexible. Many of these deliverers of broadsides of bologna would try to make us believe that this industry started with the introduction of the first PC by IBM in 1981.

Students of history will know the first completely electronic computer was invented by the English mathematician Alan Turing. This computer was used early in the second world war by the British, to crack the German communication codes. A trick which dramatically turned the war in the favor of the Allies and probably saved democracy. Turing's was not the first computer. Other electro-mechanical machines were built before that.

Although Turing defined the general purpose computer dubbed the Turing Machine, his actual computer was single purposed. The first modern general purpose electronic computer was ENIAC, designed by John W. Mauchly and J. Presper Eckert, Jr. at the University of Pennsylvania in 1946. Doing the difficult math, I find that 51 years have elapsed since the introduction of the first practical computer until now.

For contrast, the Model T Ford was introduced in 1908, about 35 years before the first usable computer. You had to be a ballet dancer to drive it, but Ford introduced this *Peoples Car* long before the Germans even thought of it. The auto industry was mature by the start of the second world war in 1941, as is witnessed by the industry's ability to become the Arsenal of Democracy overnight. That's a little over 30 years from the first practical automobile to Army trucks and tanks. The best in the world.

Some apologists may try to bull you into believing the PC is a revolution in concept and somehow separate from the previous computer industry. If you buy that, you would have to agree that the introduction of the V8 engine or the automatic transmission created a revolution and a separate auto industry. It's crap. A Turing machine is a Turing machine is a Turing machine. A Pentium class computer is conceptually no different than ENIAC. It's simply smaller, faster and more powerful. It also integrates a great number of functions which were once in the domain of software. A Ferrari is smaller, faster and more powerful than a Model T. That's evolution, not revolution and it should be smooth. A Ferrari is smooth.

From their beginnings, both industries have evolved with the introduction of improved technology in the two industries and in related industries. In computers we can cite the development of solid state electronics as, perhaps, the single most influential factor. In automotive we can cite the parallel developments of paved roads; the plastics, steel and aluminum industries and the petroleum industry. The point is, there has been no revolution in either industry. Just evolution. Thus, there is no reason to believe the computer industry should not be mature. It has had time.

Greed and power mongering are the twin engines which drive the computer industry. Rush to market is the name of the game. Get there first even if your stuff does not work. It can take the form of deliberate fraud as it did in the case of one company who advertised and sold to me backup software they did not have, then delivered an obsolete product with a certificate to send in for what they had promised, when and if they ever finished making it. They did this with the help of a marketing company who offered the product in their catalog even though they knew it did not exist. The reason they did this was the existence of a competing product which I eventually bought. It turns out it didn't matter. Neither of the products worked.

I thought about filing charges with the state's Attorney General but I forgot it when I realized how he, and the others, mishandled the AOL debacle. That settlement punished the business people who desperately needed the online service and went to extreme measures to log on. Because they were successful, they got no recompense for Case's bungling even though it cost them millions of hours of lost productivity. The weirdos and net surfers who had no real need to get online were fully compensated for not trying. They simply went somewhere else to play. In the long run it may not matter. I don't know that AOL is making good on the claims anyway. I know they have not compensated me. They have not even acknowledged my claim which was mailed several months ago.

You know! I bet it was lost in the mail.

Enough of that. Almost everyone has a PC now whether they need it or not. Here is some advice you may consider. The software makers will 99 dollar you to death if you are dumb enough to buy every upgrade they offer. Most upgrades are just bug fixes which you have learned to work around. Buy every fifth or sixth one and skip the rest. Never buy a version X.0. This is what they call a major upgrade and it will have more bugs than a Florida swamp. You'll be in a real quagmire trying to make it work.

Only in the computer industry can manufacturers get away with shipping products they know don't work. It's because they all do it and we have to buy from one of them. It's kind of like when the big three used to make cars that fell apart after the 90 day warranty. They had to stop doing it when the Japanese gave them a wake up call. I'm afraid that call will not come from the East in this business. If it comes at all, it will have to come from inside the industry. I have seen very slight hopeful signs of late.

Meanwhile, we are dealing with the biggest let the buyer beware, screw the customer, all the traffic will bear, fraud which has been perpetrated on the public since the good old days when the Government let the railroads rule the country for a couple of decades. Don't conclude that I am advocating the Government take over the computer industry or even regulate it. If you think that's a good idea, take a look at Medicare. I will advocate that the people, every human being who has had to deal with, and been screwed by, these companies, begin keeping a kaka list and not give them a chance to screw you twice. I have a list which I can document in court if need be. Please sue me! There are others unlisted because I did not keep documentation. I don't need documentation to write them off as suppliers.

When I was younger and had different interests there were names which just made me feel good to hear them. We knew it was quality and we wanted it. Zippo, Exacto, Lionel. I pray that someday there will be names in computing which will have the same impact as Lionel and Exacto in hobbies and toys; as Steinway in Music; as Porter Cable in tools or as Dresden in china. You get the idea. Just one hardware company. Just one software company. Did you ever see an Exacto knife and not want it? Did you ever fail to realize it was the best?

It's been a long time since software and hardware production has been driven by sound engineering principles. Currently, it is driven completely by marketing people. The whole thing is controlled by peddlers. Deadlines take precedent over solid design and robust error handling. The less expensive crap called online help and wizard guides take the place of documentation. They are, for the most part, useless for two reasons. First, they assume the product is functional and you only want to learn a procedure. Second, they are inane. For example, you click on the help question mark. You point to the file menu and click, then you get a help box with the inane statement, "This is the file Menu." Ain't that helpful as hell?

None of this will change until we, the users, narrow the field by only doing business with the best of the bad. By doing this, we can force a gradual improvement in the products quality. What I suggest is this:

Keep a kaka list so you won't get ripped twice by the same producer. Don't confuse marketing companies with producers even though they are also often culpable. When you get a bad product don't let your ego keep you from telling everyone you know. We have all been ripped. Protecting your ego, protects the crooks who ripped you. Do the same about technical support. When you get insulted or put off, tell everyone. When you get good help, tell everyone. If you get a good product, tell everyone. Most of all, ignore the hype. Check with your friends.

Even though I despise the computer industry on the whole, I think the model is right. It's a whole bunch of separate enterprises, large and small, making pieces which can be assembled in various combinations to create useful devices. It's called open architecture. Resent it or not, the thank you for this concept goes to Big Blue (IBM). The industry simply needs a great deal of integrity and some basic honesty in the sharing of information. These things are conspicuously absent and dilute the open architecture concept.

The cut throat mentality and the rush to market with flea market sales promotions and strategies is undermining the entire industry. As a whole, this industry has less credibility than the Justice Department at Ruby Ridge and Waco. And, like the Justice Department, they have brought it on themselves.

To be fair, I have seen some progress of late. If I were to award the Gaffer prize for product excellence in the computer industry, the hardware prize would go to Adaptec. I cannot say anything about Adaptec's customer service because I've never needed it. That's as it should be. There would be no prize for software at this time. The, "at least they're trying," prize could go to Adobe.

Finally, I feel the need to apologize for the anger which carries through in this essay. I consider anger to be a bludgeon and humor a scalpel. I would like to sharpen the edge of anger with humor so it cuts more cleanly. When the insult is current and ongoing, that is difficult and, in this case, impossible for me. Still, for better or worse, what I have said is important and needed to be said, even though I could not say it well. We need to take a hard look at this industry. I have no desire to punish anyone. I simply want these people to start behaving the way their mothers taught them, with integrity and honesty. That's all.

Produce

We love fresh produce at our house and we buy a lot of it.

So, I'm pushing this cart through Crazy Louie's produce store. I'm not going to buy that much. At my age I just need the cart to lean on.

I notice this gentleman standing in front of the cabbages.

He's saying things like, "Hello there. How are you? Nice day," and stuff like that.

I look around but no one else is there.

I can't handle it so I motion to Louie. He comes over.

I say, "Do you notice that fellow over there. He seems to be talking to the cabbages."

"I see that," says Louie.

It's too much for me. "Don't you think that's a little strange," say I.

"Well sure it is," answers Louie. "But you gotta understand. This guy has bad vision. To him it's all a blur out there."

"Oh!" says I relieved. "Then he doesn't realize he's talking to the cabbages."

"Well of course not!" snaps Louie. "Everyone knows cabbages can't talk. Actually, he thinks he's talking to the cantaloupes."

Divine law forbids a person to laugh at their spouse's humor, no matter how funny.

One Country, My Country

There is a ridiculous argument going on between the Canadian and American fishermen over the salmon catch. The posturing and threats have taken an ugly and ominous turn. It's all about some American-Canadian treaty which was not renewed. Why should we need a treaty?

I have never been able to understand why the United States and Canada are two separate countries. We have been very good neighbors for decades. To be sure, there are snotty people on both sides of the border but it's been years since shots were fired. If fact, we have fired on our own people since we fired on Canadians. Canada and the Canadian people have been our allies in every significant jam we have gotten into after 1812.

We share a common border of nearly 4000 miles in addition to the Alaskan border. What a terrible waste of people in customs staff alone. Sad, when we realize that this waste is exactly duplicated on the Canadian side. These people could be given honest jobs to increase productivity in both countries. All they do now is stand and wave cars through. Sure, they can also cause major traffic jams when one of them happens to have indigestion, a hangover or a recent spousal rejection.

We have a common language. We have an almost common currency. We have the common habits of drinking too much beer and wine, and eating too much rich food. Our art and cultural riches are similar. We also share a history of corrupt and inept governments, kept viable by the people's underlying faith in the democratic process and the institutions which sustain it. Our two countries have more in common than have New England and Texas.

As Americans, we ought to get smart and realize the only reliable allies we have ever had are the English speaking nations. Canada, Australia and the British Islands. The rest are what I call fair weather friends, taking all we give them and waiting for the chance to cut our legs off. It's the governments I'm talking about, not necessarily, the people.

Isn't it about time the English speaking governments got together and set a 20 year plan for complete merger into a single nation? This would create an economic force which could dominate the world for centuries. How does a thousand years of peace sound? The very presence of such a power would be a massive influence in the prevention of wars.

A merger would also give the British a graceful way of eliminating that silly and embarrassing anachronism, the royal family. What I would do with the royal family is pension off the last of them and turn all the palaces into public museums. Perhaps the prince could become the first curator.

I don't see any details which would not work out. What would it matter if the president were an Australian in one of those nifty hats? Could he be more embarrassing than a Texan in a ten gallon hat who drags his dog around by the ears? What would it matter whether we called him Mr. President or Mr. Prime Minister? What if we had three houses instead of two? Could the gridlock get any worse? In theory now, one house represents the states and the other represents the people of the states (wink, wink, nod, nod).

Maybe we could have a house which represents all the people at large. Two hundred vulgar, snide, rowdy, obnoxious babblers, elected at large. We could call it the house of commons. They could even sit on hardwood benches if they preferred to enhance the meanness of their spirits. We could put them on TV. Watching the house of commons could become a household pastime, much like watching our favorite evening soaps. We could select our own private heros to compete with JR and Dr. Doug on ER. There could be a "Snotty Prize" of the week for the best back bench putdown.

As to election rules for the house of commons, anyone could declare for these seats. They would have to run as independents and have a strict limit on campaign spending. One million bucks adjusted to the year of the first government. This would allow them a chance to recover campaign funds without taking graft. It would require two elections. The first would occur around the time of the primaries and would be a field reduction election. Each voter would be allowed to vote for no more than 500 of these babblers. It would be nomination by the people. The top 500 vote getters would be house finalists. In the regular election, each voter could vote for not more than 200 babblers. You can see, we will have to implement electronic voting.

We would have to think of a neat name for this new multi-nation government. It cannot be a name which would tend to exclude other nations from joining the alliance in the future. United Honky Nations would not do. I would lean toward an inclusive and noble name like Alliance of Nations United in Service (ANUS).

There would be many sticky details of government to resolve and there would be some rough spots. Yes, the English would have to learn to count money in a logical way. Americans would have to learn the difference between a stiff upper lip and stiffing a friend. American beer companies would have to improve the quality of their products in order to compete. Canadians would insist on having Cuban cigars. There would be *Beatles* everywhere. Americans would have to learn to put up with the wailing of bagpipes.

If necessary, Quebec could be offered the option of honest participation or seceding and having their own small, poverty stricken country. There is also the question of where to place the capital. With modern communication, it could actually be spread out over the four major existing locations. These are all just details to be worked out in committee.

Once the single nation was established, nothing would stand in the way of allowing other countries to apply for merger as they qualified with some kind of minimum standards of behavior. This could eventually lead to a realistic world government. In time, we could even let the Irish join if they could demonstrate a willingness to stop murdering their own relatives. How could a people with such beautiful music lay such a horrible burden of hate and savagery on their own children. I cannot believe that the majority of Irishmen want this. It has to be an insane minority on both sides.

A PVC Business Plan

You can build almost anything with PVC plastic pipe. Even a PVC log cabin. Picture it with 6" PVC pipe and elbows.

I would like to see one of the plastic plumbing companies start a hobby division. They already make most of the components needed for some great kits for older kids. They still need a few simple components in all the pipe sizes. We need a hub with spoke holes to take standard thick wall pipe. Perhaps a sphere where pipe could come off at 30 degree angles in every direction and another for 45 degrees. These are simply multidirectional junctions to complement the T fitting and the X fitting. The multidirectional ones would work for building three-legged stuff like tripods and stools and large canopy or umbrella supports. We need wheels in various sizes with slightly oversized axle holes. We also need floor flanges in various sizes for anchoring stuff to a deck or floor.

Perhaps we could even have various sized panels for making surfaces. These could be cut to length for whatever project was at hand, like picnic table planks. The panels would need snap on clamps in various pipe sizes, like pipe clamps except they snap on to the pipe and glue to the panels. The clamps would also provide an alternative way of connecting cross pipes together, if the clamps were double sided. Then we would also need double sided clamps at different angles, or just one which rotated. In addition, we should have some attractive reliable way of attaching fabrics like screen and canvas to our plastic structures. Everything I have seen for this is cumbersome and ugly. It may be OK for temporary work in plant nurseries but not in our yards and gardens.

The hobby division could build and test prototypes, then create plans for various projects. I can think of several. A bird feeder on a

PVC telescoping pole to discourage squirrels is simple. I built one of these. It works fine with the feeder supported on a 1 ½ inch pipe nested inside a 2 inch pipe. A bolt through the pipe holds the feeder up. Remove the bolt and the pipes telescope for feeder filling and cleaning. Other projects could be a picnic table, a tea cart for the deck, a bird bath, a greenhouse frame, a decorative fence, a children's playhouse, lawn and deck chairs, awning supports, rose arbors and a summer screen-house frame. I'm sure there are many others in the minds of creative folks out there. The only tools needed should be screw drivers, pliers, hack saw, adjustable wrench and electric drill.

Real men, of course, would use the plans only as starting points. They would eschew kits altogether in favor of assembling their own from components. We must understand that most men never outgrow the Tinker Toy, Erector Set mentality. Some of the happiest people I know are the technicians who support engineers by applying their creative genius to build prototypes of what the engineers conceive. These guys have rooms full of tools and parts of all kinds. It's about time some hobby manufacturer caught on to this. What you must do is give us components which make it appear we are doing something useful rather than playing. Think of the fun we could have if only there were just a few special hobbyist components to go with all the regular plumbing parts. For maximum market penetration, these components should come in several standard colors, not just white. We need at least the basic nine colors.

Now, I would not be greedy. If a plastics company wanted to pay me a small royalty for the idea, I would be happy. Of course I would also expect to receive all the plans, as they were developed, along with a truck load of components. As to the plans, I believe it would be a marketing error to sell them. The old Gillette motto would apply in this instance. He is alleged to have said, "Give them the razors. Sell them the blades." That may not be a precise quote but it's close enough to understand the concept. Give them the plans. Sell them the components. Yes it's true! I did not have Tinker Toys when I was a kid. I got them for Christmas but my brother took them away from me.

The Oracle from Peking

The Great Yee Jinx Makes Predictions.

What will be the most significant events of the next 100 years?

Elvis will be seen chatting with the Pope in the Vatican.

A 15 year old on a skate board will win the Indy 500. He will be disqualified for using nonstock components.

The stock of spice and herb companies will soar.

It will be discovered that politicians and managers consume five times the average of alcoholic beverages and toilet paper.

Laws on noise pollution will be rigorously enforced.

It will be revealed that almost as many women as men suffer hair loss which they have successfully concealed.

Baldness and shaved heads will become fashionable for women and men.

How will the telephone companies fare?

They will go belly up in the near future unless they get a piece of the web, satellite action.

What about the computer industry?

Competition will force it to become honest. Voice recognition will actually work. Keyboard, battery, electronic and monitor technology will be replaced by flexible electronic fabric technology. The whole damn computer will roll or fold up like a sheet of yard goods. You will carry them in your purses or hip pockets.

Will there still be conflict between the sexes?

Yes! Most men will realize the advantage and begin to carry large purses. Women will make fun of them.

What else can you tell us?

Alcoholism will increase.

Will there be racial harmony?

Not in 100 years. Not in a thousand years.

Why?

Rage and revenge will always rule the human psyche.

What about our future diet?

The common diet will consist of beans, rice, seaweed and processed plankton.

Can you tell us something about crime in the future?

There will still be criminals and fools everywhere. It will still be unknown which are the more dangerous.

What about art?

Nothing new. There will still be more charlatans than artists because there will be more fools to support them.

Any other scientific breakthroughs?

Safe, controlled fusion will make unlimited power available for humans to squander.

What about the political front?

There will be one world government based in Beijing.

Will it be a democracy?

No! It will be a Dumbocracy, much like the United States is now.

What will be the biggest threat to the earth?

Thermal pollution.

What will be the biggest threat to human life?

Terrorism.

Will there be a change in the musical landscape?

There will be a revival of the traditional classics. The three B's will again be fashionable.

Why is that?

People will become sick to death of loud, obnoxious noise disguised as music.

What will happen to rock?

It will fade to a small cult status.

Country and Western?

As always, on Saturday nights in cyberspace redneck bars and cyberspace bowling alleys.

What of drugs?

The illegal drug industry will continue to be the wealthiest and most efficiently run enterprise on the planet.

Communications?

All communication will be by satellite, word of mouth or smoke signals.

Education?

The same as now. Very little will occur.

Employment?

All employment will be intellectual in nature. Computer controlled machinery will do all labor intensive work.

Will we have leisure time?

Too much! Many people will commit crimes out of boredom.

What about social activities?

Most social interaction will be through cyberspace pseudo gatherings. Actual physical contact will become socially unacceptable, aberrant behavior.

Will we have families?

The family as you know it will disappear. People will live separately.

Population growth?

Population will be controlled by the government.

Space travel and exploration?

It will be abandoned. Limited resources will make it unsupportable.

House of the future?

The typical dwelling will be a 9 by 9, one room walkup.

Entertainment?

It will become more localized. There will be a renaissance in legitimate theater and burlesque via cyberspace. Bawdy routines will be popular.

What can you tell us about children?

There will be few.

Birthing a child will require a license from Beijing.

Illegal children will be executed along with their parents.

Women will not bear children. It will be done in machines, where the environment can be properly controlled. Each newborn will be perfect, per the standards of Beijing.

Children will be raised in public facilities to the age of consent.

You show us a grim future. Is there no hope?

The Oracle does not deal in hope, only in time lines.

That sounds like a riddle. Does this mean we can change our time line?

I am sometimes called the Oracle of Change.

Does this mean your predictions may be inaccurate?

They are simply projections out of the current dynamic.

OH! Thank you!

Yeah. Right. Like, now you'll make changes!

Uniforms

Most people would say they abhor uniforms and would not wear one unless compelled. Yet, if we watch ourselves, particularly the men, we tend toward a standard of dress which can only be called a uniform. Almost everyone has a characteristic uniform by which we identify them to the extent that we may not recognize them if they are out of uniform. Bill with his hat and string tie. Cuestick Eddie with his white shirt, tie, jeans, tennis shoes and baseball cap. Dave with his plain, conservative, blue suit, white shirt, dark tie and wingtips. You get the picture. Look at your peers.

I have three uniforms. My summer work uniform is shorts and a T shirt. My winter uniform is sweats. My dress uniform is a conservative suit which I wear to weddings, graduations and funerals. Other than that, I go naked. I gave most of my clothes from my working days to the Goodwill. They sent some of them back.

Mrs. Gaffer has no need to go outdoors to know the weather. She can look out and see me. If it's below 55 deg F I am wearing sweats. If it between 55 and 65 deg. I'm wearing shorts and T shirt. Otherwise .... Yes! Our home is isolated.

You know you're getting old when you start having sex free guilt.

The World of Books

I still remember the weird feeling I had when I first found *The Interpretation of Dreams* by Sigmund Freud in my high school library. I brought the book home and here I was in the parlor. My parents were there, so proud that Little Willie was actually studying. And I was sitting right in front of them reading the dirtiest book I had ever found. Freud talked about penises, breasts and masturbation, and all the forbidden words in my universe. All of this in a remarkably casual way. It beat heck out of those little Popeye flip books that all the other kids had. How are they going to look at those in the parlor. Finally, study paid off.

If one thing changed the direction of my thought and life, it was this first book by Freud. I had to learn to use a dictionary. I had to look up masturbation. Oh, I knew how to do it right enough. It's just that the word did not match any of my synonyms. So, I had to go to a library, to find an unabridged dictionary and more Freud. I had found the first book by accident while hiding from a teacher in the library. A place she would never think to look for me. To find more, I had to learn that ingenious Dewey System. I did these things all by myself with no adult mentor, except for old Sigmund himself, of course. After that I realized the world of books was just as exciting as Bare Ass Beach. After all, nothing really happened at BAB. There were too many people there. Don't ask me where it is. I suspect the kids still go there.

Mrs. Gaffer told me if I'm going to keep my head where it is, I should have a windshield installed in my stomach so I can see where I'm going.

You know things are bad when you send your old suit to the Good Will and the Goodwill sends it back.

Once a Crook

I'm in this jewelry store buying a nose ring for my wife.

She wants to have a ring put in my nose.

I don't know why.

Suddenly the door is slammed open by a guy with a silk stocking over his head.

He has a revolver in his hand.

I'm not thinking, "Oh darn!" I'm thinking something much stronger than that.

He takes a look around and points the gun at me.

I'm shaking my head and pointing at the clerk. Then I realize the clerk is not there. He is on the floor, passed out. It's just me and the guy with the stocking.

The gun is trembling. The guy with the gun is trembling and I am spastic.

"Be careful," I whine. "Just tell me what you want. I'll do anything you say."

"Fill a bag with all that stuff," he snarls.

I look desperately for a bag. There is no bag.

"There's no bag here," I babble. "No bag at all!"

"Oh shit," he shouts. "Here! Use this."

He pulls the stocking from his head and throws it at me. Just as he does it, he realizes he has made a giant mistake. His eyes are big as we look at each other.

My eyes are big too. I know he is going to shoot me.

Instead, he drops the gun and busts out bawling like a baby.

What I see, then, is a teenage kid, scared out of his wits and confused.

I pick up the gun and see that it's a toy. Not even a convincing toy, now.

The kid gives me this pitiful look.

I take a step toward him and he throws his arms around me and starts to blubber.

"I'm sorry. I didn't mean it. Please let me go!"

Actually, I'm not holding him. I pat him on the back.

He continues with his pleading and explaining. I find out more than I wanted to know about his mother, his sister, and mostly his remorse.

I can't stand it anymore and say, "for crap sake, just go, I'll tell the clerk you got scared and ran away."

He starts blubbering about how grateful he is as I push him out the door.

I go over and shake the clerk. He looks at me and whines, then faints again. I realize I still have the gun in my hand. I put it in my pocket and wake him again. I convince him it's OK.

Finally we are back to normal.

I start looking at rings again.

It's not until I go to pay for my nose ring that I discover my wallet and watch are missing.

I drop the ring and start bawling like a baby.

Profound Quotes

Yahweh:	"I am that I am."
Descartes:	"I think, therefore I am."
Popeye:	"I yam what I yam, and dat's what I yam."

In our current cultural climate, it would be impossible to create a comic strip like Popeye. I believe it would be politically incorrect, and probably against the law, to create a comic character who was appearance challenged.

Always thumb your nose at street drugs. That's a rule of thumb.

You know you are getting on in years when the glare in the mirror turns out to be the top of your head.

Hostage Consumers

Our power is out again. I was using my computer when it happened. Ten times today I got blown off while the power company's technicians experimented. On an average of once per week the power goes out. Sometimes it's off for several hours. Sometimes it's off for days. I know they will contest this because they count differently than I do. Sometimes, like today, it goes on and off at short intervals as though they were trying to damage my equipment. They will count today as one outage but my equipment does not see it that way. My equipment will count today as ten outages worth of damage.

All it takes to shut us down is a vigorous wind. Not a hurricane or tornado. Not even a warning or alert. Just a brisk wind. It's not just that the power goes out. It's also that they are unable to restore it in a reasonable amount of time. The company is so badly mismanaged they cannot respond to simple problems. Every simple outage becomes a major emergency.

It didn't have to be that way. Somewhere between thirty and fifty years ago the power companies had the technology to go underground. If they had started the process even twenty years ago they would now be invulnerable to the vagaries of the weather. In the long term, going underground would have saved billions of dollars in damage repair and maintenance costs. The short term costs, however, would have affected the year-end bottom line. Of course, they elected to maximize short-term profit at the expense of long term stability. We are now paying for that stupid greed. And still they follow the same policy. Forget the long term.

The power companies have made us dependent upon them. Then, when we need them the most, they are not here. We have to go to our private back up power supplies. They tell us to have consideration for the poor guys who are out fixing the lines and stop demanding so much. That's just a cover. The fact is, they have mismanaged to the point where they cannot respond to the problems.

Problems which are the result of previous management greed. They are trying to direct our attention away from this by invoking our human sympathy. You phony bums! We do care about the workers. Why don't you? Why did you put them in such a precarious position?

We can speculate that these companies have management bonus policies, set by management, similar to the auto industry and others. Yearly bonuses based on the year-end bottom line. Guess what that causes? Maximize this year's bottom line and screw the future. Now we find that our corporations are the most unstable things among us. They yo-yo up and down and fluctuate around, because there is no long-term planning. They talk about it but that's window dressing. Watch what they do!

The original concept of incorporation under law was to create an economic entity which would outlive individuals and thus create a long-term stable environment for economic development. American managers have found a very simple-minded method of circumventing that philosophy. By any other name, it's nothing more than short-term management greed. The finances of individual laborers are more stable than that of American corporations whose economic health jerks up and down with every vagary of the total environment.

We can take a look at what happens when a corporation must plan a mere four years ahead in order to bring an automobile to market. How often do they come up with an Edsel instead of a Taurus? How often do they see the short-term future and kill the next Edsel before we see it? In truth, why does it take four years and a billion dollars to bring an auto from concept to market? If it had taken Henry one hundredth that effort we would not have a Ford Motor Company. Yet we find the Ford folks slapping themselves on the back because they shaved a couple of months off that 48.

The entry of foreign competition into our markets has put a limit on the degree of incompetence American managers can get away with. Of course, this is not true in the hostage consumer business.

However, we can look forward to improvement even here. The phone companies and the power companies will be replaced. Overland lines, which create hostage consumers, is what they have in common.

The phone companies are already on the verge of extinction though they don't seem to realize it. A pizza sized dish to a satellite link will replace their long lines and their hostages will be freed to choose among many providers of fax, phone, TV and web access. This is already being implemented. The upside of this is competition will force a price just slightly above cost. Billing will be for bandwidth and time, not distance. Wider bandwidth will allow more phone numbers or faster access depending on how you use it. Long distance will become a meaningless phrase in communication. As an alternative to satellites, this concept could be implemented using the partially established network of cellular phone towers.

The basic unit of bandwidth will be one voice connection (VC). These bandwidth units will be dynamically assigned and recovered based on demand. There will be a basic monthly access charge and additional charges will be itemized in terms of voice connection minutes (VCM). This is important because it departs from the concept of separate permanent connections or phone lines. If you make one call, you will pay for one VCM per minute, if you make 12 simultaneous calls with 12 different phones, from the same location, you will pay for 12 VCMs per minute.

The electronic logic for these multiple connections will be in the home or business equipment, not in some central location. Record keeping will be in a central location with cross checking records in the home or business. There will be many manufacturers of this hardware and special features will proliferate as prices fall.

There will be a huge installed base of rooftop dish systems and providers will have to conform to whatever defacto standard grows from the chaotic startup. No one will be shut out because of location. Every shack in every remote part of the world will have the same opportunity for access, provided they have a power source.

Anyone who wants part of the action will conform. Users will have a choice of several providers and the difference will be quality of service not price. All users will benefit from improved service caused by competition. Users will no longer be assigned phone numbers. We will create our own IDs much as we now do on the internet. These IDs will be personal property and will go with us if we move.

It would be nice to keep the heavy hand of government out of it until the direction becomes clear. That probably won't happen. The government is outstanding in setting growth crippling standards which forever bar new technology. It's because congressmen who pass the laws are generally ignorant of technology. They are as bad as weathermen, having no understanding whatsoever of the factors and forces involved in what they are trying to predict.

Nontechnical people will worry about available channels. With the multiplexing, burst mode and packet encoding technology currently available, it need not be a problem. Gee! Look at how technical that sounds. It's called techno-speak. All you need to know are the words. It's not necessary to know what they mean. Engineers use it all the time. They particularly like to lay it on their managers. It sounds impressive.

Providing convenient power for remote sites will take a little longer. I predict within 20 years we will have portable stand alone cheap power supplies sufficient to run a home or small factory. Perhaps some form of fusion. No house or hovel will ever be isolated again. Be it the top of a mountain or the middle of a desert, communication and power will be available. Automobiles will have power sources which will outlast several vehicles.

I may have to stumble down the road of loose logic to speculate how to create this power source. I know vinegar and soda won't work. I've already tried that. It's not fusion and it's a very puny source of thrust power. It is enough to break a cheap wine bottle and it could be viable for outer space thrusters but not as a main source of power. It won't drive much of a generator and there is no way of making it into a fusion process. It could be used in sports as a thruster for outer space sailing vessels. Who knows, outer space sailing could become some kind of rich man's sport like the yearly Port Huron to Mackinac boat race.

Back to the problem. I expect a breakthrough in cold fusion to occur in the near future. Given that, a fusion generator in the fifty KW range, even with adequate shielding, will be no bigger than a modern home furnace. It could replace the furnace because it could provide environmentally clean electric heat. The best part is, it won't have to be in the house. It could be outside or in the garage. The only pollution we will have to watch for is thermal. That will be a big and dangerous one. It could flood the earth or create deserts.

Sure, it may not be fusion at all. It could be some as yet unheard of technology as foreign to us as nuclear physics was fifty years ago. Remember? I'm that old. When I was in grade school, space travel and laser technology (ray guns) was the stuff of science fiction. Only Jules Verne could conceive of some kind of mysterious power source.

This power source will come and it will be the demise of the last of the hostage consumer companies. They will fight it like mad. They will use every dirty trick in the book to get the government to outlaw privately owned power supplies. They will use every scare tactic ever conceived in the minds of man and invent a few new ones. All of this will delay the process. It will not halt it. Once we know it is possible someone will see the profit in getting it to us and they will. Edison, Ma Bell and GTE will be a bad dream. We will remember them in the same way some of us remember having to use outhouses. A necessary evil.

One big advantage to a people's power source is that the earth's remaining crude oil will be spared. It will become a raw material for the manufacture of reusable products like plastics. No longer will it be burned to drive our cars and factories. Air pollution will be reduced. Another gain is that unsightly overland lines will disappear. If the power and phone companies don't recover them, vandals will. Even internal wiring will be minimized. Factory managers will be able to spot power where it's needed, rather than route it, helter-skelter, all over the building.

Saga

If you ever wanted to write your life saga in a pop country song, here is one episode and a refrain you can start with. I hereby place it in the public domain or public outhouse. You pick! This is not real serious. It's a song to play with. The episode I wrote is just so you can see the tune and the structure. Feel free to throw it out after you get the swang of it. Then put in your own story. Each episode should be a chapter in the story of how you came to this sorry state. Write as many three verse episodes as you need. Please retain my refrain and introduction.

When I put this tune in the public domain, it means you may perform it in any medium and add to it in any way and you don't have to pay me squat. To be sure, it would be nice if you mentioned the book it came from. Also, the book is copyrighted so please do not make copies of the score for sale or distribution.

Now I wrote this thing in the key of C cause I know there are a lot of fellows out there who can only do their guitar that way. Just the three major chords. Even then, the F ain't all that easy for those of us as has arthritis. For those of you with dextrous fingers, feel free to transpose to your own key as you go. Also throw in the minors, diminished, augmented and all that fancy stuff if you feel qualified. The tune was actually written for piano but its hard to find a carrying case with a handle for a piano, so I penciled in the guitar chords. Too bad cause the F is real easy on the piano. I use it often to do my own version of Willie Doodle Dandy.

C G 7 F C F
O - - - - - o - - - - - - - - - o - - - - - - - - - - oh I'm the sad - est man you've
G 7 F G 7 F F G 7
ev - er seen cause, I got hard and I got mean and
G 7 F C G 7 F G 7 F C F
I got old and not too clean, just a pass - in through the

C F G7 C F C F C F G7 F
rec - tum of my li - - - - - - - - - i - - - i - - - - ife. Just a pass - - -
C F C F G7 C F F G7
in - - Thro -ugh the rec - tum of my li - - - - - - fe. It's all
All but last To Coda
Last
Fine
C F C F C F F F C F F
a ga - - - - - - - - - - a - - a - - as. Life is a gas. - a - - as. I think I'll pass.

Coda
Git fiddle solo - four bars ad lib
C G 7 C F C G 7
C C G 7 C G 7 F G 7 C G 7 F G 7
Now I was born in a pick - up Ford. On a coun-try road they
Lord! How could this thing a come from me? It's the ug-liest thing I
They did not dump me out on the road. On up to a town they
C G 7 C C G 7 C G 7 C G 7 F G 7 F G 7
cut my cord. My Ma-ma looked and she said dear Lord, It did not rain. It
ever did see. Dammit I just thought that I had to pee. Now all my sins came
drove and throwed me on the porch of a Nun's a-bode. They left me there and

Depending on what bar you perform in, you may want to substitute some other word for rectum. It would never fly in a Redneck bar. They would think you were talking about a demolition derby. You must be literal and not too literate with some folks. Tempo is optional also. It can be a quick 4/4 or a slow ballad 4/4, depending of whether the fools who won't listen to your great story want to belly rub or do the *Texas Two Step*. Point is, any music I write is intended to be interpreted by any artist or ne'er-do-well drifter who performs it.

Just a bit of advice about adding your words. In poetry the syllables are the rhythm so syllabification is very important. In music, the rhythm and the syllables are related but not totally dependant. For example, the word 'ever' is two syllables but can be a single beat or a double beat in music. It can even be drawn out to several beats. Not so in poetry. In poetry we use tricks like the contraction "e'er" for ever. This does not mean we can be completely careless in fitting our words to the musical rhythm. To have a smooth flow in the song we must still have reasonable agreement from one line to the next and from one stanza to the next. Our license is a bit broader but not unlimited.

This particular verse is the beginning of Short John's Saga. Short John was a friend I once knew. Not short at all, he was six foot nine. We called him Short John because, whatever he tried, he always fetched up short. Like, when they throwed him on the porch; he fetched up short. He actually landed in the hedge. He squalled and bellered real loud. At first, the nuns thought it was cats having sex in the hedge. They threw a few bricks at it and turned the hose on it. No matter. John could not go away and he did not stop hollering, so they came out to check.

They found him, right enough, but he wouldn't stop squalling even after they brought him in and dried him off. Finally, in desperation, one of the nuns opened her habit and stuck a teat in his mouth. He stopped squalling and commenced chawing. For both of them, it was the greatest feeling of their entire life up to then. Of course, nothing came of it.

Just so you'll know how he thought about it, I've added the final lines of Short John's Saga.

So I have roamed over land and sea.
Just to come and go I have been free.
I think of all that I got to see,
And know the Lord's been good to me.

You don't want to hear the rest of his story. You already know it. Everyone knows John. He's the guy at the end of the bar nursing one beer cause he ain't got another dime in his pocket but it's warm inside and there are people. He's the guy sitting on the park bench examining a hole in his shoe. You've seen him on the highway standing under an overpass, waiting for the rain to pass so he can continue his endless journey to nowhere.

If he has a couple of bucks in his pocket and you're broke, he'll buy a pack of hot dogs or a loaf of bread and share with you. If you ain't hungry, he'll buy a couple beers and share them with you. John has never begged, but if you hand him a sandwich he'll say, "thank you ma'am." and eat it real fast. If you have a six pack and have time to listen, he'll tell you some great stories.

If you know a down and outer, if you know a guy who just can't get it right, you know John. It ain't that he don't try. He just always fetches up short and he feels bad about it. Kind of ashamed.

Finally, depending on how you feel about your own saga, here are some alternate words for the final refrain. It would be nice if all stories came out with a happy ending. But, then, it's really up to us. Isn't it? Can we take the good in whatever happens and exploit it?

Sooooooooooo!
I'm the gladdest man you've ever seen,
though I got hard and I got mean,
and I got old but I came out clean,
just a passin' through the rectum of my l -i -i -ife,
just a passin through the rectum of my life.
It's all a ga - a -a as. It's a great gas.

Overheard in an auto company executive suite:
"Damn! We're not getting any publicity on this new concept car. Charlie! Call Channel 12 and have them send their spy photographers over right away."

Grandpa:
Like an ancient apple tree he was,
gnarled, twisted and misshapen.
And yet,
a friendly sight.

Task List

Because of code bloat in the software industry, I recently had to install a new hard drive in my computer. I named it "Code Bloat." Even for a practicing simpleton like me, taking the cover off a computer is scary. To ease my terror, I spent a few hours thinking about and making a detailed task list. It began with making sure everything I needed to restore the system would be available and ended with remembering to thank Minerva. Of course, everything did not go smoothly but having the list kept me out of panic and major trouble. I have always found this task list idea to work.

Installing a hard drive, writing a book or building a chicken coop can all be approached in the same manner. The task can be broken down into a series of tasks each of which can be reduced to smaller tasks and so on. We can, but seldom do, reach a point where each task is a simple single action. Calling this task list an outline will not help. It just makes a simple thing sound complicated. Calling the tasks milestones is even sillier. Silliest of all is the management notion that we can predict the effort required to do something which has never been done before and assign times to the tasks. I guessed it would take me half a day to do the hard drive. It took me a day and a half.

There is a step beyond silly called project management. It spawned an entire genre of software development. This software draws lines, circles and boxes on paper and formalizes nonsense for managers who can put times and numbers and names on the paper and pretend it means something. I knew one person who wasted most of his professional career on this stuff until he got so dumb he became a manager. In the face of project management, calling a task list an outline almost makes sense. A great number of people have earned good incomes propagating this nonsense. It's equivalent to creating software to help us do sculpture.

If you could break a task down into smaller tasks, to the point where there were no unknown elements, you could make some good guesses on timing. Making a list that refined and detailed would probably take as long as doing the task. If you want to be a fool, you can guess at times and call them milestones. You could also have a program draw lines and circles and put dates in them. You could also just go ahead, make a list and start working on the first task. Now there's a frightening thought. Just stop the nonsense and start working.

When I'm in my shop and messing around, people sometimes ask me what I am making. The only honest answer I can give is sawdust. I always have to wait until I finish before I can be sure I am making anything else. Sometimes, I finish and find that sawdust is all I have made.

America's prisons are taxpayer supported educational institutions designed to teach people to be better criminals. It works well because the ones who don't learn must keep returning to school until they can do it right. The problem is, it costs more than regular schools. In fact, it costs more to keep an inmate in a Michigan prison than to care for a patient in a hospital.

Pit Bull

Another of the frequent cases of a pit bull biting a child was reported on the news. The child was severely injured. The authorities are investigating whether the dog should be destroyed. What's to debate? If I had a dog which bit a child, I would put the dog down, regardless of the circumstances. That would be my duty. Not the duty of the state but of myself. There is nothing to investigate. It may break my heart but I would do it. In defense of dogs, I must say, dogs are not born bad. They must be vigorously, even brutally, trained to be bad. Somewhere behind every bad dog is a very bad human.

Principles of Ethical Business Practice

I expect, someday, to be a successful businessman. More importantly, I expect to operate an ethical business. Hence, I must look at, and think about, what a business should and should not be. Everyone will give lip service to being ethical. Now, what does that mean? What is an ethical business? To answer this, I will need to define the parameters of ethical behavior at all points of contact with the universe around me and my business. Broadly this consists of the five interfaces with our colleagues, customers, suppliers, community and environment. Of course these are linked and cannot be treated completely separately. Yet, each has unique requirements.

How we treat these interfaces will come out of the goals we define for the business. I believe most businesses have defined the wrong goals. Their primary purpose is to create profit for the business, the managers and the stockholders; personal, monetary gain! I respectfully submit that this is not a good reason to be in business or to start a business. Personal financial gain is the wrong reason to do anything. It is impossible to be ethical with an overriding primary goal of monetary gain. True personal gain comes from the process.

Ethical business begins with proper goals. The only compelling reason to be in business is for personal fulfillment. This can only come from ethical behavior in pursuing the four basic goals of business. These are colleague fulfillment, customer satisfaction, environmental enhancement and sound community citizenship. Clearly these are dynamic goals and are addressed on a daily basis. The total disregard of these goals is what caused the rape and near destruction of our country's resources including human resources. The rage which we see in our population is a blood descendant of those ruthless business practices.

Here are some of the patterns of behavior which will tend to satisfy our goals. First, we must be doing something useful. Then we must share the creative process with others. We must be a good citizen in the community. We must support the growth of everyone involved. We must enjoy the process. And, we must operate so as to improve rather than damage our environment. These things are like a glove. It's not very useful to put on just one finger.

In these activities and goals profit should not even make the top ten. It's only necessary to maintain a cash flow sufficient to maintain the enterprise and continue toward the real goals. I submit that a business which follows the ethical goals will not be able to avoid profit. Profit will come inadvertently. Whoring after money can create enormous wealth, but if you look at the result you will see it cripples the human spirit and takes the joy from the life of everyone involved. We see it every day in our strike bound major corporations and in our wealthiest people. I know of no way to prove this except through anecdotal evidence. We either believe it or we don't.

An ethical business must start with excitement about an idea. A fun, enjoyable, useful, exciting idea. Not with an idea just to make money. I don't care if I ever have a large profit so long as I can stay in business. If my success is not based on integrity, it's ashes in my mouth. Still, the more income I earn, the stronger the business can be and the more fun I can have bringing the joy of creativity to my associates and friends. It's simply a matter of keeping the focus on ethics, even at the expense of short term profit. Once my firm starts, others will come to zippate with me and profit will follow as surely as rats follow commerce.

Strangely enough, to my knowledge, most businesses start with the goal of personal fulfillment for a single person. Somewhere along the line, if the business begins to succeed, the goal changes. First it points to greed, then to power. There is nothing inherently wrong with seeking wealth or power so long as the other goals are not lost. Sadly, the other goals are usually forgotten or not even considered. Sometimes they are remembered and given script type lip service. The script gets read aloud by a dignitary at periodic intervals. It's usually in conjunction with the annual report or stockholders meeting.

It was a treat to listen to the last two Bendix CEO's read the script. A favorite phrase was, "People and Profits." As is normal for these people, they mistook the words for the deeds. It is common for people to mistake symbols for reality. All of us mistake money for the wealth it represents, until inflation slaps us upside the head and shows us the difference. In the end, they bungled both goals. A lot of good people followed Bendix down the tubes.

Yes! Bendix is now defunct. A small tactical error. We don't know if a nail was lost or a shoe was lost but we know the blacksmith was at fault. It couldn't have been the generals. They all rode off with big bonuses and an honor guard. The blacksmith was left hanging, it's not clear if he was actually hanged, but it must have been his fault.

I have observed and worked in many business operations large and small including the Bendix Research Labs. In my experience, the most ethical and the least ethical of these have been the relatively small enterprises. These were the print shops, gas stations, retail stores, etcetera. They are usually an extension of the personality of a single person. Larger enterprises have no personality and their sterile managers count on specialized agencies to create the illusion of a nice personality. At best we can say they are amoral.

When a small business first starts, there is usually only one or two people involved. There may be partners or spouses but there are no real employees. It may be years before the business can support employees, a conventional place of business or community involvement. Sometimes these things never happen.

Ideas for personal fulfillment sufficient to start a business can be complex or simple. Some of the simplest ones have been the most successful. A home baked cookie is an example. A special brand of ice cream is another. To write a book and make sure it gets published could be a goal of personal fulfillment. Sometimes, it's a matter of being disappointed in the way something is done. We could discover that an entire city has crappy restaurant salads because there is no good lettuce. So we buy a piece of land, learn hydroponics and learn how to grow loose head lettuce in a greenhouse. We become a restaurant supplier and we feel good. We are filling a need. Never mind that we may be highly educated. Now we are doing real stuff first hand.

If we do it well, the business will grow and we are faced with a dilemma. How do we handle the growth and still maintain our feeling of personal fulfillment. When the crunch comes, the rush of events may overwhelm us. More orders than we can fill by ourselves. More work than we can possibly do alone. We must decide in advance if we are willing to grow and how we will do it ethically.

If we decide to grow we must implement the principals of ethical behavior in our working life. Let's define these principals by outlining how we will treat with the four basic goals. As I said, these are employee fulfillment, customer relations, citizenship and environmental responsibility.

Employee fulfillment

I will start with fulfillment of employees because their behavior will influence everything else about the business. Conceptually, employees must be partners. Profit sharing, by itself, is not enough. There must be a way to make the people who operate the business into real partners. These can be full partnerships in the business or limited partnerships on projects within the business or on aspects of the business. It can also be a share of a special issue stock.

This partnership is not just about money. The employee must be a real part of the decision process. This is especially important in decisions affecting the person's tasks. I have heard managers say stupid things like, "We want the employees to 'feel' they are part of the process." For crap's sake! It's not an encounter group you sh__ head! It's not about feeling. It's about doing. It's about real control over real events.

It follows from the concept of partnership that no one must ever "just" work for me. So from now on, I refer to these folks who zippate with me as colleagues or partners. I might have used the word associate instead of colleague but, recently, some retail firms have perverted the meaning of the word by calling minimum wage lackeys associates. Creative thinking must go into how we turn workers into colleagues. It must be effective for the treasurer and just as effective for the janitors.

In the case of creative endeavors limited partnerships or fellowships can be a powerful tool. Let's consider the example of a research company. The company could sign a fellowship contract with a person to develop a fast orbital overdrive lock (FOOL). The contract would include subcontracts with the assistants and technicians required. The company would provide the capital, the working environment and any legal double talkers needed for patents and such. The "Fellow" would then direct the research to create the FOOL. Eventually, the FOOL would be marketed or the patents sold. In either case, there would be a resultant divvy of the proceeds unless the project proved unfruitful.

Yes! There would be a great number of details and each contract would be specific to the person and the project. Safeguards would be necessary for all parties. Time and cost limits would be required. However, history is rich with examples of this kind of contract, from Christopher Columbus to modern publishing. Most of the relationships between publishers and writers are of a contractual nature.

In the end, there will still be situations where people will be part of a regular staff. Depending on our size, we may need many regular staff people. These could be money management people, legal staff, maintenance folks, accountants, expediters and security. These must also be made into partners. Here is how I propose to do it.

We start by having an equitable pay scale. On that let me say if a person is only worth the minimum wage, I don't want him in the firm. I have met a lot of screwed up people and more who were in the wrong job. I have never met a person who was not worth more than minimum wage, including managers, who, sometimes, come very close. These people, if they exist, could not carry their weight and would be a drag on their colleagues.

In addition, I have never met a human who was worth forty or fifty times what another person was worth. Most officers of most companies are grossly overpaid at the expense of the workers. This would be true even if they did it well. If the company was staffed by the kind of excellent folks I want to attract or train, a pay scale ratio of two or three to one would be about right. The highest pay would be for special creative people. Not managers! We must understand, managers do not produce wealth. Workers do! Managers just brag when it works and whine when it doesn't. All hardware, tools, plant and equipment notwithstanding, the most valuable asset any company has is its colleagues. They, and only they, produce the wealth. It's about time management understood that and acted accordingly.

In general, stock holders receive a very small part of a firm's profits. They tend to agree that it's better to plow most of the profit back into the business. They must be satisfied with the growth in value of their stock for investment gain. I have concluded that colleague profit stock is one of the best ways of plowing profit back into the business. It will be returned in spades with increased productivity. It will create more growth than any other investment the company could make.

Beyond base pay, a percentage of company income must be provided as a form of colleague held stock. My guess is about 50% of profit would be the correct amount. I do not believe sharing up to half of the profit with the people who created it is an error. This kind of honest sharing can only create more profit as people bust their butts to increase their share. A number of shares of stock would be created to represent this profit. This stock would be owned by the company. These shares would be called profit shares or profit stock.

Each colleague would hold stock shares based on his perceived value to the firm. The issue would be for the colleague's term of employment. Ultimately, for this to work, the stock must return to the firm so it can be reissued. At accounting time, the firm's profits devoted to this stock would be divided evenly among the shares and paid out. Any profit for stock still held by the firm would show up on the firm's final bottom line.

This stock pool gives us some powerful tools to enhance the zippate experience for the colleagues and the firm. In a well-operated business, the stock payout could easily exceed the colleague's base pay. In addition, the available stock pool gives the firm an excellent incentive tool to attract key people. We can court the very best with confidence. Even so, the profit stock, by itself, is not enough.

Since the stock makes the colleague's income dependent upon the firm's success, she or he will demand to have real control over how the firm is run. I don't mean a stupid suggestion box where the suggestions are handled by someone with a vested interest in obstructing change and screwing the worker. I remember making a suggestion at Bendix. It won the prize a few days after I left the firm. I got squat. No one notified me. A friend informed me. I remember making a suggestion at FoMoCo. I received a letter explaining how things were fine the way they were. Many months later, the suggestion was implemented. I got squat.

There must be unassailable company integrity yielding real worker control. Specifically, the colleagues must have control over their contribution. They must define what their tasks are, the tools needed and how the tasks are done. They must be intimately involved in the planning of their work and how it fits into the larger scheme. The profit stock gives them a powerful incentive to plan well and execute impeccably.

Getting people

Running a firm this way requires the very best people, since it is they who will run the business while I show off and brag. How, in this corrupted world, do we find such people? What we don't do is try to hire big timers away from corrupted companies. These people will bring too many bad habits with them. Still, we all know a few people, personally, who we would like to have. By all means, we should court these folks.

Some folks will hear of us and come to us. These will be the disgruntled, creative folks whose necks are raw from pulling the yoke of obstructive management. I was a person like that, but there was nowhere to go. I made the best of it until I reached age sixty two and graduated. We must carefully evaluate these folks on an individual basis. We will find some jewels. However, the best way to find people is to create them through training.

We know people are the primary key to success in any business and my philosophy is very simple. Hire bright untrained people whom we can train to learn our business and run it our way. Get them before they go to college and get corrupted with the notion that they know and understand how things ought to be done. Get high school seniors or fresh outs. Once they join us, if they decide on advanced education, they must be supported in that effort. In addition, zippating with us will give them an education superior to any undergraduate degree they could acquire. If it does not, our program is flawed.

In recruiting, we must face the fact that some people are not employable. An employer should not have to be a psychiatrist, a psychotherapist or any kind of a healer. There are some people who are beyond our help. It is not a proper function of an ethical firm to treat seriously disturbed people. They need too much help. We cannot bring them into our environment and burden our associates with this emotional load.

These people will have to heal themselves. We do not have the technology to do it. We don't have the skill to soothe a worried grandmother for crap's sake. It may be possible to create a situation where we could give tentative positions, in a separate operation, to some dysfunctional people. Then we could move them into the organization if they respond. This too may require some law adjustments. It would be a public service more than anything else. Still, people should have a chance to look up from despair when we can offer it and justify it financially.

In observing people at work over many years, I believe the ideal new colleague to be a very bright graduating high school senior woman. We have to include the concept of brightness because we know some teenage women and men are inane as hell. Here's the conundrum. If a person is inane at age seventeen, they will probably die that way even though it's learned behavior. It's a behavior which was once effective and will not be unlearned without expensive help. What seemed precocious at age seven will be annoying at age seventeen and sad at age fifty. This inane behavior is not as common as we pretend. It's like any other stereotype. There are more bright young folks than inane.

Here's the rationale for young women colleagues. These are not laws and have many exceptions. They are just the sum of personal observation over time.

Women are easier to train because they are relatively free of that male ego dumbness. You know! The silliness which causes a man to nod his head and say, "Yeah I know." Even when he doesn't have a clue. He just can't let the other person start to think he is dumb. So he will go and waste time learning it by himself instead of asking questions. Young people, in general, are easier to train because they don't have so much baggage. They don't have things to unlearn. Unlearning is much more difficult than learning.

Young bright women are eager to learn. They want to understand. They listen carefully and ask questions. Women on the job spend more time actually working than their male counterparts. Here's a tough one. It's a known statistical fact that a woman will work for less compensation than a man in the same job. Many employers take advantage of that. It's a pretty short sighted philosophy. I believe an employer who pays someone less than they are worth simply because low self-esteem causes them to accept it should be summarily executed. It's unethical and counterproductive in the long run.

Low self-esteem is a likely problem with some female colleagues. Many women have a somewhat diminished ego. This is due to early conditioning. They are not as likely to speak up in group situations. They are not as likely to offer ideas even though they have an abundance. Sometimes it gets so silly that a woman will go with an inferior idea because it came from a man. An employer must be vigorous in encouraging the female colleagues to express themselves lest the very best creative talent be suppressed. This is necessary even if it means paying for the women to take a Carnegie.

Now, having made this wondrous case, I am sad to say, we must be very careful about employing young women. I keep up with the news. I have noticed the great number of cases of women and children accusing men of sexual misconduct. Some, even years after the alleged facts. Many turned out to be unprovable. Some were even proven to be fraudulent. No matter. Lives and businesses were disrupted and ruined. Because children are often involved, there is a public hysteria surrounding the issues and, as always, the situation gets polarized. Reason is lost.

To be sure, anyone convicted of sex crimes should be dealt with at least as violently as they dealt with their victims. My choice would be to put them in a hard time prison and make sure everyone in that place knew the details of what they had done. They would probably not live a year. We would not be bothered with them again. To convict a guilty person of a crime does not need a media fanned lynch mob. It simply requires a competent prosecutor.

In every charge of sexual misconduct I've seen reported, I have detected a presumption of guilt by the media, especially the visual media, toward the accused. They don't come right out and say it but you can hear it in the tone and tempo of the reporting. That stigma does not go away, even when the victim is acquitted. Most people still think he's guilty. His life is ruined.

I must think long and hard before I create a situation where I must spend as much effort making myself safe from those kind of accusations as I do running my business. No one can afford that. I cannot afford to have some prosecutor or other shyster conning some young woman into turning on me. I cannot afford to refuse a woman employment and have her, later, tell a jury, "That old cur waved his whacker at me." Even if I was acquitted, it would waste and ruin what remains of my life.

I'm trying to point out that this public hysteria and lynch mentality is going to be very costly for young women coming into the market. Sadly, it comes just as real progress is being made in securing equality in the work place. It threatens to erase the gain. When I hire, I'll probably still consider young women first but I will be much more careful than I should have to be. I will scrutinize very carefully for any hint of dishonesty. For my own safety, I'll probably also hire old geezers and grandmothers. These are, by the way, an alternate choice of ideal colleagues. It's a damn shame, but that's the situation we have come to. The day will come when we will not be able to get qualified men to teach school for the same reason. The risk is too great.

Amenities

Now we know who we want as colleagues. How about when? Before hiring people, we must make sure we can provide all of the tools and support required. A business must be profitable enough to support a staff. If we cannot pay the real and total cost of having colleagues we must not have them. We must work harder and pay as we go for services, or close the business.

It's not necessary to hire an accountant. There are firms which will provide this service. It is not necessary to have a secretary, documents can go to a service bureau. We should be able to do our own filing. An answering device and copy machine can do the rest. We can consult an attorney when necessary and use a patent firm when necessary. We should only have colleagues if we can pay the entire cost. These real costs include government mandated employee insurances and adequate medical coverage plus vacations, pensions and sick time but it goes beyond that. Safety and amenities in the work environment are involved.

We may have part time folks but we will never use rent-a-bodies. The rent-a-body industry is evil. It should be shunned completely. It treats people like material. Using them is nothing more than transferring guilt. There are two justifications for allowing part time positions. First is, if it benefits the person because they have other activities or commitments like children or personal education. The second is, if there is a real belief that the position will become full time in a reasonable time frame. If not, we must work harder or take the work to professional firms. If we need a lot of part time people, we have failed as leaders. We are not planning and scheduling the work load properly. More than likely it's because we are lazy.

Having colleagues is a serious responsibility. These people are not things to be managed, like materials or cash flow. They are not to be treated as simple assets but as peers and allies. The colleague's hopes and goals must become the employer's hopes and goals. They must have the opportunity to grow and learn. The must have the opportunity to learn the business and grow with it. They must enjoy their work. Fair pay for work done is important, but pay, by itself, is very much overrated as an incentive. Equitable treatment and creative opportunity is much more important.

The ultimate cost of cheating our people is enormous. Look at any retail firm which is paying at or near minimum wage. You will find shelves are not restocked. Articles will not be where they should be. Disarray is rampant. Service is poor. The people who are assigned to answer questions know less than the customers. Worst of all, is the generalized, "don't care" attitude of these workers. Even as they do the "Hi! How are you." ritual, you can see the anger in their frozen smile and posture. This all costs money, directly in sales. How many times do we go to another store because we could not get help or answers at the first store we chose? How many times do we write a firm off, then watch later as the CEO, with a bewildered look, announces chapter eleven? He need not be bewildered. He need only look at how he has treated his colleagues.

As I said, equitable treatment and creative opportunity is important. Colleagues must be included in all decision making. They must also have the opportunity to contribute ideas and products. When a good idea is offered, it's time for the top guy to consider offering a fellowship contract to that colleague. It's sure to get around and cause more good ideas. Some of the most profitable products in our history have come from colleague contributions. 3M Masking Tape is just one example. People must never be dead ended except by their own choice.

In addition, the colleagues must have time for quality of life and educational activities outside the work environment. They must have time for their families. Employment time schedules must be adjusted to reflect all of these realities even if it means two people sharing one job. People must also have vacations from work. Even if they want to, they cannot be allowed to work through their vacation. Change of focus is essential to human health. If they want to work, send them to Ma Waddles' soup kitchen. They will find real work and learn humility while waiting on the down-and-outs.

Along with this, personal time is private. An employer has no right to inquire about nor interfere in the personal lives of its colleagues. What a colleague does on the job is a legitimate concern of the employer. What a colleague does otherwise is not. We have a right to dismiss a person for missing work. We do not have a right to dismiss a person for getting drunk after work so long as they do their work. Drunkenness may be a legitimate concern of the community and police. Employers are not police.

Unless public safety is an issue, even drug testing is wrong. It is only reasonable for people whose work involves risk to the public; like pilots, police and firemen. However, help for colleagues in trouble should be made available if it's financially possible. Abuse recovery programs can be legitimately offered to all colleagues. Along with this, we will provide facilities or support membership in athletic clubs for our colleague's exercise programs.

In this, we must avoid even the hint of paternalism. Our colleagues are not children. There must be a very sharp line drawn between the work environment and their private lives. While we offer legitimate programs we do not interfere. Specifically, we do not make loans to colleagues, we do not provide housing for them, we do not build towns and we, sure as heck, do not have a company store. We are not a government or a father. Every time this kind of overbearing nonsense has been tried, it has backfired. Then everyone involved gets hurt.

To continue, all the legal and decency requirements must be met. There must be adequate health insurance. State and federal taxes must be handled properly. The work environment must be clean and attractive. There should be a clean, attractive area outside the work environment for people to take breaks and have lunch. This area should be off limits for any business activities. I don't know how many times I have seen some hot shot manager invade an employee break area with a business meeting. That is arrogant, shabby, contemptible behavior.

As to colleague retirement, we must set up a viable plan as soon as finances allow it. In an established firm, the ideal plan is straightforward. It must not be a fully paid company benefit. No benefits should be fully company paid. That undermines the incentive for responsible behavior by our colleagues. The colleague must be involved with contributions and with decision making. The firm should arrange a spectrum of investment options for individual colleague retirement plans. The firm should then arrange some fund matching plan where the individual's retirement contribution is enhanced by company contributions in a proportional way. Some upper limit of contributions must also be established for the firm's part. There must also be a floor contribution by the firm, even if the colleague makes no contribution. There should be no upper limit for the employee's part except as government mandates. The company must provide the administrative structure for the plan.

Within the spectrum of investment options the colleague should have full control over his or her personal fund. This is similar to many current stock plans. The most important part of this plan is, once a fund is set up the firm has no way of raiding it for operating capital when they are in trouble. The firm may be able to change the rules of its participation but it can never get back what is already invested. There should be no way a company can raid a pension fund. Preventing pension raids is a proper function of government and it's about time they stepped up to the responsibility.

Finally, we must treat worker health and safety the same as any other asset and act to protect it. Careless activities, including smoking, must not be allowed anywhere in the work environment. We are not required to provide bars in the workplace for alcoholics and we need not provide special places for tobacco addicts. I would go so far as to refuse permission to leave the premises for purposes of smoking. It's time away from work and it would place an unfair burden of our non-addicted colleagues.

All necessary safety equipment must be provided. Safety rules must be established and vigorously enforced. Most work accidents occur because the colleague took shortcuts. Because shortcuts can be short term profitable, many employers pretend not to see. This practice is unconscionable. I would rather go bankrupt.

If these requirements are met, the colleagues will be happy and rich in many ways. They will then bust their respective butts to make sure the business which creates this feeling is successful. The business will prosper and so will the colleagues.

As to parents with small children, we must make it possible for them to care for their children and still be creatively employed. Both colleague and employer must be extremely flexible about this. If it means putting a crib and a bottle warmer in a key person's office, it must be done. It could mean five people sharing four jobs so one of them is always with the children. Of course, the pay would be determined accordingly. In addition, we must get used to mothers nursing their children and not treat it as a titillating incident.

We must provide a receptive environment for children in the work place. This will probably require some easing of the laws governing employer liability. We need to give reasonable protection to everyone in the work environment but we cannot place strict liability on an employer for things out of their control, if this is to work. The grubby, chiseling insurance companies must also pick up some of the burden here.

Size of operation

If an operation has more than three levels of management, it is probably untenable. The ideal firm would have a top guy or owner and there would be no managers. There would be peers and colleagues, sometimes acting as teams and choosing their own leaders; sometimes working directly with the top guy. Thinking of this we must consider the size of the firm. How many teams and how big an operation can be viable with this theory of operation.

If you are a top person, there are two things you must know about your people. First of all, you must know their name and how to pronounce it properly. I had a Hebrew manager once whose name was Amos. In his language that's pronounced Ah-mous. He was a very patient man, for it did not make him nearly as angry as it made me when his manager and peers called him A-muss. They were just too lazy to care. You must also know exactly what your people are doing for you and how well they are doing it.

If I am unable to discern what people are doing for me, I am going to have severe moral problems. Continuously! The operation should never be so large that I don't know everyone by name, why they are with us and exactly what it is they are doing for the organization. If I don't know that, the operation is too large. Or, alternatively, I am incompetent. Perhaps both.

When the operation gets so large that we lose this span of knowledge, we must make changes. We must divide it into autonomous interacting units with top coordinators who can answer the questions. Who is this? What's he do for us? How well is he doing it? These folks work together with the top guy to coordinate activities between the units.

It's true that some industries require large operations to function efficiently. They can use this as an easy excuse for losing the span of knowledge. It need not be. Even steel mills and auto companies can have semiautonomous, interacting entities within the structure.

Another test of size is how we measure performance. If we use time, we are in trouble. It means we don't know our people or what they are doing for the firm. The only legitimate use of time as a measure of performance is in racing. If we have to resort to using time as a measure of performance in any other human endeavor, we have failed. Perhaps the firm is too large and unwieldy. Perhaps we have gotten lazy.

Managing

As to managing folks, if we get someone who thinks he needs to be managed, we must either break him of his dependency or get rid of him. I just don't ever expect to have time to manage other folks. It's damn hard enough managing my work without having people who are supposed to be helping me wasting my time. Once a person knows what needs to be done, he should not bother his employer unless he needs tools or materials or has some good ideas to offer.

Good people don't need to be managed. They must know what needs to be done and what they would like to do about it. If they are part of a team, they must know how they are sharing the project with the other team members. Once they know these things they will go ahead. The best thing a manager can do is make sure they have the tools and material they need to do the task. He can find this out by asking them. He should also make sure they get paid on time and he should vigorously approve and encourage their progress. Other than that he should stay the hell out of the way until they need something.

What amazes me it how often people get the job done even when the manager does not do the basic things. Even when they do not have the right tools or the correct material they get the job done. Most of the time they get it done even when they don't get paid on time. Sometimes they get it done in spite of the heavy handed, stupid interference of people who think they are managers. Workers are truly amazing. Meddling is what managers seem to do best.

To compete effectively requires good management. Everyone says this. It must be true. If more is better, the last place I worked had great management. At least they did when I retired. I took a count of the department wherein I worked. Here is the count from their phone book.

27 managers for 42 workers!
Honest to God.
It's the truth.
I swear!

Who did the work? They employed temporary folks to do it. Some of them had been there longer than I.

Now why can't those darn Japanese play on a level field?

Communication

In a good company, with good communication, people will know what needs to be done and do it. There must be good communication. Everyone in the organization should know exactly the state of the company. There should never be any company secrets. Proprietary information is something else. The president's pay does not qualify as proprietary information, nor does the cost of the overhead burden caused by executive salaries.

Proprietary information is process and product specifications which must be kept from competitors. No other information can be secret or proprietary in an honest company. It must all be public knowledge. If your boss says don't tell the others what you make, start looking for another job. He's screwing someone and it may well be you. Salaries are a proper subject for open discussion. All salaries.

The workers especially have a right to know if the company is in trouble or needs help. Some of them may be in a position to help. All of them will have better ideas for solutions than the "locked in, mind set" managers who created the problem. In addition, they will have a vested interest in helping, even to the extent of investing in the firm.

Overtime

About overtime problems, there is a trend in our culture, more pronounced than ever, which has gone on since the industrial revolution. That is to bully and coerce workers into working overtime for no pay. It is especially prevalent in the white collar segment where organized union protection is weak or nonexistent. This creates an illusion of productivity gains which have not really occurred. This illusion allows managers to vote themselves bonuses with only a token amount of blushing.

The problem here is the same as the one caused by the congressional trashing of presidential cabinet nominees. It will systematically drive the best and most productive people away. A truly thoughtful and creative person will not tolerate those abominable conditions. She may put up with it to learn the business or while she makes different life plans, but that's all. Many more people are moving away from the traditional loyal employee, fatherly firm relationship. Some start their own firms. They must think, "As long as I'm going to do all the work, I may as well have all the reward."

In addition, I know some very bright people who prefer to work a skilled or semi skilled trade type of job rather than give up their family time to the hallowed company. It may be mind numbing work but it only lasts eight hours. When they are done their time is their own to share with their family. If overtime is called for, they will at least get time and a half or double time pay.

This whole trend is reversed in some smaller companies where the need for family time is recognized as essential to human mental health. In a small firm where every person is a key person the individual's health becomes an important issue. They cannot buy new people with every graduating class, then trash them when they wear out. They need to nurture their people. At Wesoomi Publishing, only the owner - manager works 70 hour weeks and that pot licker deserves it. He's a hard man.

Almost all colleagues have a family and that family should be the primary focus of their lives. A great manager will come to understand this and insist that the colleagues understand it. Then he will strive to make the work interesting and fun so the person will go home to his family recharged and energetic instead of angry and exhausted. Zippating should be an adventure. The manager must make going home seem like leaving a party. Then the person will return to zippate eagerly. When management is honest, everyone wins, big time! Petty coercion and chiseling never win big time.

Company picnics are a crappy substitute for creating a viable social environment in the work place. If these kind of activities occur, they must be created and managed by and for the colleagues themselves. Management may be invited to attend but we do not initiate, finance nor control outside social activities.

Excess staff

Now we have great and happy colleagues, but even with the best of intentions the situation may change and we find ourselves with excess staff. More colleagues than we need to create our product or service. What then? Downsizing is the current management answer.

I submit that downsizing is stupid and cowardly. It's a classic, American management, cover my butt, screw all else, shortsighted, solution to a supply - demand - efficiency dilemma. The problem is, in its simplest terms, efficiency in production has satisfied demand with less people, leaving excess staff. The classic American management solution is, "Let's maximize the bottom line by screwing our people."

The ethical, honorable, and more profitable, long-term, solution would be "Let's invest in our excess staff to create new products and new demand." This solution has proved effective every time it has been tried. It's a simple, elegant solution which always works.

It is seldom tried because cowardly, college trained managers have been taught to duck and keep down. They have been taught to not take risk. They have been taught to do the tried and true, to do what's safe. They hide their cowardice by calling it conservative planning. The whole culture suffers for this shabby behavior. People who are not working do not tend to be conspicuous consumers. They are more likely to be on welfare or unemployment compensation.

To avoid downsizing, we go back to our initial premise. An ethical business must start with excitement about an idea. A fun, enjoyable, useful, exciting idea. Now we need only go to our staff and ask for ideas for useful products and/or services. We will get a plethora. All people are creative unless some physical or emotional anomaly prevents it. It is a proper function of an ethical firm to draw that creativity out of its people. We do this by telling them they are creative, and systematically insisting that they are special. Then we reenforce any positive behavior. In America, English works just fine for this.

If we do this systematically, we may never face the problem of excess staff. We may accidentally spawn an entire new industry through this action. Every great industry began with a single idea for a useful product or service. Take a look at the facial tissue industry. It's enormous.

On the other side of this issue, some colleagues, for their own reasons, may wish to leave. In that case, we must support their decision. We must always encourage attempts to grow and reach out for new experience. To folks who have been good colleagues, we must say, "Thank you for being here. We wish you every success in your new adventure. Just in case, we will leave the door unlocked." We never really lose these people. Wherever they go, they will do good things and our world will be better for it. Beneath this, also, is the knowledge that we are ever training new people.

Customers and product

Now we know how we want to associate with our partners and colleagues. Let's think about our customer and our product. To have a satisfied customer is a study in simplicity. All we need to do is give them a useful, reliable product or service at a competitive price. This means everyone in the process must do an excellent job and there must be strict accountability to our peers for errors. Not to the bosses, to the colleagues. If we screw up, we fess up and go on with the task. In addition there must be rigorous final inspection and testing so the customer never sees the errors. That's all.

What's so hard about that? It's simply a matter of everyone doing what they know they ought to do. It means everyone being accountable. It means all of us doing our best every day. It's about personal excellence. In a sound working environment, these things are bound to happen on a regular basis. It happens because everyone believes in it. It happens because people want to be excellent.

It does not matter what the product is. It must be useful, reliable and competitively priced. Useful can mean many things. A product could allow us to do something we could not do before. It could make something easier to do. It could replace a dohinkey with a better dohinkey. It could be educational or just entertaining. Although it's possible to market inane products like pet rocks, I would not want to do that.

We also offer a guarantee with our product to cover the rare situation where an error gets past us or a component proves faulty. The dreaded unforseen event.

One important point about customers. The desire to have satisfied customers does not mean we must tolerate dishonest people. The customer is not always right. A few are just plain crooks. These are in an extreme minority and we will not hurt our business if we dismiss them. In this, it's important to have a reputation for more than fair behavior toward our customers. We must also have a reputation for good citizenship in the community.

As to government as a customer, I would not accept government contracts ever. The government is just another customer. They can buy our products but they cannot be allowed to control the business. Government inspectors and government rules can multiply research and production cost by factors of ten or more. I have seen enough of it as a technician at Bendix Corporation. It was indecent. We welcome the government's business, but not under contract.

Citizenship and community

A company does owe its community a degree of public service when income justifies it. Other than taxes though, a company should not be required to subsidize a community's government and, conversely, a government should not subsidize a business, profitable or not. There should be no tax breaks if the tax is already fair. Also, I think it unconscionable for the owners of sports franchises to blackmail local governments into funding their arenas, even in part. We know that government is inherently evil. This does not excuse us for acting unethically toward the government. I consider the local officials and media people who suck up to that sort of thing to be coconspirators. It's the taxpayers who get raped and left holding the bag years later.

Community citizenship does not mean sucking up to local politicians or necessarily doing what the political hacks and media think you should do. It means being responsible to your neighbors. That's all! Perhaps the most important thing in this is to blend into the community. Appearance of the firm in the community is important. It should be discreet and tasteful. It should blend with the community and be a visual asset. Garish signs and conspicuous buildings are wrong.

Beyond appearance the firm should be in touch with the real community needs and act to support them. This could mean supporting a music program at the local school. It could mean buying books for the school library. It could mean creating a small local park on the firm's property.

We are responsible to the community and not necessarily to their government, except for obeying the law. We must make sure we know the laws of the community and set the example for compliance. This does not mean blind obedience. If we find a law to be wrong, we should work to change it. If the law becomes oppressive to our business and cannot be changed, we must move our business.

In community service, it is not necessary for us to support universities. Too many universities have become nothing more than vehicles for research grants. Beyond that, most of them are trade schools, teaching skills rather than educating people in the classic sense. A few are nothing more than professional athlete factories.

We must not forget community service by our partners and colleagues. We must set an example by allowing paid time off for community service. I would think one week per year for each person would be right. We could work with our people to draw up a list of approved services. These could include working in a soup kitchen, cleaning up trash around the city, and working with disadvantaged children. There is a plethora of things which need doing in every community. While I would vigorously encourage this community service, I would stop just short of making it a condition of employment.

Political involvement

An ethical company will never make contributions to politicians or to political parties. Of course, implicit in that is that we will never ever coerce our colleagues into political activism of any kind. That would be unethical, criminal and evil. Yes! I know they do it all the time, under the guise of getting out the vote and other slippery tricks. I believe these things are not a legitimate function of an ethical company. They should be left to civic minded private citizens.

As a matter of free speech, our colleagues will discuss political issues and support whatever position they choose. Officers of the company cannot be allowed to participate in those discussions. It should be clear that intimidation is implicit in their position. Team leaders, elected by their group, are not officers of the company.

Along with this, we do not coerce our colleagues to support or contribute to charities. Charity, like volunteering for community service, is a personal thing. Each person must make their own choice from their own conscience.

Research

As a business grows and prospers it will eventually acquire the additional responsibility to support pure research. This is community service on a larger scale. Of course, this carries with it the responsibility to decide which direction of research will be best for the business, the human community and the environment. These issues cannot be evaded and they cannot be decided by screaming picketers.

The responsibility cannot be assigned. It belongs to the owners of the business. The business has the responsibility to select the researchers and to control the funds invested. Setting up foundations does not get it. Giving grants does not get it. The business has the responsibility to be directly involved. This means the business must create its own research facility and have its own director of research.

The research must be focused and controlled. The human community will never have sufficient funds or resources to support random or frivolous research, like growing hair on silly, vain, bald men. Poor planning and lack of understanding, both in the research community and in the support community, is wasting enormous amounts of funds, people and tools. This kind of negligence must stop. Cost accounting, while distasteful, is essential. This does not mean bean counters can control the decision. It simply means they must have input and that input must be seriously considered.

I don't know why, but research facilities are magnets for problem people. Dead beats, brain dead and con artists will worm their way into the system. Once in, they are hard to get rid of. They can bring research to a crawl and funding to its knees. One way to get them out is to close the facility and open another one somewhere else. I watched one company get away with that. Problem was, the managers didn't know enough to move the right people. They ended up relocating the problem.

Environment

We must always pay the full cost of producing our product and make the customers pay enough of it to stay in business. If they won't pay it, we cannot participate. We must close the business. These costs include garbage collection such as bottle return, recovering wrappers and other garbage.

Whenever and wherever we do business: If we use water from a pond, we must put back cleaner water than we took out. If we leave a site, we must leave it better than we found it. If we operate a gravel pit, when the gravel is gone, there should be a public park or single family dwellings in its place. If we use chemicals, none should be left behind. If we had a septic field, it must be neutralized and filled when we leave. There should always be something more valuable when we leave than when we came. Any property we occupy should test as good as or better than the surrounding countryside for pollutants. If we create a lake or pond it should be cleaner than others in the area.

Other considerations

It should be clear, that a start up company will need to implement some of these concepts on a pay as you go basis. We cannot expect a firm with assets of $10,000 to support a local library. That's silly. Even so, the basics must be in place from the start and implemented as soon as possible. All the steps concerning colleague satisfaction must be implemented, in some degree, as soon as we acquire people. However, there is nothing wrong with having a probationary period for new colleagues even after we are established. This could be as much as six months.

As to suppliers, we must behave toward them the same as we want our customers to behave toward us. Our suppliers are our partners and we want a good relationship. We should shop for the highest quality at the best price but we should never whipsaw our suppliers. That's dishonest. We will not play bidding games. We won't have time for that. We must tell them, give us your best price and conditions. We are only going to ask you once. On the other face of it, if we encounter a dishonest or slippery supplier, we should write them off for good. No second chance. If we act toward our suppliers in the same way we act toward our customers, we will have few problems. Remember, they want us to succeed.

Finally, we must never involve ourselves in political pseudo wealth schemes. There's a current trend toward the nonsensical notion that non-product enterprises, like casinos and sports franchises can produce wealth in some magical way. Politicians and media seem to prefer this in place of manufacturing and basic industry. Easy solutions have become an epidemic. We should never get involved in supporting this short term nonsense. Money is not wealth. Wealth is real property. We create it by changing things into more valuable things with human imagination, energy and sweat. Enough said. A discussion of wealth and the accompanying concepts could fill an encyclopedia sized set of books.

Principles, the list

If we filter out the extra verbiage, this entire discussion produces a rather simple list of the rules of ethical behavior in business. In no particular order, here is the list.

Our product must be useful.
We must support the growth of our colleagues in all areas.
We must be a good neighbor and a proactive citizen of our community.
We must be proactive in enhancing the environment.
We must arouse and support the creative energy of our colleagues.
Colleagues must become real partners in the enterprise.
Colleagues must have real control in defining their contributions.
Colleague's base pay must be sufficient to provide a decent standard of living.

The highest base pay must be no more than three times the lowest base pay.
Half of the firm's profit must be directed into colleague's profit shares.
Women and men must be compensated equally.
Casual overtime is wrong. All contributions must be compensated.
Temporary situations which require overtime work must be corrected immediately.
The top person of the firm must vigorously solicit colleague ideas for products and operating improvements.
Any colleague must be able to talk, publicly or privately, to the top person without unreasonable formality or delay.
We must have a training program to train colleagues on the job.
We must not mix emotionally disturbed people in with our regular colleagues.
Colleagues must have time for home, family and personal activities.
We must never invade the colleague's private life.
We must make abuse recovery programs available for colleagues in trouble.
We must obey all laws without exception.
We must provide a clean and attractive work environment.
Colleagues must have a dedicated lunch and break area away from their work place.
There must be a participating pension plan for colleagues secure from company raids.
Colleague safety must be rigorously enforced.
We must provide employment opportunities for parents with small children.
We must know our people by name, what they do for us and how well they are doing it.
In evaluating colleagues, we must never use time as a measure of performance.
Colleagues must know all of the business of the firm. Nothing is confidential.

Colleagues must receive a detailed statement with their pay showing every cent which was expended on their behalf and where it went. No general fund crap.
We must support our colleagues in making the work experience an enjoyable process.
We must act vigorously to avoid staff reductions.
Customers have a right to expect a reliable, honestly priced product.
Our product must be guaranteed.
We will not accept contracts which give the government control over any aspect of our business.
We will not subsidize the local government nor ask them to subsidize us.
We must support our colleagues in community service without requiring it.
The firm will never involve itself in political activity of any kind nor will it express political views of any kind to anyone.
When economically feasible, we will invest in and direct pure research.
We must treat our suppliers just as we treat our colleagues and customers.

Will you have an employee billiard room?

Bellies and stuff

These are some things I wrote when I was younger and more athletic. I think it's time they saw the light of day, while I can still remember why I wrote them.

About Bellies:

I like to feel the funny vacuum
which has its play,
when my bare belly moves on yours
in a certain way.

And Sweat:

Folks get it in moments of stress,
when wearing their best Sunday clothes.
Honesty makes them confess,
perspiration it's called I suppose.
It's barely wet.

What covers your body and mine,
when rollicking naked in bed
and suctions our bodies together,
must be what proper folks dread.
I'd say it's sweat.

And Odors:

When we come together with clean unperfumed bodies
and we've intercoursed,
our juices and our sweat have mingled.
We lay beside by side each one to the other.
Fingers barely touching - each one another

whisper touching - gently;
There is a perfume about us
which we have made together,
different than either alone,
and better, I think.

And Skin:

Thank God for skin,
and fingers,
and gentle love.

And Bodies:

If I didn't have fingers to touch you
and a body to be touched by you,
I would only wish
for a way to weep.

And Left Field:

Somewhere in this universe,
there must be a place
called Ortonville.
Although
I can't think why!

There was this thoughtful, but slow minded, young woman who came to the adult education registration to sign up for basic mathematics. She explained she had been told by her preacher that the bible instructs us to go forth and multiply but she just didn't know how.

The Master's Wisdom

A simpleton was on the roof of the Ashram making repairs when he slipped and fell over the edge. He managed to grab the gutter as he fell and found himself dangling two stories above the flagstone courtyard. His arms grew quickly weary and he began to pray loudly.

The Master heard and came out to see what all the fuss was about.

He looked up at the simpleton and demanded, "What are you doing up there?"

"Master!" cried the simpleton. "Please do not jest. I am in dire danger."

"Of what?" demanded the Master.

"Oh please dear Master. My arms are weak and I am in danger of falling. Please help me."

"Are you frightened?" asked the Master.

"Oh yes, Master. Yes!"

The Master said, "Do not be afraid my son. Let go. All will be well."

The poor simpleton closed his eyes and released his grip, whereupon he plummeted to the stones below, breaking both legs.

In agony, he looked accusingly at his Master. Tears filled his eyes.

"How could you do this to me?" he demanded. "You said all would be well, yet I am in agony."

"Yet," said the Master gently, "you are no longer frightened. All is well."

The simpleton closed his eyes. He had no desire to contemplate the wisdom he had just received. Years later, perhaps.

Once we understand that life is a merry-go-round, it no longer matters if we are ahead or behind.

Perry's Story

Perry was a ne'er-do-well drifter I once knew. He had been married and had helped produce children to which he owed an inordinate amount of money. This according to the Friend of the Court, who tried desperately to make him pay. There were, of course, two sides to the alimony story. Aren't there always? I have heard Perry's side many times but I have never heard his ex-wife's side. I make no judgement. As people like Perry would have said. "My dog ain't in that fight!"

It is another side of Perry I would like to address. He was a fellow you could not help liking though you knew he was a drunkard and a bum. It's quite simple. He could play a guitar and sing. He would stop and have a drink or several any time. He would always drop what he was doing to help a friend or a stranger. As far as I could tell he had never hurt a soul and would not. He liked dogs and children and was good to them with the possible exception of his own. As I said to that charge I withhold judgement.

Above all of these things however is the real reason most folks liked Perry. He was a great storyteller. He was just the type you could sit and listen to for hours as he wove his words. He was also the type who would cause my spouse to frown when he showed up, for when words get wove drinks get drunk and so do men. Here is one of the stories he told me. It may be true. It may be! But I like it anyhow.

Perry was residing as a guest of the Oakland County Sheriff in the Pontiac jail, not for the first time. In fact he was a frequent visitor. It was through the actions of his ex-wife with the help of the Friend of the Court, that an almost permanent warrant for his arrest existed. The charge was always the same, nonpayment etcetera.

Perry did not mind his stays at the jail. The food was OK and it was a good enough place to dry out. Since he rarely had a decent job, he had no job to lose because of absenteeism. In addition, he got along well with most, not all, the deputies. He was, in fact, as close to being a trustee as one can get in a county lockup. He whiled away his days in the staging yard washing and cleaning the police cars as the deputies brought them in. He probably could have walked away but, heck, they would just pick him up again and maybe not so gently.

It was a nice summer day with the sun shining warmly into the yard when deputy Steve wheeled a car into the wash area and stopped sharply, with the bumper about 3 inches from Perry's trembling knees. Steve was one of the "hard-nosed" deputies who did not like bums like Perry.

Steve stepped out quickly and snapped over his shoulder, "Clean it up punk!" as he walked away.

Perry said nothing. He picked up a vacuum and opened the passenger door. There to his surprise was a sheriff's twelve gauge resting in the door holster.

Closing the door quickly, Perry turned and yelled, "Hey Steve!" Then he whistled.

The whistle got Steve's attention. He turned and stalked back toward Perry. His face was a whitened mask of pure rage. He grabbed Perry by the belt and shirt and slammed him, full body, into the side of the car. With his nose an inch from Perry's and the odor of his cheap lunch flowing into Perry's space, he snarled, "You God Damn F------ Punk! Don't you ever whistle at me again. Not ever!"

The "not ever" was enforced with a backhand to the head followed by a forehand and another backhand. Other officers noticing the action turned their heads away. They didn't want to see or know.

Again Steve slammed Perry into the car then turned and stalked away. Perry slid to the ground to catch his breath. He was terrified and trembling but he knew what he had to do. He opened the car door. He took the shotgun out of the holster. He turned toward the building where Steve had entered.

Then, holding the gun by the barrel over his head like a flag, he walked into the staging office and hollered as loud as he could.

"Hey Steve, old pal! You forgot your gun!"

There was an enormous silence in the office as Perry carefully placed the gun on the desk.

Perry was very good at story telling and I know some of the stories he told were of the manufactured variety as opposed to a recital of actual events. I suppose I will never know which variety this one was. I do know that as he told me this story, he suddenly excused himself and strolled quickly into the woods behind my house. It was then I saw a sheriff's cruiser sliding slowly by. He had seen it before me but I was not watching for it. The driver was a flinty-eyed fellow who gave me a hard look. Or did I imagine that?

A short time after that, Perry's sister told me he had left the area, probably for good. She also said, "Good riddance!" Not very profound but honest. If the story is true, it was probably a good decision on Perry's part. After all, who would care if a ne'er-do-well bum was found dead in a ditch somewhere?

Maybe I would.

Do all writers feel this way? I feel like my mind is like a field which has been covered with manure then freshly plowed. It's quite fertile and I know seeds are blowing in from all around. I know some things will grow. I have no idea what they will be. It's not predictable as to what might sprout.

A friend of mine made a product. He called it **Chuck's Soothing Sorbable Sulphur Syrup.** ***Good for digestion and liver ailments. Uncle Louie took it for years. He died anyway but we had to kill his liver with a stick.***

Crisis at Creek City

It's two o'clock in the morning. A light still shines through the window of the little computer room on the prairie. Occasional shadows loom as Greg or Naomi move across the room to get a listing or flow chart. The old computer whirs and clicks restlessly as though waiting for their attention. A single desk lamp creates gloomy shadows around the room, matching the mood of the pair, as they crouch over the desk.

Greg raises his head wearily and speaks:

"I don't know what's wrong Naomi. The payroll has run on this system at least 50 times, and now ---"

Greg shrugs and looks at Naomi but she has nothing to offer. She sighs deeply.

"If only it would print an error message instead of going into that stupid loop!" he says.

She sighs again and touches his hand. "I don't know what we're going to do Greg. The Creek City Silver Mine payroll is due in six hours."

"I know," he says rubbing his forehead, "and the men will be furious if they don't get their checks before Saturday. They're liable to tear up the town and we'll be to blame."

"They're liable to tear up our computer too." she adds.

"Oh God! I never thought of that," cries Greg, striking the desk with his fist. "We need help."

He buries his face in his hands for a moment then looks up with a tear making its way down his face.

"I'm sorry," he says. "I just can't stand the thought of those ruffians wrecking our installation. If only I'd listened to papa and become an M.E."

Naomi stands and cradles his head against her body.

"There, there," she says. "Whatever happens we'll have each other."

"Oh! You're so strong Naomi," he sobs wiping his nose on her sleeve. "I don't know how I'd manage without you."

Just then, the door bursts open and a tall masked man strides into the room.

"Oh God! They're here already," cries Greg.

Naomi, moving quickly, has snatched the sawed off shot gun from behind the line printer. With her lips curled into a mean little sneer, she swings the gun up to cover the man's chest.

The stranger extends his hands, palms out, in the universal gesture of peace.

"Easy, easy little missy," he says, in a beautiful deep baritone. "I'm not here to hurt anyone. I thought I heard a cry for help?"

"Oh!" says Greg, red faced. "That was me. I get a little emotional sometimes."

"Well! Was the girl hurting you?" asks the stranger looking sharply at Naomi.

His hand is poised over the ominous looking holster at his hip.

"No! No!" hurries Greg. "Nothing like that. It's just that our computer won't run."

"And it's due in six hours," adds Naomi. "The payroll. And if we don't deliver the checks -" "They'll - They'll," stammers Greg.

"They - the miners. They'll be angry," says Naomi.

"And they'll wreck it," adds Greg.

"The computer," continues Naomi. "And even if they don't -"

"What?" shouts Greg. "What if they don't?"

"We'll lose it anyway cause we'll lose the contract."

"Oh God! I never thought of that. When we lose the contract - Yeah! Old Silas Banker! He'll want his money."

"And we won't have it and he'll take the computer," finishes Naomi.

Greg stands up and looks appealingly at the masked man.

"We're out of business," he says, "and all because that old beast," indicating the computer, "decides to quit."

The masked man seems to notice the computer for the first time.

"Why!" he says. "It's an old I-BEAM 360, with a drum memory no less. Wherever did you get such a cute antique?"

"Laugh if you will," snaps Naomi, "but it's all we could afford and it's served us well until now."

"No offense little missy. Just teasing," says the stranger quickly. "I'm surprised because I haven't seen one of these in a while. They replaced it with a 370 cause the 360 didn't quite work."

He pulls a pair of black suede gloves from his belt and snugs them onto his hands as he swaggers purposefully toward the computer. He walks behind the cabinets opening panels and poking around.

"Wait a minute!" he exclaims. This is not a 360. Inside it's a 370!"

"Oh," says Naomi. "Well, Greg is good with things like that."

"But, however did you know to rewire these things?"

"Heck!" says Greg proudly. "It just seemed obvious."

"Good work young man!" says the stranger.

Greg glows for a moment and then says dejectedly, "Yeah! If only I was as good with software."

"Well, let's have a look," says the masked man.

He steps in front of the master control console, poises on the balls of his feet and flexes his fingers. His eyes glint from behind the mask and he pauses briefly.

"The boot load's at octal six thirty," he remarks over his shoulder. "Right?"

"Right," whispers Naomi with admiration. "However did you know that?"

"I've been around," he smiles.

Naomi lowers the gun and edges closer as the masked man confidently thumbs in the boot loader address. He toggles the clear and then start.

"Rat a tat a tat."

The console device slams out a question mark.

Greg jumps, startled, then sits down grinning sheepishly.

"Some day we're gonna replace that with a CRT," he says.

"Nothing like hard copy for keeping track," says the stranger.

"Diablo!" he voices loudly. "Bring my briefcase."

A shadow moves away from the window and Naomi shudders, realizing that she has been covered all the time. She moves over and replaces the gun behind the printer.

The door opens silently and a short, dark wrinkled man shuffles into the room, carrying a black leather briefcase with silver hinges and buckles. He places it carefully on the desk.

"Orb gouda sans bana na mit cheez?" he queries the masked man.

"Pasta un knepp mit won ton," answers the masked man.

"What did he say?" giggles Naomi. "What'd you say?"

"Oh!" says the stranger. ""He asked me, in his own language, what to do next. I told him to stand by."

"It must be one of those new higher level languages," remarks Greg.

The masked man merely smiles. His assistant melts into a shadowed corner of the room and becomes almost invisible.

Suede covered thumbs push back on silver buckles and the brief case snaps open. It is impressive. There are three fold down pockets with memo pads and scratch paper. There are two pocket protectors with pencils and colored felt pens. There are seventeen ball points in assorted colors clipped on the lower pocket. There is the latest model engineer's pocket calculator. There is a paperback copy of *I'm OK You're OK.* There is a deck of crib cards for every computer and operating system ever built. There is a copy of yesterday's *Wall Street Journal* and a volume on structured programming. There is a volume of standard math tables, a *Schaum's Outline* on *Linear Algebra* and the requisite tuna sandwich with a package of "Twinkies."

Greg sniffs and turns his head while Naomi jealously fingers the case and its contents.

"Oh wow!" she whispers.

The masked man seems not to notice as he demands. "What's the name of your payroll program?"

"See see ess em pee pee," Greg spells out.

The stranger's fingers flick over the keyboard like busy humming birds. The drum whines, lights flick and flash and the console raps out:

"READY"

"You have a test deck?"

Naomi gets up and opens a card drawer. She takes a deck from the back and riffles it before she sets it in the hopper. The stranger, meanwhile, has pulled a crib card from his deck. He hooks a stool with his English leather riding boot and pulls it under his butt as he hunches over the console, looking not unlike a flinty-eyed eagle.

Again his fingers flick over the keyboard. The reader gobbles the cards and the masked man slaps down hard on the computer halt switch. He stands up and begins flipping the front panel switches rapidly, referencing his crib card occasionally.

"Where's your source listings?"

Naomi rummages on the desk and pulls out a listing. She hands it to the stranger. He looks it over with many a "Hum" and "Uh huh." He flips more switches and then he sits down at the console.

"What are you doing now?" asks Greg.

"Hush," says Naomi.

"But I was only -"

"I know dear but be quiet and let the handsome stranger work."

"Reload the deck!" orders the masked man.

"Naomi jumps to comply.

The night wears on with Naomi running and fetching, Greg sulking and the masked man snapping questions and orders, while playing the computer with practiced ease.

Finally, near dawn, the deck is gobbled and the console bangs out a cryptic message.

"AHA!" shouts the stranger.

"Diablo! Where is my punch?

The wrinkled man shuffles out of the shadows mumbling softly, "It on-um your belt you dumb honky."

"What's that Diablo? Oh! Never mind. Here it is on my belt."

Diablo retreats to the shadows.

The masked man's hand flashes to his holster and he whips out a pearl handled, chrome plated, portable paper tape punch.

"Made it myself," he says proudly, holding it up. "You got a reader?"

"Only the one on the console," says Naomi, "but we've never used it."

"Let's hope it works. I'm making you a temporary patch. What you have is a core failure at location 17334. The failure caused that location to look like a jump instruction which caused a store and index loop, which overwrote the program."

He talks as his clever hands manipulate the punch.

"This patch should keep you in business till you can get replacement parts. If you can get parts!"

A few minutes later he says, "That should do it."

He cuts the tape and feeds the lead end into the reader.

"Load the test deck!"

Greg jumps ahead of Naomi to do it.

The masked man calls up the payroll program and then reads in the paper tape patch while Greg and Naomi take notes. He punches the start sequence. The cards are gobbled, lights flash and all eyes turn to the printer. Naomi holds the answer sheet for the test run in her trembling hand.

The ancient printer rattles and bangs. Paper spews forth and Naomi rushes forward. She grabs the output, compares and then she shouts:

"This is it! These are the right numbers! Oh thank goodness."

"Get the payroll deck!" shouts Greg and he rushes to get the accountable paper from the safe. With shaking hands he feeds the check forms into the printer.

Naomi puts the payroll deck in the hopper while the stranger resets the program. Greg puts his thumb up. Naomi smiles. The masked man punches out the start sequence. The cards are read, lights flash and paychecks spew forth. Greg watches and begins to cry with joy.

"Thank God! We're saved. Oh thank you masked stranger, he says turning to the console but the man is gone.

Greg looks at Naomi.

Naomi looks at Greg.

"Who was that masked man?" asks Greg.

"Damn!" says Naomi. "I forgot to ask his name."

Suddenly, the short dark wrinkled man appears from the shadows startling both of them.

"What you think-um that?" he says, pointing to a small item on the desk. Then he slips through the door.

Greg rushes over to the desk and touches the thing.

"Why, it's a silver floppy!" he exclaims.

"Silver floppy!" shouts Naomi. "Why - - why, that must be -"

" It is! It is!"
"It's the Lone Byte - Whacker!"
"They say he leaves a silver floppy wherever he goes."
Both of them freeze as they hear a call drifting back from the trail.
"Hi Ho Ansiiii, Ha-wa -a -a - y."
Then a softer, "Get-um up Scsi."

Wynton Marsalis

In a previous incarnation I had this friend who was into jazz. He made the comment that Wynton Marsalis is a great jazz musician. I hate to contradict my friends but I felt compelled to take exception. I argued that Marsalis is a great musician who, of course, plays blues, jazz and everything else. In truth, I believe Marsalis is the greatest trumpet player who ever lived. I came to that conclusion when I heard his CD, *Portrait of Wynton Marsalis* and, in particular, his breath control and triple tonguing on *The Flight of the Bumblebee* by Rimsky Korsakov. Until then, I thought Harry James was pretty damn good.

In Detroit, there is a mural of a football player which takes up the whole side of a tall building. Deliberately or not, this player is held up as a role model for the kids of Detroit. I'm sure he is a fine person, just as he appears to be. What I want to know is, where the heck is the mural of Wynton Marsalis? Does anyone come close to understanding the dedication and superhuman effort it took for him to achieve what he has? It ain't just natural talent folks. Talent is where it starts, and, in most of us, ends. The great ones enhance the talent with a lifetime of work and sweat.

It's nice to start work early in the morning. By the time you wake up you have half a day in.

Time

Your time is a commodity which you can use, trade or waste. Time is also a nonrenewable resource. A point we usually don't realize until it's too late. We can tell when people are on the verge of realizing it's too late. They will use phrases like, "It seems like only yesterday....." Time is your most valuable asset. It's really your only asset. All the wealth and power in the world cannot buy back one minute after you have piddled it away. This is why I keep books in my bathroom. I never do number two without a book. "Don't waste time when you make waste," is my motto. The divinity can move back in time because she stands outside of it but we cannot. Sometimes she lets us see through time, as a kindness, but she does not allow us to recover time nor move in it except as we normally do, toward temporal death. I wrote this ditty when I first started to understand about time.

Clock a tock clock a tock.
Hurry hurry clock a tock,
scurry scurry clock a tock.
Get there first. Beat the flock.
Don't be late. Punch a clock.

Click a tick click a tick.
Time is wasting click a tick,
minutes chasing click a tick.
Stitch in time. Stitch a lick.
Don't waste time. Do it quick.

Chunka chuck chunka chuck.
Keep a plodding chunka chuck,
never pausing chunka chuck.
Follow through. It's not luck.
Do not rest. Show your pluck.

Measure time measured time.
Once upon a treasured time,
it was I who measured time.
Time to play. Pleasure time.
Time to rest. Leisure time.

Finally, finally,
I have found by God's decree,
it is time which measures me,
measures me,
measures me,
measures me,
relentlessly.

A simpleton, while sitting at the feet of the master, presumed to ask a question. "Master." he begged, "All that you teach indicates you disagree with the President's policies, yet you say he is a wonderful man. How can that be?"
"It is because he has such a marvelous sense of humor." replied the master, kindly.
"What do you see, Master, which makes you approve his sense of humor?"
Snapped the Master, "He laughs at my jokes you dolt. Now go and contemplate this while you polish my silver and gold serving ware."

One time, when I was a Ford employee, my management person called a full staff meeting in a very small room. This time, instead of everything coming out of his mouth as usual, he had an actual flatulence attack during the meeting.
Boy! Was that fun!

Humor

Government and established powers hate humor because it is inherently subversive. That is the nature and purpose of humor. It must examine the way we look at and think about ourselves, our culture and our institutions to be effective. To the entrenched establishment, this examination will necessarily be regarded as an attack. Good humor must be subtle enough to make any retaliation by the establishment seem absurd. Humor can never be violent or crude. An old lady falling down the stairs is only funny to a very sick mind. An old Democrat falling down the stairs ----- well-l-l---? However, an old Democrat falling from power can be hilarious.

A culture's humor is its most important asset. It tells all we need to know in one packet. Notice that Nazi Germany had none. Most aggressors have none, be they nations or individuals. In many midwestern towns, it is possible to become a police officer simply by proving, beyond any reasonable doubt, that you have absolutely no sense of humor.

I have noticed that people who emigrate from other countries to join our culture have success here in proportion to two key factors. First, of course, is their willingness to do menial things for long hours while getting established and planning. No less important, however, is their ability to acquire our sense of humor. Think about how difficult this is. A culture's humor is deeply embedded in the most subtle nuances of the language. There is nothing universal about it at all. If you have been looking for the common denominator in humor, stop looking. There is none. It takes an extraordinary intellect to acquire an alien sense of humor.

There is another class of immigrant who wish only to emulate our most gross qualities. Arrogance, pomp, power-mongering, effluent affluence, and especially *Joe Camel* and *The Marlboro Man*. These folks do not understand our sense of humor and see no need for it. Like most of us, they live here and take the benefit of citizenship but they are not outstanding.

In this sense, I have noticed no difference in the ability of folks from reasonable cultures. Some seem eager and able to acquire our humor and some seem incapable. Strange though, when I told two friends, one Indian and one Jordanian, that I saw no difference between them, they both completely lost their sense of humor. It's as though they had never acquired one. Neither ever spoke to me again. Perhaps I worded it wrong.

While most of us will agree that humor is unique by culture, we must also look at the idea that humor is very personal. We notice this when we tell a joke and someone doesn't get it even though they were raised in the same culture as the people who do get it. Usually, they will want us to explain why the joke is funny or what's funny about it. Of course we can't do that. It's the same catch as being asked to explain to someone why they failed a particular test. If they could understand the explanation they would not have failed. It is impossible to explain a joke to someone who doesn't get it. So we find that a sense of humor is sometimes very personal. Thus, when someone asks, "What's so funny about that?", the most honest answer we can give is, "To you nothing."

This helps to explain how humor which works fine in one place will not work in another. A stand up comic who is funnier than heck in a red neck bar may fall flat on his face as a television comedian. On the other hand George Burns would not go over at all in a red neck bar. It's not because the folks in the bar are drunk or anything like that. They simply have a different mind set than people sitting in their parlor or family room. It's always very refreshing to meet a person whose mind can appreciate the subtlety of Mark Twain and still enjoy a rowdy round with Jeff Foxworthy.

My own sense of humor was tested very severely when I was ill. I remember a family friend visiting me at the hospital. She said, "I just came from the church where I said a prayer for you."

"That's nice," I gasped.

"You know," she continued, "Reverend Dufor is getting quite feeble. I just hope he doesn't die before you. I don't know who we will get for you if that happened."

"How thoughtful," I wheezed.

Well, not to worry,"she said patting my hand. "I'm sure we'll find someone nice."

"I can't wait," I whispered.

"There's a good sport," she smiled.

I closed my eyes and she eventually went away.

Luddites

The anti-technology folks. It does not matter what mantle they wrap themselves in. They are silly under any guise. The universe is changing. The divinity is changing. The absence of change is death. Life is change. One thousand years ago there were Luddites resisting the development of metal tools. Then there were Luddites resisting the industrial revolution. Now there are Luddites resisting the use of automobiles and tractors. One thousand years from now there will be Luddites resisting the development of N-dimensional, point-rotational, instantaneous, intergalactic travel. Oh well! Let them be. They do no harm, except to their own kind, and they do nice needlework. Change will eventually roll over them.

If your business is about humor, don't do your own income tax. Hire a CPA. There is nothing can destroy your sense of humor faster than a *&%$#@ tax form.

For those women who need a way to compete with a Corvette for their man's attention, Maybelline has the answer. Give yourself a new paint job.

Whipsaw

When a person writes a check and gives it to a merchant, the merchant deposits it to his bank. The check is cleared and accounts balance in a matter of hours, sometimes seconds. All of this is done through a clearing house system established by the banks to make banking possible and to make commerce flow well. The cost of this entire transaction is measured in mills rather than cents. It would seem crazy for a person to write a check and then have it rejected at every turn in the system causing him to have to follow it up with letters, phone calls and harassment from various banking institutions until finally getting the check cleared weeks or months after it was first written. No one in our culture would think that was rational. The cost would be enormous and commerce would stagnate.

Given that, why do we believe it is rational for medical insurance claims to dysfunction the way they do. For any family which has medical insurance, and especially families that are covered by more than one insurer, including many senior citizens, there is an ongoing whipsaw effort by the insurance companies. This requires the insured people and providers to follow up almost every claim with letters and phone calls and harassment from the institutions until finally getting the claim settled weeks or even months later. The cost is enormous and the system is stagnant. It smells stagnant.

Whipsaw creates a bloated bureaucracy of claims adjusters and clerks ad infinitum. Just the cost of wasted paper forms is beyond measure. The cost to our forests is sickening. The waste of human energy is staggering. The hope of the institutions, of course, is that the insured will give up and pay the bill just to end the struggle. The stupidity is the institutions spend enormously more than the value of the claim in their whipsaw effort. I believe the whipsaw effort is deliberate and systematic.

There is no reason whatsoever why the medical insurance industry cannot work the same way the banking industry works; smoothly, quietly and quickly, behind the scenes. What's needed is a medical insurance clearing house, using the very efficient bank clearing house model. This clearing house would act as the processing center for all claims. It would be a federally regulated, not for profit service set up and supported by the insurance companies. A company's contribution would be based on the value of the insurance they had underwritten. As sources of some of the most blatant abuses, Medicare and Medicaid would be required to participate. Regular audits by independent companies would assure that the government regulators were doing their job. Just like in banking.

Being the processing center for all medical insurance claims, this facility would have all the information of all the insurance companies and a set of rules to decide which company would pay how much of what claim. These rules would be constant for all claims. The decisions would be final. The companies would pay. Any noise about privacy concerns is a smoke screen. The argument is no more relevant than one about privacy concerns in the banking industry. If we hear this argument, we can check the people making it. They are probably double dipping - a practice almost impossible to track in the current system. This center would surely put a stop to that.

All claims would be submitted to this clearing house by the providers. No claims could ever be submitted anywhere else or by anyone else. The clearing house would have information on all providers. Each one would have to be listed to be legitimate. For each claim a single itemized statement would be sent to the patient showing in plain English what service was provided, how much it cost and who paid for it.

The statement would have a boldly listed hot line number to call if a person thought the claim was fraudulent. Who do they call now? In many cases, the alleged patient does not get a statement at all. Health Alliance Plan never sends statements if they happen to pay, only rejections when they don't. How does a patient know if a fraudulent claim has been made? Along with this, we need a new law to protect these whistle blowers against unreasonable prosecution and retaliation for pointing out what they might reasonably suspect is fraud. This allows the patient to become the policeman, filling a void in the system. The patients, I suspect, would much prefer to do the harassing rather than be the victims of it.

The providers would get a single monthly summary as would the insurance companies. Accounts would be balanced daily by computer. No checks would be written. The providers would start to get paid on time instead of waiting months for a check, but they would get only one payment for each service provided. Excesses and fraud would show up very quickly in routine analyses of pay outs. The penalties for stealing from the health care system should be very long, hard time. It's unconscionable.

The claims centers of the individual companies would be eliminated with a considerable cost savings. The patient would never get whipsawed by the companies with that old, "Someone else is your primary provider" game. "It's them, not us." The blizzard of paper which flies around the country because of that whipsaw would be eliminated at a considerable savings. An enormous burden would be lifted from the post office. There would be a single on line computer form for submitting claims and a single printed patient's statement for the results.

There would be an easily understood regulated appeal procedure for people whose claims have been denied. This procedure would be simple enough to not require attorneys until it reached the legal process. There should be at least two levels before court; a state level and a federal level. There could also be a binding arbitration level for those who desired it.

If there is a co-pay, the patient will get that information as part of his statement after, and only after, the claim has been processed. The patient would not be required to pay anything until that time. This would make it very difficult for providers to charge both the patient and the insurance company. It would eliminate that particular double dip.

Most insurance companies whipsaw the patients. They do it because they know if they force the patients, who, by the way, are ill and already under enormous stress, to deal with it long enough, a large number of them will give up and pay the bill. The insurance companies know the providers are also harassing the patients for their money because they do not have the courage, the resources or the knowledge to go after the insurance companies.

While banks have bankers, many of whom are inherently dishonest, the banks themselves, as institutions are usually not dishonest and banking as an institution is generally honest. The bankers do not control the system. Medical insurance companies also have dishonest people within their ranks. The difference is, in insurance, the managers do control the system to the extent that the institutions themselves and the institution of medical insurance becomes inherently dishonest. This whipsawing and evasion results in an enormous increase in the cost of insurance as the individual companies, including Medicare and Medicaid, struggle to shift the burden of payment to other companies. A central claims clearing house would resolve this problem. Therefore, we can be sure, the companies would oppose it.

I believe an insurance claims clearing house would save more than enough money to provide an adequate level of medical coverage to all the people the congressional and administration hand wringers would like us to fret about. That is its strength. Its weakness is, it would be almost impossible to implement because it would take power away from the insurance companies and all their petty clerks. It would put a number of bureaucratic free loaders out of work. The insurance lobby would fight it vigorously.

Let the Games Begin

Today I went through a classic, though different, example of HMO tactics designed to withhold treatment. Call it stonewalling. Tomorrow I am scheduled to see my orthopedic surgeon, who has replaced both my hips. It's a yearly checkup to avoid expensive and health threatening complications.

He advised it and my primary care physician (PCP) agreed. The PCP's staff initiated a referral action several weeks before the appointment. Today, the day before the appointment, I got a call from the surgeon's office, saying no referral had yet been made. It took six more phone calls to convince the HMO that I was going to see the surgeon before they gave in. I will keep my appointment tomorrow. Both of these doctors are participating in the same HMO.

You might think this was just a simple mistake except for one thing. The same deliberate stonewalling has occurred every time I have had to see my orthopedic surgeon. It has been going on for six years. I believe the procedure is calculated and deliberate with the intent of causing me to give up. It's similar to the procedure which almost killed me eight years ago, when I actually had to go outside the HMO and pay for treatment to save my life. It was too late to save my health entirely. I firmly believe these HMO corporations would prefer to maim or even murder their victims rather than pay the legitimate cost of their health care. I still have the documents which go back about ten years.

We had to make one phone call. We had to stay home, by the phone, and wait while my doctor's staff people made five more calls. It was not about straightening out a glitch. It was about forcing someone to do what they had accepted money to do. It was about forcing the HMO to behave honestly and fulfill their contract. We spent an entire day being stonewalled and whipsawed by these people.

We are not patients. We are not even subscribers. We are victims of the HMO's. They are all the same. It does not matter which one you use, it will be the same. This particular one is based in Detroit. It exercises control over major hospitals in Detroit and Grand Blanc plus a number of smaller facilities. Doctors used to run hospitals. Now HMO's run hospitals and control doctors while greed controls HMO's. This is not progress. HMO is supposed to mean Health Maintenance Organization. It practical fact, it means Health Menacing Organization.

Point Matrix Theory

In my reading, I came across Dr. Einstein's *Theory of Relativity* and learned almost nothing. From the little I understand, that wise gentleman describes a universe of four dimensions, with time as the extra dimension. There are confusing concepts where space curves back upon itself and time is not constant, but changes relative to the velocity of an object. In this strange universe, if we could travel fast enough, we could come around and see ourselves from behind before we left. Even if I could do that, I'm not sure I would want to. I hear snickers from behind often enough without having to witness it myself.

After the famous physicist came others whose names I forgot. They wondered about dimensions and space and theorized that there are not four but eleven dimensions. These eleven, they conclude, are necessary and sufficient to describe the universe. I thought about that and it did not make sense. My question was, "Why stop at eleven? Why should we limit the description of the universe in any way?" I thought, if we can have eleven, why can we not have an infinite number of dimensions? After all, linear algebra allows for it. Normally, clever educated people say, "If something exists, we can create a mathematics to describe it." I surmise the converse, if there is a mathematics to describe it, it must exist.

With this idea, I go beyond fuzzy logic and stumble down the trail of loose logic to a premise. To wit:

The universe has an infinite number of dimensions such that every point in the universe is adjacent to, and at right angles to, every other point in the universe through some dimension "N."

I call this the Point Matrix Theory. Given the premise, if we could rotate around a given point in the proper dimension, we could move from any point in the universe to any other point in the universe instantaneously. We could disappear from one place and appear in another just as did Wesoomi. If we find this theory to be valid it could solve the age old conundrum: "How did our mothers always know when we were screwing up?" Clearly, they have the power to see through N dimensional space. They really can see around corners!

The simple task which remains is to determine the energy required for the rotation in the proper dimension. Given that, any bicycle mechanic should be able to build a machine to do it. Practical space travel could be upon us.

Detroit is Cultured

Detroit is known around the country as a great sports city and indeed it is, if you accept that Detroit means Metropolitan Detroit. The area supports four major league franchises. Two are based in the city proper and two are not.

What the rest of the country does not know is that Detroit is a cultured city. It is a lunch bucket, rust bucket city, but it's cultured. Here is the evidence I know of.

In addition to two universities the city supports a number of excellent local Shakespearian Theater groups and many outstanding small repertoire theater groups. It also attracts most of the Broadway first run companies for long stands in some excellent classic theaters. That's just the beginning. The city supports a vast public library system, an outstanding art museum and a world class symphony orchestra. This orchestra has attracted some of the greatest conductors of our time.

When the great conductor Dorati was with the Detroit Symphony I decided to do a little survey, to test what correlation I could find between the support of sports and culture. I took a small card, wrote "Mess" on it and stuck it in my hat. I did not want to be accused of impersonating a fool so I did not write "Press". I do not have to impersonate. I am perfectly capable of being a fool on my own. Then I took my tape recorder with a mike and went to the ball park. I had no problem. No one questioned my credentials. I had one question. I stopped people at random and asked, "What do you think of Dorati?"

After recording the following eight answers I gave up and returned home to study the logo on a cereal box.

1 Oh they're ok. I like them with hot sauce best. To tell the truth, I prefer Burritos.

2. Huh?

3. It's ok but I like lasagna better.

4. I only buy American.

5. What's a Dorati?

6. It's not something to eat. I know! You're trying to trick me.

7. Listen! My neighbor bought one of them. He only drove it about five thousand miles then he got rid of it. He went back to Chevrolet.

8. My wife bought a bottle of that once. Said it went with spaghetti. I tasted it. Threw it out! It was bitter. I'll stick with Bud, thank you!

Trivia

"You don't have to believe to belong," said the snake.
"You don't have to be small to belittle," said the harpy.

Why is the hood latch on every make and every model of every car different? Why do you have to be a cryptographer to open a car hood?

The great Booboo says, "Books are better than bricks. Both can act as a doorstop but you really can't get into a brick."

There seems to be some kind of immutable law of the Midwest. For each church built, a bar must be opened and vice versa. Go out and count some time. Go to any map-dot town. Count the churches and the bars. The numbers will be very nearly equal.

A policeman arrives at a bar which has just been robbed and asks the bartender for a description of the suspect. "Well," says the bartender, "he had a short antenna sticking out of his head and seven fingered hands. That's all I remember."

"OK," says the cop. "Just think now. Was there anything really unusual about him?"

"Oh darn," says the bartender. "Yes, there was. You know! I should have known he was from out of town when he ordered Bud on the rocks. None of my regulars drink it that way."

Recently, I stopped worrying about whether I was right or wrong. I'm a bit slow but it finally came to me, I was going to get beat up either way. It was only a matter of who beat me up.

We must assume everything is sentient unless we can demonstrate beyond question it is not. It's simply the decent thing to do.

A young lady asked her father what he would say if she shaved her head.

Said the father, "I would say, 'stay out of the sun.'"

What I ask of my spouse is that she enjoy her life and be here for me. I promise to do the same. The being here part is natural. The part about enjoying life is not so natural for us folk whose formative conditioning consisted of cod liver oil and the puritan ethic in equal parts. We kind of have this sense, if life doesn't taste bad we must be doing something wrong.

When you were born, the doctor or midwife grabbed you by the hind legs and slapped your butt. Then they looked you right in the eye and said, " Life is going to be fair!"

Isn't that right? Isn't that what they promised? We know darn well it didn't happen, so why are we always bellyaching about things being unfair?

I don't care if life is fair.
I just want a free lunch!

Never let your sense of morality prevent you from doing what is right.

Natural and common! Many of us get confused about those two concepts. Many of us think that what is common is necessarily natural. For instance, is it natural for women to have emotional responses and for men to be stoic? Is it natural to find empty beer cans in our parks and forests?

My manager at Ford had an outstanding nose. It was hand-picked.

Did you notice that politicians always ask for more money for more cops? Would you be surprised if one of them asked for more money for better cops?

It's about time someone stood up for us old, senile, crazy people.

I've been down the hard row followed by a short visit to easy street. The hard row is more interesting and educational. Just the same, I hope I'm done with it. I'd just as soon stay on easy street. If I hoed the entire hard row, others might be cheated out of the experience.

As to ticks, if it were not for lunatics and politics, I wouldn't have any!

A fellow I know went into a motel and stole one of those Gideon Bibles. He said he wanted to study and become more Christian like. Made sense to me!

Here is a way to rid a city of rats.

First, discover an odor they cannot resist. Probably the smell of soiled babies or sour milk.

Second, use a small fan to blow this odor though a small tunnel into the open air wherever there are rats.

Third, put a hair trigger trap door in the tunnel with a fast spring recovery.

Forth, put a pair of 50 KV capacitor charged electrical plates beneath the trap door so that the rats must slide between them.

Fifth, place a very large bin beneath the plates.

Sixth, every day, empty the bin and take the contents to a fish food or fertilizer processing factory.

These giant rat traps would be inexpensive and effective if, and only if, the people clean up the garbage in the city. The government can provide the traps. The people should not count on the government to clean up their garbage.

I look at Mrs. Gaffer's cat and ask myself, "How could anything look so noble and regal and be so absolutely stupid?"

On comparing old fashioned village cultures with modern metropolitan cultures, I come to this question. Would I rather have neighbors who know all my business, keep an eye on me, tattle on me and gossip about me, or neighbors who close their door when they hear screams for help?

Yesterday was sunny.
I was up, up, up!
Today is overcast.
I am down, down, down!
What a Yo, Yo, Yo!

Mrs. Gaffer said she was going to put a new belt on the vacuum. I told her to wait until I could help. She just can't swear good enough to do it by herself.

Mrs. Gaffer has suggested a new device called the purple pill. It will be given to everyone in the world and will turn all of us purple. Thus, there can never again be discrimination based on skin color. After that, she has a neuter pill so we can't have any discrimination based on sex. Then we must have a teenage pill so we can't have age discrimination. Ad infinitum. We will still find a way.

Poor Baby!

Another news item. A sixty three-year-old woman lied to get into a fertility program and gave birth to a six pound baby. Everyone is marveling at the wonderful miracle. The Gaffer asks, "Does ego know no shame? Who will raise that child? Who will hug it, love it, change it and nurture it? And, if it grows up as selfish and sick as its mother, who will care?" Children are uncared for and starving the world over and researchers are figuring ways to make more children to satisfy their own insane egos and the deranged egos of their clients.

Now we find the government proposing a tax incentive for indiscriminate fornication. There is to be a $500 or more yearly tax deduction for poor people who make more babies than they can afford to care for. How in the world can we justify the government's subsidizing of population expansion even as the *Four Horsemen* bear down on us?

There are enormous numbers of women in this world who happily produce children and, in most cases, happily care for them. We expect this and approve it. Still the world's population is gradually increasing. Isaac Asimov, physicist and author, noted for his great science fiction works, made an interesting calculation about population. It was unique in that the calculation was based on mass rather than numbers of people. I have lost the reference but the point was not lost on me. He calculated that in the very near future given the current rate of population growth the total mass of humanity would exceed the total mass of the universe.

Of course, that will never happen. The Malthusian Specter is upon us. We don't see it in the United States because we don't want to but we see its effect in many other places of the world. There is important work to do. Do we really have research and tax dollars to throw away abnormally increasing the world's population by extending the productive cycle and subsidizing childbirth? Would we not be better off doing research into food production for the world's starving people? Isn't anyone thinking of their grandchildren and the world of limited resources, with rampant starvation which they will face?

Autumn

Red apples, cider.
Pumpkins, dried corn.

Tractor over fertile earth
turning rich furrows
in the field of dried stalks.

Tough cabbage,
still green after a hard frost.

And Asian children
Gaunt and starving.

What more
could a healthy American want?

Change and Progress

Mrs. Gaffer and I do not argue. However, we do have occasional, very loud, possibly heated debates. Our most recent debate was precipitated by television news coverage of a local home and builder's exhibition featuring kitchens of the future. Remember the old Bendix washing machine? They made a front loading washing machine sound like a revolution in design. Why would anyone put a washing machine and dryer in the kitchen? They also featured a Rube Goldberg sink which doubled as a cooking surface. I could not help laughing. I likened the progress in kitchens to the progress in the automotive industry where, I contend, nothing significant has occurred since the Model T Ford.

Mrs. Gaffer took immediate exception citing the windshield wiper and washer, anti-lock brakes, turn signals and many other gadgets. After a period of debate, I concluded that we had a disagreement about the meaning of the word significant. I consider the word, in this context, to imply some sort of revolutionary advance while she considered it to imply merely useful. With her definition, I allowed that there has been steady progress and improvement in the automotive industry, especially in the area of drive train performance. This I call evolution.

I did not allow that there has been any progress in kitchens. I remember sitting in Mother Gaffer's kitchen fifty or more years ago. That kitchen had everything our kitchen has and one thing which our modern kitchen was never able to duplicate. It had a warm toasty feeling which just felt great. I don't know why I expected Mrs. Gaffer to concede there has been no revolutionary change in either industry. She simply lifted her chin, turned her back and crossed her arms. That was the end of that.

Faucets only drip at night.
Managers run off all the time.

The great Booboo says, "Watch out for bible thumpers coming into the fields. They like to pretend they are the Lord's reapers. In fact, some of them are just hoe-ers."

Mrs. Gaffer says, "The Swiss bankers of WW II were no different than the carpet baggers of the American Civil War.

Trapped Inside

Someone I love had a stroke. He cannot talk. His entire right side is paralyzed. He tries hard. I thought about how he feels. This is what I thought.

I'm still here.
They think I'm dumb or senile or that I've degenerated.
They don't know I'm still in here.
They think I'm gone.
I can't make my body work. I can't talk.
I say it but it doesn't come out. Noise comes out.
I know that. I know it's noise.
I didn't do noise. I did words. Just like I always did.
Just like I always could do.
Oh God!
I can't do words.
It's me.
I'm in here.
I'm trapped inside.
God help me!
Someone please help me.
I'm here.
Please tell me I'm here.
Please tell me you know I'm still here.
Don't leave me in here.
Don't leave me alone!

It's a damn shame that a nice person like me has to have a conscience. There are so many things I could have and do if it were not so.

On Being a Simpleton

Anyone who thinks the world can be neatly divided into just two categories or sets is a fool. There are, however, opposed extremes of some human conditions which can be defined with the proviso that we will not find these extremes in their pure form and they are only part of the human's makeup. A perfect fool does not exist, although, those who know me say I come close on occasion. A complete simpleton is likewise a mythical character though it may be a condition to wish for. The spectrum from fool to simpleton is large and most of us find our place along that spectrum.

Now that I have muddied the water sufficiently, let me give my definition of a fool and a simpleton. A fool is a person who believes he has significant knowledge and makes no distinction between temporal knowledge and cosmic knowledge. Many bible thumpers are fools insofar as they believe they know about God. A perfect fool believes, further, that everything is knowable.

A simpleton is a person who begins to understand that he has no significant knowledge and, baring some cosmic event, is not likely to have any. This understanding, that he doesn't know crap, is the beginning of wisdom. He then sees no reason for pretense and, using what temporal knowledge he has, begins to simplify his life. A perfect simpleton is a creature of complete faith who is connected to the Divinity. His life has been simplified to the point of simply doing the next task, impeccably. One Eastern name for people in or near this condition is Sufi. A simpleton is usually effective because he has no pretense or dependency on outcome. He is simply task oriented.

One cannot strive to be a simpleton. It is a position of acceptance, not achievement. We must not mistake this as being passive or weak. A simpleton can plan precisely and execute impeccably. The best way to tell a simpleton from a fool is that a simpleton will not crow when the results are good nor misdirect blame when they are bad. A simpleton notes the results and proceeds to the next task.

At first there is the Divinity, the Simpleton and the next task. The Simpleton opens to the Divinity and begins the task. As things proceed, the Simpleton and the Divinity begin to lose their separate identities. Then there is just One, performing the task. Then, the One becomes fully identified with the task and there is just the task doing itself.

Now, you can sit back and roll your eyes. You can whistle, snort and fart. You can say, "The Gaffer is off the deep end." You can say, "What kind of metaphysical bologna is this?" You can do all of that. But, if you are honest, you will not deny, what you just read has happened to you a couple of times. Please admit also that it was a great if weird experience, even if you would not want it to happen again.

People who write describe this experience as the point where the book begins to write itself. An artist will say, "The painting took control of me." You need not be an artist or writer. The experience can strike while we are mowing the lawn or sweeping the porch. It's a perfect synthesis of Divinity, doer and task, a perfect meditation. It's a moment of Grace. When the task is doing itself, there is no stress! It's a fact that a simpleton lives a relatively stress free life. I wish I could be one.

I know there are people who will say they never had an experience like this. If that is true, it means we could duplicate that person with a piece of machinery. Our connection to the infinite is the only thing which separates us from machines. To have lost that connection is a tragedy of the highest magnitude.

There is only one person in the world who can make a fool of you.

You can always identify a highly educated man. He will be the one with all the answers and no solutions.

Ghetto Blaster Blaster

The last frontier of the human decencies of the world has disappeared. There is no peace and quiet left anywhere. It has gone the way of large front porches, squeaky screen doors, real lemonade, and porch swings. I suspect it will never come back. There is nowhere left to go. There is nowhere in the world where some audio thug cannot assault us with hundreds of watts of audio sewage spewing into the sound spectrum. These thugs claim it's their right.

Our culture is developing into an individualistic, arrogant, sociopathic cesspool. Never in human history has there been such wide spread personal disregard for the people around us. This manifests in many ways but in particular, the last frontier of human decency. Respect for peace and quiet.

Whether it's Beethoven, Baez or the stuff called hard rock, punk rock, pop rock, slop rock matters not. When you spew it out over the audio spectrum at a volume which can be heard for miles, it is not music. It's a vicious assault on your neighbors. I don't care if the noise comes from the scum bag across the street, a public concert or a summer camp for kids, it's unconscionable.

I never thought I'd say it. We need another law. When I become God Emperor, we will have a Ghetto Blaster Blaster law. This law would empower the police to issue special hunting permits to citizens which would allow them to fire a shotgun into a ghetto blaster. The law would not allow the hunters to injure people but it would allow them to order a person to stand clear of his ghetto blaster. If a person refused to stand clear, the law would empower the hunter to enlist the aid of bystanders in making a citizen's arrest. The charge would be obstructing justice.

The law would define a ghetto blaster as any device being operated whose primary purpose is to produce sound and can be heard more than 50 feet away. This would include in-car stereos. The permits would be restricted to predesignated areas including public parks, residential neighborhoods, and tranquil rural areas.

Of course, before we can get the police to issue Blaster permits, we must first get them to care. How is it where you live? If we have an emergency where I live, we can dial 911 and get a very rapid response. This system is wonderful. On two occasions it saved my life, when I had serious heart problems. The local volunteer fire rescue people came in a matter of minutes. It was fire rescue people who responded, not police. That's great! The problem is, what happens if you don't have an emergency?

A short distance away from us, there is a local summer camp for kids. Last month, when they were spewing noise out over the audio spectrum at about 1000 watts, I could hear it in my bedroom, about two miles away, at 10:30 PM. It was keeping me awake. If I had called 911 they would have been justifiably cross with me, so I called the State Police mini station on their regular number. It rang down to an answering machine and I got a recorded message.

Whoever set it up did not know how to do it or did not care. I suspect the latter. This is the message I heard. "Will dispatch a unit to your home. If you would like to leave a message for an officer noise - noise - noise - noise after the tone. . . . 'Beep'." I hung up. You may notice that the message started with an incomplete sentence and ended with garble.

Two weeks later, I called the same number again at about eleven PM. This time the answering device functioned properly. I left a message complaining about the noise from the camp and about the lack of police presence. I have received absolutely no response from the Michigan State Police.

The truth is, we can get a total emergency response from 911 or no response at all. Nothing in between. Governor Engler is real proud of these guys. A real caring, community support team.

Pawing Children

Young people are human beings. They are not pets. They are not toys. They are not oddities. They are human beings with rights to privacy in their own person and space.

Why is it that people think they have a right to interfere in the lives, privacy and space of children? I sat in a restaurant and watched an old crone walk up to a family she did not know and start cooing and pawing a three year old girl. She got in the kid's face and told her how cute she was and all that adult to child babble designed to make the old bitch feel good. The child was very uncomfortable, but the old bag did not notice that. She was very much into her own trip. She gurgled and babbled while the child shrank from her touch. The kid's parents seemed, for some reason, to be helpless. They should have told the babbling old fool to get away and let them eat but, although they were clearly uncomfortable, they did not. They nodded and half smiled and looked uncomfortable.

There seems to be some insane notion among adults that children have no rights. We all subscribe to the idea that a person has a right to privacy in their own person except when it comes to children. With children, any babbling fool adult can invade the child's space and privacy with no rationale at all. Just because they want to. It's as though the child were not really human but some kind of pet or toy.

If I had walked up to that old bat and got in her face, pawing and stroking her while telling her how cute she was, she would have screamed bloody murder. She would have called me all kinds of awful things. OK! The truth is that meddling old bitch is all kinds of awful things, getting her kicks by abusing the rights of a helpless girl. And yes! I think there is something overtly sexual in it.

How about we get an agreement, among adults, that the age of a person has no bearing on their right to privacy in their own person and space. Let's agree once and for all that children are human and have rights even though they don't have the power to enforce them.

Let's stop babbling old bags from fondling and running their stuff on children.

In the case I related above the child was defenseless. Her parents seemed unable to protect her and she had no physical or intellectual tools of her own. I could have wished that I could loan her my intellect for just a few seconds. Then this might have occurred:

When pawed by a kinky old crow,
a young girl spoke up and said, "Whoa!
Ma'am, please use your head.
Unhand me," she said.
"Just go home and use your dildo."

Greenhouses Gurus and Meditations

I have a lovely greenhouse where I sit for a few minutes each morning and open my heart to Minerva. That's a thing I use to start my day in peace. It works for me.

Each path to peace is individual. No one can tell you the nature of your path. It is for you to learn, as is the method of opening to the Divinity. Many will try to tell you how to pray or meditate and how to gain wisdom. At best, they are telling you a technique which worked for them. At worst, they are telling you something they have been taught which has yet to work for them. There are no rules or guaranteed methods.

It is better to let your own heart guide you. I spent years trying to follow rules laid down by ones masquerading as teachers until I realized they did not know. Then I looked in my heart and found a link to the Big Guy in the Sky. It was there all along.

I live in the real world. There are many things to do and many things to learn. I really don't have time to hang around with people wearing robes. I don't have time to shuffle along in sandals with my head bowed and my hands folded. I don't have time to sit on hot rocks, or cold rocks. I don't need to shave my head. My hair fell out. I don't have time to spend hours sitting with my knees folded under me. The last time I tried that, Mrs. Gaffer had to take me to emergency to get me untangled. It was painful as heck. I have arthritis.

I'm a real person, living in the real world. Enlightenment will have to come to me. I just don't have time to seek it out. I refuse to waste my life acting mystical when there are so many interesting, exciting things I have not done, seen or learned. I prefer to spend my life doing the next task. Whatever turns up. Meantime, I'll check with Minerva each morning. She is very helpful in starting my day right.

Another way Minerva helps is in problem solving. The solution to most problems is implicit in a clear statement of the problem. Here's how: Sit down, center and set aside the noise in your head. It's there, but set it aside. Open to that deep well of peace and wisdom within yourself. Make a clear concise statement of the problem. Don't try to solve the problem, just state it as perfectly as you can. Relax for a few minutes. Then forget it. Go about your business and don't think of the problem. Usually, within one day, you will have an elegant solution to the problem. Always check with your internal wisdom. In my case that's Minerva.

Sometimes I don't have time to sit down and be peaceful and all that stuff because the crap is coming right at me. Then I may just scream, "Minerva! For God's sake help me!" or some such panicky nonsense. Then, if it's necessary, Minerva will put her hand on my heart and stop the pounding. She will bring a calm into my mind. Then my heart and eyes will see differently. Sometimes I will see that the problem was imagined and sometimes I will see that what is about to happen is OK and sometimes I will see a way to handle it. Other times she just watches and snickers while I take it in the ear. In that case, I must assume I'm just getting what I deserve.

Top Guy

When you have a problem or complaint, go to the top person involved. Don't mess with tweeners. If the top guy can't or won't handle it, there is no chance of getting it handled. If you are mad at Ford, write to Alex Trotman. If you're mad at the Governor or the President, write to his wife. Always go to the top person. The truth is if you don't get a response from the top guy, it's simply because that company does not care about your business.

From experience, I can assure you if you complain to Alex Trotman you will not receive a reply from him or any of his people. The letter will be opened by one of his flunkies, who will buck it down to the people who bungled in the first place. It will then be forgotten by Trotman's people. About one month later you may receive a response. I had two complaints when I wrote and I discovered the United States Post Office was to blame in both cases. Of course! Why didn't I know that?

This gives us an idea of how woefully out of date some managers are. While it used to be fashionable to blame the post office every time we screwed up a communication, we are now expected to blame a computer. It was a computer glitch. Most people are happy to believe either excuse so long as they are allowed to use it too. Why don't we get honest and admit that the performance of the post office is, in general, outstanding.

Every time I have complained to an auto company, the same thing happened. They did not respond or follow up. They bucked it down to the people who screwed up and expected them to make it go away. What really went away was their customers. I don't think they understand yet! It is that kind of behavior which allowed foreign companies to penetrate their markets. Why would they ever think the people who caused the problem would have an incentive to do anything but shift the blame? What I get from this is that no one in the big corperate management cares enough to follow up.

I have had much better success going to the top guy in small and mid-sized companies. Enough success to keep me doing it. The general rule is, "The larger the company, the less they will care. The smaller the company, the more responsive they will be." A conclusion, "If possible, give your business to the smallest company which has the resources to do it correctly."

Along the same line, the only thing worse than no response is a response that is totally irrelevant to the problem or request. Did you ever send a request or file a complaint with some company or bureaucracy, only to receive a form reply which was totally unrelated to your input? Like, when I sent a book which I wrote to the *Ford World* house organ asking them to review it. I receive a form letter back saying, "I am sorry. We discontinued *Second Wind*. If you sent a photo, I am returning it." Honest to God! I saved the letter. I still have it. Would you ever pay attention to or do business with a group like that again? Me neither!

Here is a great follow up on Ford. Today, I received an empty envelope from one of the departments I had complained about. It was a mass mailing which had been stamped and addressed but not stuffed or sealed. Now why can't that post office get things right?

About human value and earning, The Great Booboo says, "There is no way one human being can be worth 100 times more than another human being."

There is not necessarily intellect in all red necks but there is a little red neck in all intellects. It's the part that wants to cut loose; the part we try to conceal with a collar, tie and thoughtful expression. We used to affect a pipe but that's no longer fashionable.

Mrs. Gaffer says I have attention deficit disorder. I never listen to what she says.

Michigan Law

The crazies are at it again. Michigan legislators and educators are trying to implement a new law for teens. The essence of the proposed law is, "Go to school or lose your driver's license." I suppose the theory is we can use social privileges to blackmail someone into doing something we think is good for them. If that is so, I don't see why we should stop so short of perfect. How about, "Eat your broccoli or lose the right to vote." How about, "Brush your teeth or don't use the public parks." Why should there be any relationship at all between the blackmail and the goal? If we have power, let's use it!

In Michigan we make the law,
no matter how stupid and raw.
you'll do it our way,
or else you will pay,
with privileges which we withdraw.

The Scientific Method

The scientific method consists of just five steps. It is not creativity. It's a method for developing thoughts and ideas in research. All of us do the first two steps. Everyone!

1. We observe something and we have an idea or thought about it.

2. We formulate a theory or opinion about the observation.

This is where most people quit. The crazy and the lazy quit here. They formulate their opinions as though they were conclusions and they publish the opinions. Often the publication only consists of shouting the theories and opinions in bars and restrooms. For a true scientific method, the following steps are most important.

3. This step consists of designing a test, experiment or set of experiments which will test and challenge the theory.

4. The test or experiment must then be executed. Sometimes this requires building equipment or designing a questionnaire. Whatever is required must be done to execute the experiment. The only output from this experiment will be information. The experiment cannot fail for it will provide information. Hopefully the information will tend to prove or disprove the theory.

If the experiment proves the theory we go on to step 5 which is to publish or use the knowledge gained.

If not, we go back and modify the theory to fit the facts discovered and design more tests. We do not modify the test results to fit the theory; although, sadly, we find that being done of late by alleged scientists. Science does not lie. Unfortunately witnesses sometimes do and scientists are witnesses. We cannot call that science. It's just plain flat out cheating and is worse than the fools who shout their theories without testing them.

A more likely possibility is the experiment's outcome will be inconclusive. In this case we devise more and better experiments to fill in the missing data.

So, we design experiments, gather data, modify the theory or create a new theory: we design experiments, gather data, modify the theory or create a new theory: we design experiments, gather data, modify the theory or create a new theory: and so on. This is how the scientific method moves our knowledge incrementally forward. It is very tedious and boring. Not glamorous at all. And it is definitely not creativity.

Creativity is a different thing. I dare say the scientific method is not how Einstein arrived at his theories. It is how they were later confirmed. The theory itself was a leap of inspiration in a great mind. None of the great breakthroughs came from the scientific method. I believe they came from some kind of internal connection which these great minds had with the infinite. Most of us are not so blessed, so we increment along with the scientific method.

This process has also been called Dialectic Materialism by some communists who pretend they invented it. Who knows why? Much as I hate to face it, the method was probably developed by some French aristocrat in the early great days of scientific inquiry when hard science was evolving out of metaphysics and astrology. In those days, France really was great.

Finally: If you only want to do the first two steps like the crazy and the lazy do, another good place to shout your theories is from the pulpit. You could also write a book like this.

Visualizing

America seems to have lost some of its inventiveness. I wonder if we have lost our ability to visualize and imagine because of television. I remember radio. It forced us to visualize scenes and objects. Now, instead of making us create our own pictures, they show us their pictures. We get homogenized. We fret over the loss of morality and family values and tend to blame television, at least in part, for this. I wonder if the loss of our inventive facilities might become the higher cost of the tube.

I remember seeing a TV film of *The Lone Ranger*. It's hard to describe my disappointment when I saw a rather ordinary man with a mask riding a rather ordinary horse in place of the larger than life heroic figure I used to imagine when I heard the finale of the famous overture along with, "The thundering hoof beats."

Visualization I believe, is the way we create solutions to problems. In a previous incarnation I had a friend and associate, Chuck, who did this visualization so quickly it appeared more like a revelation than a process. He would hear a problem and lay out a bullet proof solution with hardly a pause. No one, on such short notice, could find fault so we would have to go with it. It was embarrassing and, sometimes, frustrating for his associates. Before they got to participate in the creative process, it was over. I never lost my awe of that guy. I finally got myself off to a different group where I could be creative a little more slowly. I have to stare into space for a while.

Spouses and managers have a serious problem with that part of creativity which consists of staring into space. If they cannot see motion they conclude nothing is happening, even though this is the very part of creativity which most people are unable to do. The creative process is not about having ideas. Ideas are ten cents the dozen. The process consists of visualizing how an idea becomes a reality. This is not about white papers. It's about a reality, in the form of a usable product, process or service. This requires having a blank expression and, sometimes, appearing to be comatose.

A silly little man had a pretty stone which he called an amulet. He kept showing it off and waving it about and thrusting it toward people. One day the village bully got annoyed and took the stone away from him. He threw it into a hog pen whereupon one of the hogs ate it. Now that stone must have had some power to change things for shortly thereafter, that hog became pork. Miracles are everywhere.

They say you can't beat somebody with nobody. Not true. You can beat anybody with nobody if your timing is impeccable. You must simply publish the right lies at precisely the right time. This is how politics is done.

Solicitors

I believe it would be possible for a person to win public office on the single issue platform of putting an end to telephone and E-mail soliciting. Make it a punishable federal crime. An invasion of privacy equivalent to wiretapping. Start with fines and go on to prison term for chronic incorrigible offenders.

The candidate could just take moderate positions on all other issues of the day. They would pale into insignificance compared to this invasion of privacy. Bear in mind that the really noisy issues are issues of minority groups which don't affect the large voting majority. A candidate need only take a moderate position on these issues. The louder and more polarized the issue, the less important it is to the candidate. No matter the screaming demands of these extreme minorities and the insistence of the media. These noisy people are small minorities whose main power comes from making us believe otherwise through loud and obnoxious behavior.

The main issue for the middle class majority of voters is the steady erosion of our quality time which is based on privacy in our own home and person. The marketing assault on this quality time has become an epidemic.

Of course the candidate would win in spite of the massive financial investment toward his defeat by the communications and marketing industries. He would win but it would not matter. The lobbies of these industries would be much more effective with Congress. A bill with any real teeth would never make it to the floor. It's a good enough idea but Congress would never have the courage to stop these swine from invading our lives.

In truth, we could stop them ourselves simply by making it completely unprofitable. All we have to do is never respond to a telephone or E-mail solicitation regardless of the source. A successful business will notice a negative cash flow quickly and stop doing whatever caused it. If they don't, the business will soon become unsuccessful. Not even GM can sustain a negative cash flow forever though they seem to keep trying.

Exercises

I have a set of physical and mental exercises which I do at least four times per week in the morning. The routine takes me about one hour. When I tell people about this, I get some real strange statements, mostly in the nature of, "How in the world do you find time to spend one hour a day on that?" I consider that to be the same as asking how I find time to eat, get enough sleep, bathe or shave.

Exercise is one of the most important elements of human health. It's not something to find time for. Like proper nutrition, proper rest and hygiene it is essential to good physical and emotional tone. It's what makes all else I do a joy instead of a chore. It's what lets me dance, prance and waltz through my day rather than drag. It's the foundation for all my good feelings about myself and the world. Folks who question that have their priorities backwards.

So I do the exercises, I eat right and I get plenty of rest. After that I find time for other things as I can. Try it! Take care of yourself. Then, if you have time, you can mow the grass. If not, you can get a goat. The goat will even give you gifts for the garden. Then you will need a goat poop scoop to transfer the gifts. Also, if you have time you can do the laundry. If not you can go naked and stay inside. If it's summer and your home is isolated, you can go naked outdoors. God doesn't mind. That's the way she made you. With your sweet, uncovered buns hanging right out there. Don't let the bible thumpers confuse you with their skin/sin syndrome. That's an emotional problem, not a real one, and it's unique to them.

I get plenty of exercise by fighting the phone company. Don't you just hate the phone company?

About Lard Butts

Everyone who is fat knows what made them fat. From one step back, the human body can be seen as a heat engine which operates the same as a Ford V8 gasoline engine. It converts fuel energy to motion and heat energy. The difference being when you overfill an auto fuel tank it simply runs out on the ground. When you overfill a human fuel tank the fuel gets stored in millions of tiny expandable tanks called fat cells. Most of these spare tanks are on our bellies and buns. That's what makes us fat. If automobiles had that capacity, they would look like blimps, same as us.

We put in more fuel than we use. We know that. No sense fibbing about it and making up nonsense about metabolism imbalances. Not only do we know it, each one of us knows exactly which of our addictions is the culprit. For me it's beer. For Uncle Louie it's sugar products. For others it's burgers and fries. Junk food, called fast food. All this stuff is addictive in that the more we get the more we want.

So let's stop the bull about it and either enjoy being fat or do what the Great Buddha said. "All things in moderation." We don't have to quit drinking beer. We just have to stop being irrational about beer or pasta or sugar etcetera.

Here's one of the reasons I am a lard butt. There is a difference between beer and diet pop in addition to the fact that beer tastes a great deal better. The difference being that while beer goes to belly, the pop goes to pee. This is, of course, the reason we sometimes drink diet pop and pretend we like it.

Attorneys are like Easter eggs. They may appear to be different because of color or decoration but they are all pretty much the same on the inside.

Never Pray on Sunday

Praying to God on Sunday is like trying to call home on Mother's Day. On Sunday, there are a great number of folks in churches all over the world shouting out their hallelujahs and hosannas, begging for mercy and one thing or another - world peace - tolerance - a better wine for the communion. I'll drink to that! The point is, all this traffic tends to tie up the trunks, exchanges and net nodes. The lines are busy and you won't get through. Just like using AOL, you'll get a busy signal. The difference with praying is, you won't know you're not getting through.

Week days are a much better time to pray, or call home. Fact is, you should do it more often anyway. Not just on designated days. Some days are better than others. Monday and Tuesday are OK. Thursday and Friday are good too. Wednesday is poor because you will be competing for air time with all the medicos on the links, shouting and waving their fists at the sky. On Saturday, Jehovah will be quite busy with the Hebrew folks and the Seventh-Day Adventists.

Steve Case advised his victims to try using the AOL service in the off hours. Perhaps he meant they should stay up all night in the hopes of logging on. It would probably work. I suspect this would also work for communicating with the divinity. Praying, I would guess, is a bit of a better reason for staying up all night as opposed to fooling around in the world's biggest arcade.

Now praying in the off hours does not guarantee you will get a hearing or an answer. A clear channel is very rare. If you ever get one, you will experience an instant of grace unsurpassed by the sweetest orgasm you ever had. To get a clear channel, you must be very quiet and listen. God does not ordinarily shout. Really! You wouldn't want her to. It would mean she was angry.

One more thing: **Call your Mother!** Years from now, you'll be glad you did. There are many of us who wish we had a mother to call.

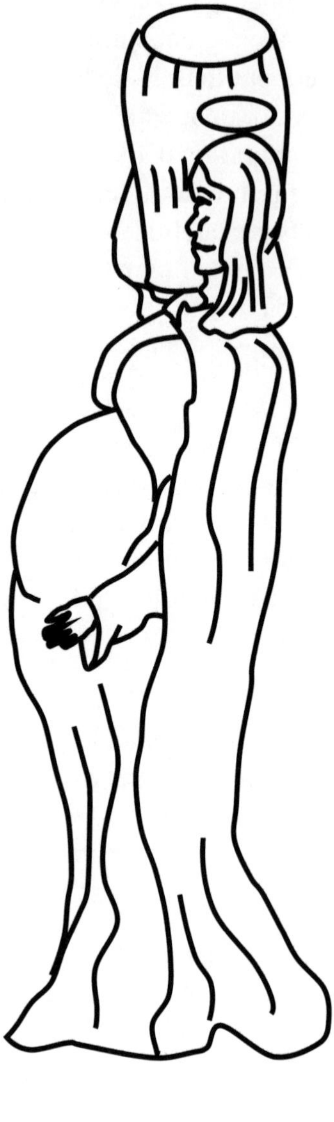

Him and his damn holy ghost!

Finish Here

All things, good and bad, must end. I hope you have enjoyed what I presented. Now I'll just pick up some loose ends. I must speak for the record, least I leave you with a wrong impression. I am not Tom Trueheart. In years past, I have done many of the things I have criticized or condemned in this book. I have been a coward and I have caused people pain; not always by accident. I have lied, cheated and pilfered. Fortunately, I could never escape my conscience. It would never let me enjoy the fruits of those sins. I do marvel at those people who can suppress their conscience to the point where they can derive pleasure from dishonest behavior. I cannot.

I have learned from these failures. Somewhere along the line, I got smart enough to stop doing those things. Seeing what that kind of behavior did to the psyches of other people helped. I have watched human beings change from normal folks to something less than human. I could look in their eyes and at the way they stood or walked and see the pain. The way they carry themselves and hold their bodies tells it all. Wealth does not mitigate the damage.

Bad behavior is simply not healthy. None of those things work in the long term. In my experience, they did more damage to me than to my victims. I could never have made a career of that kind of behavior. It is not enough to pray, go to confession or whatever and put money in the poor box. That's just ritual. By itself it's crap. I must realize that what I did really was wrong and stop doing it. It has less to do with any church or ritual than it has to do with my own peace. Now I still make mistakes but that's what they are. Mistakes, not deliberate acts.

A recent mistake I made concerned someone at PC Magazine. I affronted someone and I don't even know his name. Because I acted without thought, I owe someone a sincere apology. Here's what happened.

I had been having an annoying but non-fatal problem with my computer. The operating system interrupted what I was doing, at random times, to refresh it's knowledge of my system. It did this without any explicit request from me. I simply had to wait for it to finish. I did not know how to fix this so I went to PC Magazine. They publish a section called "Ask Our Advisors" wherein their technical people answer reader queries. I sent them E-mail describing my problem.

A few days later, I received a phone call from a person at PC Magazine. It came after a frustrating series of telephone solicitors interrupting my work at sporadic intervals. No excuse, but the frequency of these interruptions has been escalating exponentially for years until its more than an annoyance. It's a visible bottom line cost, worse than spam. Without thinking, I assumed another solicitor and brushed off a person who had called only because he wanted to help me. I hung up on him.

I took about four seconds to realize I had made a stupid mistake. Too late! I did not know his name or his phone number. I have spent some time thinking about how to apologize. I could have sent E-mail, but to whom. Dear person who I insulted? I finally figured as long as I had to go public I may as well do it big time. So here it is.

"Dear person who I insulted at PC Magazine. I have no excuse. What I did was dumb and boorish. I sincerely apologize.

Willie Gaffer:"

If having to do that does not make me a little more thoughtful, nothing will. I cannot suspend thoughtfulness even for an instant. Once done, the damage is not repairable. In addition, I still don't know how to fix my computer. Bummer!

As to this book, you may think a great deal of it is bologna. I will say, it might surprise you to discover how many of the stories in this book are based on essentially true facts. It may also surprise you to learn how many Tabby Treats it cost me to get Booboo to answer all those questions. That does not matter. More to the point, if you want to take exception to any part of this book or if you just want to weigh in with a thought or suggestion, please write to me.

Willie Gaffer
C/O Wesoomi Publishing
P. O. Box 656
Ortonville, MI 48462

You may suspect that I am not qualified to discuss most of the things I have discussed herein. That may be true. If you want to take exception to my theories or my logic, please do. Send me your most vigorous arguments. If I can learn from you, I will ask Minerva to bless you. If you have any thoughts about the principles of ethical business, by all means, send them along.

Write, even if you only want to call me a hypocrite or a lard butt. Tell me anything you want. I'll try to read it. Albeit, some criticism is probably not worth your time. For example, I already know this work contains incomplete sentences, for their effect. In addition, I know that the following are not words in most people's dictionaries even though I have used them. My dictionary is unique, in that it contains some special purpose words which I borrowed from the street or invented for the occasion.

Irregardless, buzzap, brainer, kaka, nuniness, wavicle, dohinkey, duffus, dumbocracy, Macintush, blooey, tweeners, and schmallop.

There are probably others. I do insist, however, that Zippate and Verbosalitis be accepted as real words. They put useful handles on concepts which, until now, we had no good way of expressing.

Fajioli really is an Italian word meaning bean and Pasta Fajioli is bean soup with pasta. I have heard fajioli pronounced as two and as three syllables. The Italian folks I know give it two syllables sounding something like "fa-joul". The I is silent unless they think they are speaking English, in which case they tend to throw in an 'a' wherever their tongue feels the need. Fajioli would then be pronounced "fa-joul-ah".

Kundalini is an Eastern religious term. Literally, it means spinal energy. When properly aligned this energy brings the devotee nearer to the Divinity and enables special powers.

About questions you may have, if you have profound questions, send them to me. I will pass them along to The Great Booboo. He will answer in time. If you have questions which are not so profound, send them to the government. They are very good at inane solutions. If you have questions which are very simple, send them to me. I like simple questions because they are very difficult to answer. Simplicity is the ultimate elegance and elegance is the ultimate simplicity.

I have sprinkled some of the concepts of the Eastern religious philosophies throughout this book. If you want to hear Eastern religious philosophy at its corniest and most profound, contact the Hanuman Foundation Tape Library and buy some Ram Dass tapes. The prices are very reasonable. Ram Dass is currently known in the United States as Ram Dass (Servant of God), religious teacher and philosopher. Earlier, he was known as Dr. Alpert, friend and associate of Timothy Leary. Ram Dass recently suffered a massive stroke. The extent of his recovery remains uncertain at this time. Hanuman is also a Servant of God, sometimes. At other times he seems to be just a mischievous monkey.

Hanuman Foundation Tape Library
Suite 203
524 San Anselmo Avenue
San Anselmo, CA 94960

Discounts on this book are available for bulk purchases.
For information contact:

Wesoomi Publishing
P. O. Box 656
Ortonville, MI 48462